What is Rhetoric?

What is Rhetoric?

Michel Meyer

OXFORD
UNIVERSITY PRESS

Great Clarendon Street, Oxford, OX2 6DP,
United Kingdom

Oxford University Press is a department of the University of Oxford.
It furthers the University's objective of excellence in research, scholarship,
and education by publishing worldwide. Oxford is a registered trade mark of
Oxford University Press in the UK and in certain other countries

© Michel Meyer 2017

The moral rights of the author have been asserted

First published 2017
First published in paperback 2019

All rights reserved. No part of this publication may be reproduced, stored in
a retrieval system, or transmitted, in any form or by any means, without the
prior permission in writing of Oxford University Press, or as expressly permitted
by law, by licence or under terms agreed with the appropriate reprographics
rights organization. Enquiries concerning reproduction outside the scope of the
above should be sent to the Rights Department, Oxford University Press, at the
address above

You must not circulate this work in any other form
and you must impose this same condition on any acquirer

Published in the United States of America by Oxford University Press
198 Madison Avenue, New York, NY 10016, United States of America

British Library Cataloguing in Publication Data

Data available

Library of Congress Cataloging in Publication Data

Data available

ISBN 978-0-19-969182-1 (Hbk.)
ISBN 978-0-19-884723-6 (Pbk.)

Links to third party websites are provided by Oxford in good faith and
for information only. Oxford disclaims any responsibility for the materials
contained in any third party website referenced in this work.

The desire of being believed, the desire of persuading, of leading and directing other people, seems to me to be one of the strongest of all our natural desires. It is, perhaps, the instinct on which is founded the faculty of speech, the characteristic faculty of human nature.

Adam Smith (1759)

Of all the talents bestowed upon men, none is so precious as the gift of oratory.

Winston Churchill (1897)

Contents

Acknowledgments	ix
List of Tables and Figures	xi
Prefatory Note	xiii
Introduction	1
1. The basic features of the history of rhetoric	14
2. The question-view of *logos*	80
3. Rhetoric and argumentation: the unity of the field	99
4. The common operators in figures and arguments	121
5. The argumentative structures	131
6. The elements of rhetoric *stricto sensu*: the figures of speech	141
7. The foundations of literary rhetoric	158
8. The rhetoric of the arts	180
9. The role of *ethos*: the voice of values	190
10. The role of *pathos*: from argumentative responses to feeling and emotions	203
11. The negotiation of distance or the embodiment of the interpersonal	216
Conclusion	225
Glossary	229
Bibliography	233
Index	241

Acknowledgments

My deep gratitude goes to Paul Earlie, who has read and reread this manuscript with kindness and determination. I would also like to thank Jaś Elsner, of the University of Oxford, and Nick Turnbull, of the University of Manchester, who played a major role in the correction of my English, suggesting new formulations as well as improving those existing ones.

This book was commissioned for Oxford University Press by John Davey and brought to completion under his successor, Julia Steer. I thank them for their kind patience throughout these years of writing.

Without my secretary, Tonina Salis, this manuscript, revised and retyped so many times, would never have turned into a book. She also deserves my deepest thanks.

Last but not least, I wish to say how much this book owes to my wife, Corinne Meyer, whose unwavering support and love have been so essential.

Michel Meyer

Brussels, February 2016

List of Tables and Figures

Table 1	The major theoreticians of rhetoric of the twentieth century	50
Table 2	Table of the basic correspondences between trope, figures of thought, and arguments	129
Table 3	How logical arguments are generated on the basis of the operations of discourse	136
Table 4	Table of strategies and operators as a function of the level of problematicity	156
Table 5	Literature in Aristotle's time	185
Table 6	Greek fine arts	185
Table 7	Greek fine arts and literature	185
Table 8	Table of collective values	194
Table 9	The first two lines of the table of values as an instantiation of its logic	195
Table 10	The general table of values	197
Table 11	The negotiation of distance: discrepancies and adjustments	220
Figure 1	Toulmin's model	67
Figure 2	Diagram of rhetorical strategies	110
Figure 3	The argumentative responses	134
Figure 4	The basic catalog of figures	147
Figure 5	Opposed scales of approval (or agreement) and disapproval (or disagreement)	155
Figure 6	The catalog of figures and the inner working of the four operators on tropes as examples	155

Figure 7   The transformation of emotional distance   205
Figure 8   Distance in law and politics   212
Figure 9   Translation of politics into law   212
Figure 10 Translation of law into politics   212
Figure 11 The space for political and legal debates   212
Figure 12 The projective and the effective: the arrows of
           distantiation   220

Prefatory Note

Rhetoric is a complex matter in a complex world. It emerged more than two thousand years ago in Europe and in Asia, but it survived and developed only in our fragmented Western world. Rhetoric itself underwent fragmentation: there is rhetoric as literature, rhetoric as debate, rhetoric as everyday conversation, rhetoric as art. In sum, rhetoric can be found everywhere, yet it fails to evince an underlying principle which would account for this diversity of usage, as if rhetoric were by its very nature deprived of any unity.

Rhetoric has thus many specificities, a fact which renders its boundaries all the more fluid and uncertain. Our universities do not usually have special departments devoted to its teaching. Sometimes courses in rhetoric are taught in English or French Departments, sometimes even in Philosophy, Linguistics, or Literary Criticism, as if rhetoric did not exist in its own right. Nothing is more misleading with regard to the nature of rhetoric than this multifariousness of usage. Would rhetoric therefore be a science without a definite object or a specific method? Rhetoric seems to be a ductile technique, adaptable to circumstances and to individuals but with no rationality that could transcend all its usages. Some people use it to convince others, to impress them, to affect their emotions and their judgments, to persuade them to act in a certain way, to please them, or to provide them with what they think to be the right arguments, especially in court. Others resort to rhetorical or figurative speech as a way of conveying indirect messages or constructing narratives or creating works of art, thereby suggesting what cannot be literally expressed. What do all these usages have in common, which would still allow us to affirm that they belong to the same discipline called "rhetoric"?

In spite of this glut of formulae, an answer emerges: what they all have in common is the fact that they bear upon the problematic.

Rhetoric unfolds what is problematic by presenting it as solved or simply as something which raises questions for us, as readers, spectators, or interlocutors. We are challenged and questioned by art, literature, narratives, political speeches, or simply by other people whom we must then question in turn if we are to make sense of what they say and go beyond what is literally asserted. But if rhetoric is the "art" or the "science" of the problematic, it is not concerned with every kind of problematic. Science too deals with questions, but most of the time it at least purports to solve them. The problematic at work in rhetoric is meant to interpellate, to impress, to move, think, question, to create debate, and even to charm others. In other words, through a given discourse, rhetoric deals with what is problematic insofar as it unites or divides human beings in various ways. We have thus discovered a unifying principle which accounts for what rhetoric is in all its diversity. In brief, rhetoric is the dialectic of identity and difference among human beings, as groups, as individuals, or both. Rhetoric is the negotiation of the distance between protagonists on a given question which divides them or brings them closer, the question being a measure of their difference and as such expresses the distance from one another.

What does the past tell us, if not of the importance of rhetoric when the problem is to create a political meaning for common action? Rhetoric has enabled Roman emperors to display grandeur in their Arches of Triumph or in the columns they erected in the center of Rome to impress the people and imbue them with a feeling of togetherness seldom attained in their agitated history. Rhetoric has been used to reinforce the identity of communities through common stories such as epics, thereby going beyond the task of settling disputes (for which it was also intended). But now the question is a philosophical one: how might we harmonize heterogeneous notions such as conflict and persuasion, conviction and emotion, reasonable judgment and rhetorical inference if not by relying on a single conception of the problematic in human affairs? Perhaps this focus on questioning imposes itself today because questioning permeates everything in contemporary societies: it characterizes the Other, who is a question posed to us by its very existence, its projects, its ambitions, its wishes, leading to potential confrontation as well as to an equally possible agreement and closeness. But questioning is also the key to the understanding of art and literature, which have always been considered as emblematic of what rhetoric does. Questioning characterizes contemporary literature and art, increasing their enigmatic features as the pace of history accelerates, submitting them to our constant questioning as interpretative readers or spectators. It also characterizes political debates, in which each participant claims to have the right answers. And finally, rhetoric affects most aspects of our everyday life, which is punctuated by questions, trivial or not, which need to be constantly tackled.

Rhetoric would not have grown so extensively had our society not continuously oscillated between the putting forth of old, obsolete answers, which have become problematic, and proposing new answers validated by solid arguments. Sometimes the two are intermingled in order to manipulate the audience by playing on the possible confusion between them. Is this not the origin of the difference, in rhetoric itself, between rhetoric as argumentation and rhetoric as eloquence, or if one prefers, between Aristotle and Plato?

Today rhetoric as a discipline is the study of the various ways in which questions are at stake in our exchanges with others, giving rise to the possibility of disagreement but also of proximity. Every rhetorical encounter has a social aspect. This means that behind the particular questions in negotiation, there is often another problem to be confronted: distance itself. It is through distance that social structure impinges on rhetorical relationships. This is why rhetoric could also be defined as the negotiation of identity and difference, notably by resorting to symbols such as flags, national anthems or other argumentative means of affirmation and differentiation. Rhetoric confirms itself as a powerful weapon in our dealings with others, enabling us to resort to confrontation and emotion, to difference and proximity, and finally, to rejection and harmony.

All these possible variations of distance are embodied within rhetoric, not least in the cherished fields of literature and the arts because they play on such distinctions. Novels, poems, and dramas enact the various dialectics of identity and difference which relate and sometimes oppose characters, while exerting an impact upon their readers and their emotions. That too is rhetoric.

Introduction

What is rhetoric? This question is one of the most pressing in contemporary thought, not only in philosophy or linguistics, but in many areas where interpersonal relationships are at stake, from persuasion to seduction, from marketing to literature, from media to politics. The problem is always the same: how can discourse impact others and how does it achieve this impact? These questions, and of course their answers, confirm the importance of rhetoric in everyday life, as well as its status as a new matrix in the humanities. Indeed, in most social and human sciences—in political science (and in politics) where debates are relentless; in history, where documents and witnesses, even recent ones, are often problematic; in psychology, where rationalization is often at work; in sociology or economics, where "rational" agents operate more often than not under uncertainty and risk, with only partial knowledge and likely evaluations at their disposal; in literary criticism as in aesthetics in general, where distance itself may raise problems of interpretation and arouse discussions; and this list of thematics using rhetoric as argumentation or not is, of course, itself inevitably incomplete—we find not demonstrations but reasons and arguments, whose conclusions vary to a greater or lesser degree in their probability. In these disciplines, there is no certainty as there is in the mathematical sciences, nor is there experimental control, as in the natural sciences. The force of reasoning, the relevance of certain facts and the negligible significance of others are a matter of argument, and sometimes even of presenting the issue in a certain way. This is why, as said before, rhetoric has now become the new matrix of the humanities, as linguistics once was when the structuralist model of the 1960s was dominant. A generalized recourse to rhetoric in public

What is Rhetoric? First edition. Michel Meyer
© Michel Meyer 2017. First published 2017 by Oxford University Press

life has become widespread following the fall of the Berlin Wall in 1989, if only through the increased dependency of the public sphere on the media, without which democracy would scarcely be possible today. Even in our private lives, we need to convince and please others rather than impose our views on them. As psychoanalysis has taught us, the unconscious remains more or less hidden from us, thanks to its being coded through metaphors and metonymies. As for our professional lives, hierarchies increasingly require the willing assent of all. Rhetoric does not seem to be merely personal, but has in many ways become social and political as well.

But what precisely do we know about rhetoric? Is rhetoric merely a scientific name for the whole gamut of language use in interpersonal situations? Plato was the first to stress that language could lead to the manipulation of minds, long before the concept of propaganda became a major political weapon. If rhetoric can lead to such manipulation, it is because rhetoric deals with questions and alternative viewpoints, each of which can be equally likely. The accelerated pace of history also creates potential confusion between obsolete answers, which become problematic, and new ones, which seem unquestionable. It is easy to play on the similarity of these types of answers to influence audiences with wrong answers according to Plato, since they are formally identical with the true ones. Rhetoric enables the speaker to vindicate alternative viewpoints, even if these viewpoints are opposed, in contrast to philosophy or science, which for many centuries have been identified with each other and in which discourse is meant to rely on univocal truth in excluding either A or not-A. Aristotle entertained a broader view than Plato, however. For him, discourse cannot be limited to the necessary conclusions of science. Other types of discourses exist, differing in the likelihood of their results and the problematic character of their conclusions. Indeed, it is this kind of language-use which is most widespread in everyday life and in politics, not to mention forms of speech which are better characterized by their beauty and eloquence than by their verisimilitude. Narratives must be captivating, poetry is expected to move us, and political arguments should be persuasive. Nonetheless, in order to capture these varieties of speech and writing, Aristotle divides rhetoric into two main forms, with two distinct goals. One is Dialectic or argumentation, in which people debate conflictual issues; that is, they defend A or not-A and try to reach some agreement on one position over the other. The other use of rhetoric is not based on arguments but on stylistic elegance, as in the case of literature or even casual discourse. For literature, Aristotle has in mind theater and epic poetry as much as eloquence in general; literature also covers various forms of everyday language and conversation. The latter is meant to be pleasant, charming or de-problematized, as in funeral speeches. If the goal is to influence the audience in a given direction, to impress or have any impact at all, speech must be eloquent in its own way. Rhetoric, in this latter case, usually resorts to well-put narratives, stories, and examples, from which the charmed audience will draw conclusions or will simply appreciate or approve what is said or written, according to its tastes and emotions. Such discourse usually resorts to figures of speech to convey an answer and achieve its impact. Is this manipulation? It could be, but it certainly does not have to be. There are many cases in which one does not want to be persuaded but rather enchanted, captivated, or reassured as to the intentions of the speaker, as is the case in matters of love, literature, and even politics.

After Plato's emphasis on *pathos* (the emotionality and suggestibility of the audience), Aristotle's vision shifted to a new anchor point, namely *logos*, focusing on style and reasoning, even if failing to harmonize them into one single view. The Roman rhetoricians added a third viewpoint: a final *ideal-type* of rhetoric, to use Weber's terminology. It was not rooted in *logos* above all, nor in the audience (*pathos*), but rather in the speaker, hence the major role played by the latter in Roman rhetoric. The speaker, with his own particular views of the world, society, and himself within society, was the key figure in this new type of rhetoric. The Greeks called this speaker *ethos*. *Ethos* refers to the place occupied by the speaker in society, to the values required to be trusted, or to his authority in delivering an answer to certain questions. This varies according to his knowledge, whether he is solicited for his expertise or rather simply as an exemplary human being who defends, for that purpose, humanistic values (hence the transformation of *ethos* into ethics). The speaker is consulted or listened to simply because he is regarded as having right and authoritative opinions on a given issue, his authority being moral or technical due to his role in society or his profession.

Ultimately, then, we are confronted with three broad types of rhetoric. The *first* focuses on the audience, with its emotions, passions, and prejudices or more simply its problems. The Greeks spoke of the audience as *pathos* because of the importance of the emotions which, for Plato, could give rise to the manipulation of minds, as in propaganda, for example. But focusing on *pathos* is not a negative thing in itself, since rhetoricians must take into account the audience's various states of mind in order not only to please but also to convince. What is negative in Plato's response is the reduction of his *pathos*-centered view of rhetoric solely to manipulation, which is just one possibility of rhetoric among many others.

The *second* type of rhetoric is based on *logos* as the medium through which the speaker and the audience communicate. Such a *logos* can be eloquent or composed of rational arguments; it can be more "rhetorical" or more "argumentative," according to its purpose, in the same way that seduction differs from confrontation. Aristotle calls the former type of rhetoric *epideictic*, while the latter is more aligned with legal debate in court. The *third* type of rhetoric, which became characteristic of the Roman era, has its roots in what is expected from the speaker. His *ethos* refers to his character and to his knowledge, but also to the trust the audience places in his respect for their common values. The Roman world favored a rhetoric based on *ethos* because the right to speak on a given topic was socially anchored. Roman society was essentially aristocratic and not democratic as in Classical Athens. For the Romans, the speaker can never be just anyone; he must be somebody who has the right to speak on a given issue. If the speaker is called *ethos* by the Greeks, it is because one cannot convince anyone without first having legitimacy of one type or other, even if that is simply technical (i.e. based on expertise) to do so. His authority, moral or social in this case, in other words his ethics, gives the speaker the status of a specialist and an exemplary person. But even then virtue (*ethics*) is the universal resource for anyone to *respond* on common issues, giving answers for which he is therefore ultimately *responsible*. This is where *ethos* is most closely associated with *ethics*. But for many questions, such as in law or health, lawyers or physicians are legitimate in their answers because their knowledge or expertise inspires faith in them. Their "ethics" lies in the possession of the virtues (capacities) needed to provide an answer, but also in their possession of virtues more generally, which render a person of authority responsible toward his audiences. This has a compound effect on the trust we place in the speaker, since trust is the corollary of these virtues.

With these three types of rhetoric, based respectively on *pathos*, *logos*, or *ethos*, we have a tripartite basis that has made rhetoric what it is and has been since the Greeks. The problem, however, is that the flourishing of these different lines of rhetoric makes us lose sight of what rhetoric is as a well-defined and unified discipline. As a result, its boundaries seem too fuzzy, a fact which has enabled some authors to affirm that rhetoric is the study of the figures and devices of literature, while others have claimed that rhetoric should be conceived of as argumentation, whose specific aim is to resolve disagreements, most notably those which occur in court or in politics. Through this dispersion of views, each favoring an autonomous rhetoric, grounded either in *ethos*, or *logos*, or in the primacy of *pathos*, we all sense that there is no clear common ground for one rhetoric encompassing all of them in one single field we could call "rhetoric" as such. Rhetoric has been traditionally divided into the rhetoric of figures and the rhetoric of conflicts. Their models were law and literature. A trial, which is dominated by conflict, and literature, which is based on eloquence and style, are of course different; if both nonetheless claim to make use of rhetoric, in either case a distinct type of rhetoric is in question, which makes it difficult to see basic common features or a common form. Since Aristotle, however, they have been the two major ways of seeing rhetoric, as a theory of literature or as an extension of reason.

Rhetoric, as loosely understood, is nevertheless present in both. This is why an effort should be made to bring out firm principles and establish an area of thought with clear boundaries.

Rhetoric is a discipline, but it is also a practice that the Greeks divided into *genres*, such as law or politics. What is relevant for the purpose of unification is that each use of rhetoric relies on the same components of the interpersonal linguistic transaction, namely *ethos*, *logos*, and *pathos*. Someone (*ethos* or the locutor) speaks to someone else (*pathos* or audience) on a given topic or question (*logos*) which interests either one or both parties. But does this imply that we should continue giving priority to one of these components, *ethos* as in Cicero, *pathos* as in Plato, or *logos* as in Aristotle? Why should privileging one of these three components be identified with the "right" rhetoric? Why should we favor *ethos*, rather than subordinating it to *pathos* or *logos*? All subsequent theories of rhetoric have done precisely this, however. Hence the obstacle to integrating all three aspects of rhetoric. This is in itself, however, an insufficient reason to stop pursuing that line of thought. As we shall see, rhetoric is indeed grounded in *ethos*, *logos*, and *pathos*, but the three should be given equal footing.

First, we must find the right definition that allows us to implement such a view. The one I propose is the following: *rhetoric is a negotiation between individuals—ethos and pathos—on a question (logos) which divides them to a greater or lesser degree or purports to abolish or at least diminish their distance*. Rhetoric is what allows us to take measure of the distance which separates individuals and to work on this distance through language and other symbols. Rhetoric is the discursive embodiment and the indicator of our social relationship with others; it can be used to express our distance from them, to diminish or increase it according to the circumstances. Disagreement stems from distinct and opposed evaluations of what that distance should be. The process starts from a particular question at stake, which divides people or brings them closer together, or simply enables them to position themselves with respect to one another, given the distance between them. By negotiation, we mean that the speaker wants to express an answer to that particular question in order to increase, maintain, or diminish the original distance. An agreement is meant to diminish the distance between interlocutors by offering a single answer, with more or less nuances, to both questioners who, at the outset, defended different or even opposite viewpoints. Agreement with someone is always limited in scope, because it hinges on a definite question or set of questions. Because of its impact on distance, argumentation, hence agreement, and persuasion is favored by those who want to idealize society through some kind of harmony or complementarity of individuals. The negotiation is nothing but a working upon the distance separating individuals who must deal with one another. The question raised, then, is in a way the measure of their interpersonal distance; it makes this distance, effective or merely desired by the speaker, known to the interlocutor. A highly problematic question divides *ethos* and *pathos* more than a less problematic one, i.e. one meant only to nourish conversation, as is the case with small talk. This is why we usually avoid speaking about religion and politics in casual encounters, which are more divisive issues than speaking about the weather, about which nobody will feel in question.

We can say that we now have an integrated definition of rhetoric, since this definition incorporates the three possible and traditional anchor points of rhetoric—*ethos*, *logos*, and *pathos*—*without diminishing their respective roles or putting one of them first*. We can therefore include all the possibilities developed so far in the history of rhetoric. Our definition will be systematic if we are able to develop each of those three dimensions into a wider scheme, articulating the three components of the rhetorical relationship which give sense to the various techniques, goals, and usages of rhetoric required by such an articulation. We do not want to have one view of rhetoric amongst or against others, but an understanding of the principles underlying them all as a consequence of our general definition. However, we must go one step further in order to unify these perspectives. Rather than a viewpoint, we might speak here of a foundational view. What might this foundation be? As we shall see in Chapter 2, I propose that this foundation is called the *question-view of language and reason*.

It is based on a simple and widely acceptable principle: if we debate or write, or speak in general, it is because we have a question in mind, one for which we want to express an answer that we wish to share, or which we want to raise and ask an interlocutor to answer for us or with us. On the one hand, if nothing were problematic, we would not need to address others; everything would be clear for them and silently "readable" from the start. On the other hand, if everything were problematic, it would be impossible to talk to one another. So the truth lies in the middle, between these two extremes. Some things are problematic while others are not, hence the usefulness of rhetoric: it allows us to build a bridge between the problematic and the non-problematic, for us or for others.

In rhetoric, then, as in any other use of language, we have a question in mind which animates the speaker. He may expect to get the answer from his interlocutors, or he submits it to them by addressing a question of shared interest or by creating that interest with the question raised. That question in rhetoric usually recalls or brings to light the *exordium*, also called the opening speech. What is inherent in rhetoric is that such an answer remains more or less problematic and can even be further problematized and debated, if doubted or rejected by the audience. As a result, the audience—and in court, distance is formalized right from the beginning—feels all the more distant and separated from the speaker and his viewpoints. This is why rhetoric is the problematic viewed as interpersonal and relies on a given distance that speakers or audiences want, directly or indirectly, to modify or to maintain. A telling example is that of the physician, who wears a stethoscope wrapped around his neck while on duty, although it is not particularly useful to put it there. He does so in order to show that he is a physician and not a nurse, since hospital staff indiscriminately wear uniforms of the same color. The physician wants to attest to his status in spite of the undifferentiated color of staff clothing. His place in the hierarchy of the hospital has to be recognizable and recognized. In doing so, he negotiates this distance by evincing it without any possible confusion. Recognition needs rhetorical devices to express the social role we embody in our professional lives.

Rhetoric, then, plays on the distance between individuals. It is a question-and-answer game in which the question does not have one unique solution. The answer is seldom pursued as an end in itself. It may be useful, likely, pleasant, or convincing. It has an impact on the audience, and it is what the speaker wishes to evaluate beforehand. The impact he makes as a speaker, the impact of the question, the impact his speech makes on the audience, all this depends on his answer, giving rise to consensus or dissensus, agreement or disagreement, or emotional responses such as love or hatred, or, to follow Aristotle in his analysis of calm, mere indifference.[1] Finally, rhetoric has no other grammar than the processes by which we pass from the non-problematic, which is obvious to the protagonists (or presupposed as such), to a proposed resolution of the problematic. Dialogues, arguments, figures of speech, images, and even gestures render rhetorical the interpersonal relationships we entertain in our social and private lives.

How are we to proceed if we are to construct a consistent and generalizable framework for rhetoric in the largest sense? Let us recall the definition of rhetoric proposed earlier which integrates all the other definitions and captures the reality of what rhetoric is:

Rhetoric is the negotiation of distance between individuals, the speaker (ethos) and the audience (pathos), on a given question (logos).

This definition draws attention to the fact that the subject matter, direct or indirect, debated or spoken about by the interlocutors, is a specific question, which can divide them sharply or unite them, if they share the same opinions (or even prejudices) about it. What is shared and presupposed here is called the "unproblematic." In non-problematic questions, we speak, for instance, about the weather or the family of each participant in the dialogue, in order to reinforce or simply to create the interpersonal relationship, as when we enter a shop, take a cab, or say hello to our colleagues in the morning. As we

---

[1] Aristotle, *Rhetoric*, tr. W. D. Ross in J. Barnes, *The Complete Works of Aristotle* (Princeton, NJ: Princeton University Press, 1984), 1380 a5.

can frequently observe, it is distance itself which is very often the object of that rhetorical relationship.

This treatise will unfold by working out each element contained in the definition of rhetoric I propose. Its strength lies in the fact that it will give rise as much to a new conception of rhetoric as it will integrate the preceding ones.

We shall begin by recalling the essential aspects of the history of rhetoric (Chapter 1). In spite of the foundational importance of Aristotle, we shall also briefly consider Plato's view of rhetoric and also what rhetoric has become in the modern era, more particularly in contemporary times. A flourishing of perspectives and theories can be observed in the twentieth century, from Toulmin to Perelman and Habermas, amongst others.

Then (Chapter 2), we shall define, or rather redefine, the three basic concepts of *ethos*, *pathos*, and *logos* contained in my definition in terms of questioning, since rhetoric deals with the problematic as it is embodied in our interpersonal relationships. *Ethos*, *pathos*, and *logos* are the components of our relationships but they also nourish the ways of dealing with questions raised by these relationships. The notion of resolution as the outcome of the negotiation of distance is the key to the rhetorical process. Agreement, which is essential to argumentation, is only one aspect of rhetorical questioning. Agreement could be summarized with the following formula: "one answer, two questioners." Questions that are more or less problematic are the subject matter of rhetoric and the theory of questioning is what allows us to find a common root to all the conceptions of rhetoric produced so far.

Each part of the definition of rhetoric given above needs to be carefully analyzed. This is what I intend to do in this book. We shall begin with a new analysis of *logos* based on questioning, before concentrating on the ways in which *logos* handles questions and answers. The most common internal debate in rhetoric is between rhetoric *stricto sensu* (or figurative language) and argumentation (or debate about alternatives). These two views of rhetoric can be integrated within a single discipline called "Rhetoric" thanks to the question-view of language and thought, which provides two complementary ways of dealing with the problematicity of questions. From the beginning, *logos* as inference and *logos* as style have given rise to two classical branches of rhetoric; these branches have divided rhetoric and developed independently throughout the centuries.

In fact, rhetoric *stricto sensu* and argumentation still constitute a prevailing opposition within rhetoric itself. On the one hand, there is argumentation (which Aristotle calls *dialectic*) and, on the other hand, rhetoric *stricto sensu*, in which the aim of fiction or everyday conversation is to convey a message rather than to argue in its favor or against it. Rhetoric, conceived of as a figurative mode of speaking, is often considered by contemporary scholars as the "true" rhetoric, leaving argumentation to psychologists, linguists, or logicians. However, rhetoric can be found in a variety of arguments: in advertising, in politics, and in everyday life. Rhetoric and argumentation present many similarities and the underlying unity of both will be developed in Chapter 3, providing established boundaries to the whole discipline as such. We shall establish laws proving that rhetoric and argumentation share the same foundation, due to the common underlying presence and role of questioning in both types of rhetoric, even though they embody different strategies of resolution. I shall also examine under which constraints or requirements either strategy is adopted. We shall see (Chapter 4) how the underlying unity of rhetoric *stricto sensu* and of argumentation is based on four operators, which can be found throughout the history of rhetoric, from Aristotle to the Group Mu. This will lead us to analyze how these operators define the structure of argumentation and generate the basic types of arguments (Chapter 5), as well as the corresponding elementary figures of speech in rhetoric *stricto sensu* (Chapter 6). Figures of speech (or style) appear as the "counterpart," in the Aristotelian sense, of arguments, and correspond to each other in both number and quality. This perspective will enable us to rationalize the overabundance of figures and arguments by reducing them, in the last analysis, to four main classes. The numerous divisions and catalogs that have been produced conceal the unity of both areas of rhetoric.

These catalogs rely on a scholastic complexity which has the insidious effect of concealing that unity and that correspondence. This is in addition to the fact that all existing lists of figures and arguments are very often arbitrary, for the most part, as any detailed handbook or dictionary of figures of speech or arguments shows.

The interesting aspects of the question-view of language can be found in disciplines as diverse as pragmatics or psychoanalysis, because questioning underlies all forms of human thinking. In argumentation, as in logic, questions and solutions are arranged in certain ways. But this is also the case in literary rhetoric (Chapter 7), which has often served as a paradigm case for rhetoric. Literary rhetoric is based on a specific law, called the *law of inverse problematicity*, on which we shall linger in due course. Comparisons with other forms of rhetorical usage will need to be made, for example, with political discourse or with advertising, but also with the various forms of arts which have coexisted or competed with literature as a way of questioning the world (Chapter 8).

After *logos*, my definition of rhetoric will lead us to focus on *ethos* (Chapter 9) and *pathos* (Chapter 10). After examining the resources linked to *ethos*, we shall devote our attention to *pathos* as the *reception-effect*. As just mentioned, emotions, passions, feelings, but also intellectual responses are the constitutive elements of that impact and influence. Rhetoric as negotiation of distance between individuals on a given question will lead us to analyze how the speaker negotiates (and what exactly he understands by that) and what resources he mobilizes to that effect. These resources for questioning and answering he relies on are usually called *values*, and even if he does not negotiate them, he negotiates *with* them. They provide a common ground from which to suggest a conclusion or to infer one, a conclusion which has a more or less strong emotional impact (*pathos*). That is why *pathos* is so often identified with the audience *or* with its emotions (or passions). Values are to speakers what emotions are to an audience, and the negotiation of distance between them is a way of rendering values emotional and emotions valuable to individuals. To negotiate the distance, through dialogue or through contradictory debate, to get nearer or farther from others, can even be the very object of the rhetorical relationship. Values are less conclusions than they are premises of all of our rhetorical reasonings. In the end, they are reinforced in their "value" by virtue of rhetoric itself.

In the last chapter, the question will be how to explain the negotiation process between individuals, spawning agreement or disagreement, emotion or distantiation (Chapter 11). In fact, distance is the mainstay of our definition of rhetoric, and is at work differently in some important "genres," as they have been called, or "problematics," as we should now consider them.

Ethos and *pathos* themselves bear the weight of distance and they are conceived of differently according to the distance prevailing between them. The speaker manifests himself through values that are more individualistic and passionate at short distance and the reception-impact linked to *pathos* differs according to proximity with the speaker. The impact is less passionate when the distance is great and more emotional when the distance is small. *Ethos*, *pathos*, and *logos* vary in content with distance and are modified in their contents and resources when it is short or long.

Our final chapter is then devoted to the negotiation of the distance between individuals. It will focus on the changes linked with these variations, modulated by increasing or diminishing distance. It will take into account the clash of values and emotions, of values between themselves, of high-level problematic questions and low-level ones, thereby bringing about the synthesis envisioned from the beginning.

1
The basic features of the history of rhetoric

Plato's rhetoric as *pathos*-centered

Plato's conception of rhetoric is mainly to be found in a famous dialogue called the *Gorgias*. It is true that other dialogues embody, directly or not, Plato's obsession with rhetoric as a counterpoint to philosophy. As James Golden and his co-authors have noted:

We have found that the general subject of rhetoric is featured with varying degrees of emphasis in every dialogue that Plato wrote. In these writings, he touched on all aspects of human discourse. Insights on the nature of eloquence, the need for ethics in communication, and the use of pathos are discussed in the *Apology*; rhetoric as a means of generating meaning and knowing in *Cratylus*; criticism and taste, speech introductions, ethos, humor and persuasion in *Laws*; learning and recollection in *Meno*; first principles and dimensions of intrapersonal communication in *Phaedo*; types of speech forms and recommendations concerning the length of speeches in *Protagoras*; the cardinal virtues, ideal forms, audience analysis and adaptation, and the notion of conversion in the *Republic*; genuine and sophistical discourse, and refutation in the *Sophist*; model speeches by Agathon and Socrates in the *Symposium*; the use of examples and analogies appeals to the motives in *Statesman* and the noble lover, probability, and knowledge versus opinion in the *Theaetetus*.[1]

---

[1] James Golden et al., *The Rhetoric of Western Thought*, 7th edn. (Dubuque, IA: Kendall/Hunt, 2000), 22.

What is Rhetoric? First edition. Michel Meyer
© Michel Meyer 2017. First published 2017 by Oxford University Press

There is nonetheless a peculiar feature of Plato's remarks on rhetoric that deserves mention since it appears to entail a certain degree of backsliding in the critical view of rhetoric he generally espouses. In the *Phaedrus*, Plato seems to leave room for something like a "good rhetoric" which is a far cry from what we—or even Aristotle—would understand by rhetoric today. This rhetoric is supposed to be animated by the quest for truth but in this respect it does not really demarcate itself sufficiently from what Plato understood by philosophy. The real question is whether truth is by itself convincing and thus has no need of rhetoric or whether what we call "good rhetoric" is the dialectical instrument advocated here by Plato as a means of eliminating the false answers and reaching the true ones by the division of opposites (see *Phaedrus*, 257c–279c). To conclude, "in the *Phaedrus* rhetoric holds a slightly better position. There is here a more positive evaluation of its role. This does not mean that there are radical changes or substantial differences in the theoretical framework in which it is set."[2] Good or bad, equated or not with the philosophical method, for Plato rhetoric remains throughout a matter of *pathos*, just as Roman rhetoric is essentially a matter of *ethos* and, for Aristotle, mainly a question to be settled through *logos*. The fact is that Plato's obsession with a *logos* completely anchored in *pathos* (hence the dialogical form of his works) compels him to differentiate the various possibilities of *logos* in function of the diversity of the souls, i.e. their "quality," their intentions, their virtues, and so on. This seems to impede Plato from characterizing philosophy in intrinsic terms, independently of the effects that discourse may have on the soul. As Marina McCoy rightfully summarizes that position: "Dialogues such as the *Phaedrus* affirm the presence of the forms as forces that literally move the soul through our human desires, even as our recovery of the truth is partial and limited. At the same time, philosophical discovery is always a process of becoming and not being: any expressions of truth will always be in part poetic, historical, and

---

[2] R. Barilli, *Rhetoric*, tr. G. Menozzi (Minneapolis: University of Minnesota Press, 1989), 9.

limited rather than presented in a transparent, ahistorical, and complete *logos*. For this reason, the philosophy within Plato's dialogues is always rhetoric."[3]

Legal rhetoric is also a preeminent, if not indeed the original, form of rhetoric, at least when the latter is conceived of in terms of argumentation. Legal rhetoricians were called *Sophists* and they could defend any thesis equally, including opposing ones, provided they were sufficiently paid to do so. Why did such manipulation of truth work? *Pathos* is animated by our passions. What moves the audience is all the more convincing if the speaker uses arguments that play on the audience's emotions. By granting a greater say to emotions, the speaker reinforces them. The Sophist responds by enacting the following sequence: *pathos* → *logos* → *ethos*, which means that the impact on the audience guides the way he chooses and organizes his arguments with respect to what the audience is sensitive to, even if to defend everything and anything implies cynicism.

All this would not have been possible if words could not be ambiguous. Words often have several implied meanings, on which the speaker can play, sometimes simultaneously. At least, that is the way our unconscious proceeds. For all these reasons, we can see why *pathos*, i.e. what the Sophist wants the audience to think about a given subject matter, is the factor that subordinates *logos* as well *ethos*. The Sophist's sole requirement with regard to *ethos* is simply to win the case, even if it means flattering the audience and belying truth.

Plato's position, as briefly recalled above, has long been the source of the standard criticism leveled against rhetoric, namely that its essence is manipulation. Why such a conflation? How did the status of rhetoric emerge as a question in itself? In ancient Greece, as in later periods of history, there is a moment at which old answers became problematic and coexisted with new ones which were not problematic. The difference between the two types of answers is hard to establish since they mingle and very often have the same formal appearance.

---

[3] M. McCoy, *Plato on the Rhetoric of Philosophers and Sophists* (Cambridge: Cambridge University Press, 2008), 19.

This can lead to confusion. Hence Plato's negative reaction towards opinions as unjustified answers. He wanted an unquestionable criterion to decide what would count as a true answer. His situation is in many ways comparable to what happened in the sixteenth century, when the old theological–scholastic model collapsed, or to what later occurred in the twentieth century, when the Iron Curtain collapsed in favor of generalized forms of democratic debate. Democracy, we know, has led to more and more debate on issues of public and even of private life.

The three main periods of renewal in rhetoric have been due to Aristotle, to Italian Renaissance humanism, and to the New Rhetoric founded by Perelman and Toulmin. Plato did not go that far. For him, the line of demarcation between answers—between the obsolete answers and the valid ones which ought to replace them—is difficult to draw outside of science, and it is this very fact which can give rise to the manipulation of minds. Descartes, in similar circumstances, with the same predilection for geometry, adopted the same attitude and rejected both types of answers, the false and the probable ones, as equally doubtful or "dubious." He later went on to look for a new foundation for unquestionable discourse in philosophy, such as implemented in mathematics, where the truth of A *necessarily* (i.e. without doubt) excludes not-A. Plato and Descartes thus share, without explicitly presupposing it, this same ideal of *apodicticity*.[4] This is in effect a shared unquestioned and unquestionable conception of *logos*. It amounts to reducing the norms of validity and the criterion for truth in discourse to those of science. Both philosophers have the same conception of discourse as hinging on the elimination of the problematic view of alternatives which have been left to the sterile and endlessly ambivalent field of rhetoric. Their *problem* is to make *problems* disappear, but it is a paradoxical starting point, given the result they wish to obtain. In order to succeed nonetheless, they must develop a view of Reason which must be sustainable by itself,

---

[4] A proposition is apodictic if its opposite is impossible. If I am in London at three o'clock, it is impossible that I am in Oxford at the same time.

and the necessity of such a position should be seen as a self-evident necessity in itself. Is propositionalism not based on an ideal of resolution which can never be thematized as resolution, because as such it would appear contradictory? Paradoxically, propositionalism is the model of thought to be grounded yet which also serves as its own ground.

Plato, however, praised Socrates' view of the problematic, called *aporia* (i.e. a question that remains without solution at the end of a debate), which is nothing less than a *contradiction that alternatives become when translated into the language of answers*. This has an interesting consequence. To avoid such circles and contradictions, Plato ceased to speak of *answers*. For him, a question must rather be expressed as a certain kind of proposition. As a consequence, opposite propositions cannot refer to two defensible viewpoints but can only express a contradiction. An answer which excludes any reference to the question from which it arises and to which it responds can no longer be called an answer, but must be seen henceforth as a *proposition* or as a judgment. This concept of proposition has been chosen because it is neutral with respect to what it expresses, which can be a question or an answer. It affirms something and this is what really matters. Its own answerhood is repressed. The question–answer difference does not appear in the notion of a proposition, which is an "asexual" concept (meaning that the difference between question and answer is obliterated) with respect to this basic difference of thought, that of the question and the answer. A consequence of all this is that propositionalism has imposed itself as the new or as the only possible right conception of reason since Aristotle, who codified it in many respects. It stipulates that the judgment or the proposition is the most basic unit of thought, and the truth, A *or* not-A, as the implicit suppression of alternatives (i.e. of questions), is here viewed as the criterion of any "solution" of true judgments. A, as an entity or as the object of a proposition referring to it, is what it is and is nothing other than itself. A is a proposition saying A is true, and therefore, its opposite, not-A, is false. A cannot be anything else but A: it is its essence (*eidos*) which makes it what it is, namely A; this *essence* is its *reason* for being A rather than not-A. The world of essences is thus born; it is also the world of identities and reasons. In counterpart, the world of *answers* as such and therefore of Socratic questioning is dead as a possible foundation for philosophy. With propositionalism and the disappearance of questioning as such, through which one can express alternatives via answers of a specific kind that I have called *problematological answers*, rhetoric too disappears as a valid enterprise. If one defends A, and your interlocutor defends not-A, it is now seen as a matter of ignorance because one should know that both cannot be true at the same time. Rhetoric focuses rather on the problem at stake in the opposing views. For Plato, this is a weakness of reason, a deficit of rationality and science, based on weak (i.e. equivocal) identities, usually referred to as metaphors, analogies, similitudes, because they are approximate ways of expressing what in fact one does not literally (and then truly) know. Plato assimilated the poets to rhetoricians because they constantly resort to allusive and enigmatic discourse, susceptible to several interpretative answers. For Plato, they are both indifferent to truth, which must be apodictic, like geometry.

In contrast to his predecessor, Aristotle took rhetoric seriously. Unlike Plato, he does not think that the common good of a society can be imposed from top to bottom, by a narrow ruling elite supposed to know what is better for all inhabitants of the City. For Aristotle, the common good is always a matter for discussion and collective debate between citizens, and if indeed such debate occurs, there must be the possibility of contradictory viewpoints, let alone of differences. As a corollary, rhetoric is essential to civic life. In political assemblies, it is necessary to convince the majority of the members of the group gathered around the table by using arguments in favor of what is deemed to be the right solution for all. Before being a theoretical issue, rhetoric is a political one. What is the origin of this divergence between Plato and Aristotle? The brutal acceleration of history, which led to the end of the Greek city state in part explains such a difference. With Aristotle, even if obsolete answers (obsolete because they have become problematic) mingle with new ones indifferently (which are now the real answers, hence the possibility of sophistic), it is nonetheless possible to demarcate the two. How is it possible to establish a difference between both types of answers, which are, for the most part, formally alike? Aristotle's response is quite unambiguous. In order to draw a line of demarcation between the problematic propositions and the unproblematic ones, one must justify the latter. It is the necessary condition for them to become accepted and recognized as such. We must *argue* for what are considered to be the true answers. Otherwise, answers will remain problematic in the eyes of opponents who will reject those arguments by affirming that they are, as we say, "mere rhetoric." They will not even be seen as answers, even if they seem to be so by being arranged with style and eloquence. From this attitude derives the famous distinction between *rhetoric* as pleasant discourse and *argumentation* as composed of reasons and inferences.

Aristotle's rhetoric as *logos*-centered

Aristotle's contribution to rhetoric is essential: to him we owe the first treatise on rhetoric. In contrast to Plato, rhetoric exists as a useful and *sui generis* discipline. Since then, it has become impossible to write anything in the field without referring to Aristotle's work in some way or another. Why is his book so important, besides the fact that it was the first?

Aristotle's treatise on rhetoric, which in English is simply entitled *Rhetoric*, is composed of three parts. The unity of the whole has often been questioned. Each of the three books hardly displays any continuity with the two others. Each section deals with a different theme, even if each part (or book) is itself an important contribution to the rhetorical relationship. The *first book* is concerned with the definition of rhetoric as *logos* composed of reasoning and inferences, while the third bears on another use of *logos*, founded on style, such as that found in literature or everyday conversation, or funerary oratory. This second use of logos is meant to impress or please the audience. This is called rhetoric *stricto sensu* and, alongside argumentation, they both form the core of rhetoric as a discipline. Argumentation or dialectic is a discourse which has to decide explicitly between alternative statements through inference, which Aristotle calls the *enthymeme*. This technical word has been imagined to indicate that a conclusion is not asserted but is implied by the context which is composed of other statements, said or presupposed. This context is made of missing premises. Etymologically, *thymos*, in Greek, refers to the bodily site of our spontaneous use of the mind, as a kind of inner source enabling us to transform our feelings and "subjective" judgments into objective ones with a certain degree of likelihood. *Enthymeme* is characterized by Aristotle as missing certain premises, allowing the blanks they create to be filled by the audience itself, which is in need of a conclusion and which often reacts emotionally. The audience is then influenced and pleased by reaching that very conclusion. This could explain why the *second book* of the *Rhetoric* is devoted to the emotions or passions, i.e. to the reactions of the audience when confronted with a speaker or with an enthymeme.

Apart from the *enthymeme*, which is a deduction, we also find in Aristotle another type of reasoning, called induction, in which we usually compare two cases treated as examples of something more general, on the basis of similar features which draw attention to a more inclusive proposition. From these similarities, we infer that the consequences of the second case will be similar to the first. The most famous example given by Aristotle is that of Peisistratus asking for bodyguards. The generals who have done so in the past, and have even kept their army after a military campaign, have eventually seized power and subsequently suppressed civic freedom. So the Assembly of free citizens is distrustful when confronted with such a request: "The man who asks for a bodyguard is scheming to make himself a despot,"[5] let alone one who asks for a whole army. One need only look at what happened to Bonaparte after the Italian campaign: he kept his loyal army with him in order to exert pressure on parliament, the *Conseil des Cinq Cents,* and to grant him full powers. Caesar did much the same with his army on his return to Rome after the war in

---

[5] Aristotle, *Rhetoric*, tr. W. Rhys Roberts in J. Barnes, *The Complete Works of Aristotle* (Princeton: Princeton University Press, 1984), 1357 b37.

Gaul. Now, when a famous French general, who surrounded the General Assembly with tanks and soldiers, demanded full powers from parliament, then we can conclude that he, too, will be vested with Emergency Powers. This, indeed, is what De Gaulle did on May 13, 1958. If some powerful leader wants to keep a personal guard, by induction, we are justified in fearing that he will also try to obtain the same full powers. Democratic assemblies should be careful, then, not to allow this to happen if they want to spare their citizens from a possible military coup.

Linked to Aristotle's conception of the *enthymeme* is another famous theory, that of the *topoi* or commonplaces. A *topos* is a rejoinder that enables the speaker and the audience to find common ground to discuss and, a fortiori, arrive at a particular answer. This non-problematic feature of inference or acceptance can even itself be a rule of inference (such as respecting the principle of non-contradiction), but it can simply be some answer supposed to be shared by the speaker with the audience. This *topos* can also be an obvious saying or even a sentential platitude (e.g. "It is better to be in good health rather than to be ill"), invoked to stress the obviousness of the conclusion ensuing from it ("Then, we should avoid eating too much meat"). Finally, a *topos* can consist in a specific answer linked to a specific question or domain. To be inclusive of all these meanings, let us say that a *topos* is a reductor of problematicity (or *problematological reductor*), a bridge between *what* the speaker says and what the audience thinks or knows about what he says.

Among Aristotle's other achievements is the clarification of what dialectic, rhetoric, and sophistic distinctively are. Since Plato, dialectic has always been characterized as a verbal confrontation, in which one person defends A and his opponent, not-A. This is a view dating back to Socrates. The aim of the questioner is to refute the answerer, so that only the opposite solution remains. This solution obtains either because the opponent has invalid arguments, or because they are weak, or even because they rely on erroneous presuppositions. In all of these cases, the initial proposition A cannot be declared true. The aim of such a game is to win over the opponent, without necessarily supplementing this argument by a right argument thereafter. This is why, for Plato, one must distinguish sophistic, which is refutational, from dialectic; dialectic being predicated on the best arguments and being assimilated to science. Sophistry, in contrast, resorts to any argument, since it may defend weak or false ones. It often plays on words to achieve this and the relative indeterminacy of meaning allows for the most paradoxical conclusions, the important thing being to bring victory to one's client. For Aristotle, dialectic is not science and, like sophistic, it belongs to rhetoric. But sophistic is simply bad rhetoric: it upholds views that are just as false as their contrary, while dialectic is a confrontation between alternative viewpoints in which only one true solution can emerge.

For Plato, as we saw earlier, rhetoric and sophistic seem by and large to be identical. Their common aim is to manipulate the audience by flattering its emotions and by taking the clothes of reasoning, whereas in reality, they only play on words, on associations, on similitudes in sound or content. For Aristotle, in contrast, rhetoric is a serious discipline, based on reasoning (enthymeme or induction), while sophistic is not, because it is misleading, playing on the homonymy of words, for instance. Rhetoric, when defined as argumentation, uses reasoning whose conclusions are likely. And when defined by style or eloquence, it has an emotional impact on the audience, by causing pleasure or displeasure. Dialectic is no longer the question–answer relationship that Socrates saw at work in science and which Plato even identified with science. Rather, for Aristotle, dialectic is the question-and-answer duality as it is found in human confrontation, speaker and audience each taking the role of the other in turn. As for rhetoric *stricto sensu*, it is made of narratives to be recounted with eloquence (or elegance: the two words have the same root), of answers to questions which are thereby presented as solved, as if they had disappeared through the magic of discourse. Problematic statements may sound correct and non-problematic ones still questionable, hence the need to provide reasons and arguments to make the distinction between the two, in a world of historical acceleration which often mingles them when the pace of time is too fast, especially in political life. For Aristotle, rhetoric as argumentation is surely less ambitious than rhetoric as dialectic for Plato, but it "sticks" more to what happens in practice between people. And above all, rhetoric presents a rationality of its own, weaker than in science but surely more useful in many contexts of social, political, and everyday life in which the premises are left implicit. It even has a rationality of its own, based on deduction and induction, on the enthymemes and exemplification, respectively. Rhetoric at large includes rhetoric *stricto sensu*, based on style and eloquence, and argumentation based on reasoning. They are for Aristotle two sides of the same coin, far from sophistic which will always deceive people by inducing fallacious conclusions and speaking fine words. Rhetoric in its largest sense received from Aristotle a new dignity denied it by Plato, who focused on the manipulation of the audience rather than on the inner resources of language and reason, in which Aristotle placed rhetoric's new legitimacy. If rhetoric thus acquired a dignity in itself, its boundaries were nonetheless rather imprecise from the start, because it could be dialectical, argumentative, but also made of narratives, arranged in such a way as to be pleasant and eloquent. These are different modes of discourse and if there is rationality in eloquence, it is surely different from that of the enthymeme. We shall have to discover an underlying foundation to both and thereby supersede their division in order to provide the discipline with well-established boundaries and a unity which makes rhetoric a discipline in itself. This can only be achieved if a new conception of language and reason is favored, one based on questioning: I have called it *problematology*.[6]

For Aristotle, if sophistic plays on words by using homonymy (same sounds, different meanings) and ambiguity or impreciseness of definition to create identities or differences where there are none, it is because real life is *economical*: it would be tedious to clarify everything we say, specifically each of our words each time we use them. Interlocutors too have an imprecise knowledge (if not a relative

---

[6] For problematology as a new approach to philosophy, see M. Meyer, *Of Problematology*, tr. D. Jamison (Chicago: University of Chicago Press, 1995).

and variable ignorance) of each question at stake. Dialectic is different from sophistic in that it plunges us into the language of oppositions and, in a court of law, of confrontation. It requires clear arguments to win the case. Rhetoric, since it plays on language, seems more similar to sophistic than to dialectic, because it does not refute answers but is meant to offer answers of its own. Its conclusions are not necessarily refuted as in dialectic, i.e. as answers, they can be simply nuanced, completed, or re-qualified, sometimes even rejected. Even disagreement is not seen as a victory over an opponent but as one voice to be listened to, especially in the political sphere. Most of the time, rhetoric wants the impact of its discourse upon the audience to suggest another answer, but also simply to please the audience so that the audience will remain under the speaker's spell until the very end. If there is no refutation without argumentation, both are absent in rhetoric insofar as it is composed of narrative and productive discourse. Dialectic deals with the problematic in order to achieve a solution which ultimately eradicates the problem, while rhetoric operates on what is problematic on the basis of eloquent answers which enable the audience to gloss over or "repress" what is problematic. The "cause" is then also won, even if the audience could, formally speaking, take some distance of its own.

In the opening sentence of his *Rhetoric*, Aristotle offers one of the most enigmatic sentences of his entire corpus: "Rhetoric is the counterpart [*antistrophos*] of dialectic." What does he mean by the word "counterpart"? To begin a treatise supposed to shed light on a difficult subject by writing so obscure a sentence is probably not the best strategy. Yet Aristotle did precisely this. If he wrote such a sentence, it proves that things must have appeared sufficiently clear to him. In fact, the resolution of this enigma is not too difficult to find, if we accept the fact that rhetoric deals with the problematic in human affairs. Dialectic, or argumentation, and rhetoric *stricto sensu* are the two alternative ways of dealing with the questions faced by the rhetorician. They are two approaches the rhetorician can offer concerning these questions. Either, on the one hand, he directly faces the question, as in the law courts, where parties are confronted with explicit alternatives opposed according to the accusation and the defense. Or, on the other hand, he deals indirectly with questions by providing his answer without debate, acting as if the question had been eliminated by virtue of directly answering right from the start as if, as a result, the problem no longer existed and had thereby already been solved (as its corresponding implicit question shows). *One has only two strategies when faced with a given question*: either one puts it "on the table," so to speak, in order to grasp it directly and provide arguments in favor of what one counts as the right answer, or—and this is the second strategy—one puts the question "under the table," as if it is no longer at stake, because one directly offers some answer to it, without referring to the question. The approaches which consist in beginning with a question or in beginning with an answer are the only two possible ways of handling a question. This explains why Aristotle has affirmed that dialectic, which deals with an initial question explicitly as such, is the counterpart of rhetoric, which purports to begin by offering a discourse as answer and, in order to achieve this, to express this answer with the best possible elegance of style (also called eloquence) in the arrangement of things. This is where seduction or manipulation can occur, but most often discourse is merely pleasant. The difference between dialectic and rhetoric is thus a question of starting points.

Can we provide examples of rhetoric *stricto sensu* in the sense just defined? In this case, the speaker offers an answer to an underlying question as if that question had thereby been solved. This particular question, however, remains present in the background of the discussion as its underlying rationale.

One of the most compelling examples is drawn from advertising. Let us consider a famous instance: that of the mythic perfume Chanel N°5 (created in 1921 for Coco Chanel), the subject of many successful advertising campaigns. Each campaign was more eloquent than the preceding one, since each adapted its narrative to the vision that women entertained about themselves at the particular time. The difficulty with perfume advertisements is that they must convey the attractiveness of a scent through spectacle alone, i.e. through the television screen, from which no scent can emanate. This problem seems difficult to solve rationally. How, then, did the advertising agency proceed? The solution adopted was deduced from the problem itself, which is that a fragrance cannot solve any real-life problems. The goal of the advertisement is nonetheless to present the fragrance as a solution. But how can a fragrance abolish the problems of real life? It cannot do so unless the ad presents itself in the genre of a fairy tale, as a fiction, because in fairy tales all problems are solved or disappear magically, in contrast to real life. One of the advertisements for Chanel N°5 dramatizes Little Red Riding Hood who, having put on the perfume, tames the wolves who have come to eat her. Conquered by Chanel N°5, they all leave together to conquer Paris. A door suddenly opens upon an illuminated Eiffel Tower, as if Paris, symbolized by the Tower, were awaiting their charming presence. All this, of course, is impossible in real life, and no perfume can make impossible dreams come true. Fragrance as a solution may just be a fiction, but it is nonetheless a pleasant one. We would love to believe it to be true, hence we love this advertisement. Life's problems seem to have disappeared in the elegance of the message, if not in the elegance of the characters now pacified, specifically the subjugated wolves who were preparing to eat Little Red Riding Hood. The eloquence of the given answers is the rhetorical device through which a problem, though originating in real life, comes to be presented as solved even though this solution is a fiction. Rhetoric functions by swallowing problems through elegance and style. This is why it can create a pleasant feeling (or resolution), if not an illusion everybody would want to believe in. And this is also why all the campaigns in favor of Chanel N°5 have been so noteworthy and have worked so well. Rhetoric here purports to make all the problems vanish by magic, through the resort to fairy tales.

 Another important contribution of Aristotle's rhetoric is his vision of *pathos* as an emotional response. Aristotle's conception of the role of passions is paradoxical, in the sense that his rhetoric is essentially based on *logos*. Is it a revision of his theory? We can also interpret his analysis of emotions as the different kind of answers to a given *logos*, or envisaged as an enthymeme, or as an eloquent speech. In any case, he draws up a list of passions, of *pathè*, explaining the multitudinous responses open to an audience facing a speaker, or of a speaker analyzing his audience. For Aristotle, emotions are subordinated to *logos*, affecting and altering the judgments of the audience, if not of the speaker himself. Such an emotional response is still, however, a matter of *language* and of its impact.

The *Rhetoric* details fourteen passions: anger and calm, shame and impudence, love and hatred, fear and confidence, benevolence and pity (compassion), indignation and contempt, emulation and envy. These are the seven couples of antithetic responses which express our reactions to our social relationships, according to the inferior, equal, or superior status of our interlocutors. Let us consider an example: "The Princess takes a bath naked in front of her servants." She would feel ashamed doing so in front of the Prince because he is a prince, but she does not mind appearing undressed (impudence) in front of the people she considers inferior, as they are mere "things," lacking social existence in her eyes. Several emotions are close to one another in Aristotle but what marks their difference is the fact that the person for whom we feel something is equal, inferior, or superior. Contempt, for instance, addresses itself to those whom we consider as inferior. We would never react in such a way if we considered our interlocutor as superior or equal. Indignation, by contrast, is directed towards an equal, whose fate is viewed as undeserved, while anger would be impossible if expressed in response to someone who is viewed as superior. Benevolence is a friendly attitude towards an equal, while compassion is reserved for those who are felt as inferior, such as the homeless person we help in the street. The conclusion is that emotions are states of mind we publicly express to indicate to others what we think (or feel) about them and even about what they think (or feel) of us and of the relationship we have with them. In a sense, emotions serve as the correctives of interaction, when needed, as the indicators of what is deemed of that interaction. *Pathè* alter the judgments which would normally ensue from vested social relationships. An emotion is then a reflection of the relationship we pursue with each other, but is also a message about what to be done about it.

Distance, greater or smaller, is the usual response. In the history of philosophy, at least until Hume, passion was often recognized as the pristine form of subjectivity in a world where subjectivity could not be thematized as a philosophical concept per se or as a social reality, as will later become the case, with Descartes, Hobbes, Spinoza, Locke, and thematically, with Kant.[7]

As a conclusion, Aristotle's *Rhetoric* is undoubtedly the cornerstone of any study of rhetoric. Nonetheless, the impression that remains is one of incompletion and perhaps even of inconsistency in Aristotle's definition. Rhetoric seems separate from argumentation, as if they were two isolated and autonomous disciplines, even if one is said to be "the counterpart" of the other, for reasons Aristotle left unspecified. The core of Aristotle's rhetoric is certainly the prominent role he gives to the *enthymeme* (also known as an incomplete or truncated syllogism). Taken as a whole, Aristotle's view of rhetoric places greater emphasis on reasoning than it does on passions, at least if we grant the leading role to the first book of his *Rhetoric*. In the second book, the reverse seems to be true. Considering the importance he bestows on the *enthymeme* as the privileged form of reasoning in rhetoric, this second book appears to be a step backwards. If Aristotle attributes an important role to the emotions, to *pathos*, whose nature is to modify our judgment when faced with a particular conclusion, we could interpret the role of passions consistently in spite of the paradox of their role in a rhetoric dominated by *logos*. We can do so by holding the view that *logos* is a compelling force for both the speaker and the audience, by virtue of the inner force of reasoning alone, whatever the audience itself may feel as a result under specific circumstances of reaction. Aristotle often stresses the revolutionary character of his approach to rhetoric, especially when speaking of his predecessors, who failed to single out the role of the enthymeme and of *logos* in general: "These writers, however, say nothing about *enthymemes*, which are the substance of rhetorical

---

[7] S. Lukes, *Individualism* (Oxford: Blackwell, 1978) and, more recently, L. Siedentop, *Inventing the Individual* (London: Allen Lane, 2015).

persuasion, but deal mainly with non-essentials. The arousing of prejudice, pity, anger, and similar emotions has nothing to do with the essential facts."[8] Why, then, should we concede any substantial importance to the theory of emotions in rhetoric, if they do not result from *logos*? What is noteworthy in this approach, however, is that, contradiction or paradox aside, Aristotle is the first to grant the emotions a positive but subsidiary role in rhetorical theory that still deserves to find its place in a *logos*-centered view of rhetoric. Emotions and passions thereafter pertained to the field of psychology, philosophy and, since Hobbes, politics. Without the *pathè* or the emotions, how could the differences between speaker and audience be established?

The birth of propositionalism as *logos*-centered and its impact on a rhetoric without questioning

What is Aristotle's precise definition of rhetoric and what are its consequences for *logos*? If we look closely, Aristotle's definition is not as clear or self-evident as we might expect. "Rhetoric," he writes, "may be defined as the faculty of observing in any given case the available means of persuasion."[9] Aristotle seems to have in mind here a distinction between the use of the means of persuasion of an audience and the reflexive rhetorical discourse—called rhetoric—on these means. In other words, Aristotle's definition bears less on persuasion itself than on the study of how persuasion obtains. For Aristotle, rhetoric is not persuasion as such, nor is it, properly speaking, the study of persuasion; rather, rhetoric is the analysis of the means of persuasion that *logos* can provide. What exactly does Aristotle mean when he draws these distinctions? Once again, let us see if this problem cannot be clarified with the help of a view of rhetoric based on questioning. A question is at stake. An argument,

---

[8] Aristotle, *Rhetoric*, 1354 a14–18.   [9] Aristotle, *Rhetoric*, 1357 a23–25.

or even a figure, operates as a suggestion of an answer by asking the audience to infer this answer. In other words, a question and an answer is a duality which, in rhetoric, gives rise to another duality, that of the literal and the figurative, generally used in rhetoric *stricto sensu*, just as in argumentation we have an inference from the known or the given to the resolution of the unknown through reasoning. At the argumentative level, the process at work can be seen as an implication, in which A is a reason to think B, or is even the cause of B. At the rhetorical level, A can be seen as the figurative meaning of B, as a way of expressing things differently from common usage. In both cases, in rhetoric *stricto sensu* as in argumentation, when someone says A to convey B or imply it, then he is employing rhetoric. By affirming that *to say A is to say B*, he raises a question about the real link that can exist between A and B themselves, beyond the fact that to say the first is to say the second. Does B follow from A because the utterance B has followed from the utterance A or because B and A are themselves in a causal relationship? Both conclusions are distinct. "To say A is to say B" does not imply that A is the reason or cause of B, because A is only a reason to say B, though it also could be the reason for B itself: "Socrates has a temperature, thus he has fever" is a good inference—a persuasive one at any rate—but nobody would say that A is the cause of B, that high body temperature is a cause of illness, but nonetheless it is a good reason to infer that Socrates is ill (or may be ill). The reverse, however, is also true: illness is a cause of fever. Sometimes, however, "to say A is to say B" because A is the cause of B (or if you prefer, "A, then B"). For instance, if I say to my child that it is cold outside and that he should put his coat on, the reason to dress more warmly is the cold weather. It is a cause for B and a reason to say B. Rhetoric, for Aristotle, is the study of these different forms of relationship between A and B and the ground on which they can be established. Inference (or causality in general) is one among others. Identity, especially when based on words, also retains his attention in several of his treatises on contradiction. Persuasion, for Aristotle, means inferring an implicit conclusion inscribed within the structure of *logos* rather than having a given state of mind, although we can suspect that he is equating the two.[10]

Rhetoric, according to Aristotle, is not the means by which we persuade; it is rather "the faculty of discovery" of what has been used to generate that state of mind. In this sense, rhetoric is probably reflexive because the reflexive act of finding what will lead or suggest the conclusion sought belongs to the rhetorical practice itself, and ends up with a given rhetorical strategy. But are we so sure that Aristotle always clung to this view? In any case, he maintained this definition of rhetoric as an analysis of the means of persuasion through *logos*. Today we would instead say that rhetoric is made up of arguments and figures of speech meant to be arranged in some discourse (for example, a narrative or an argument) with the aim of influencing others, of persuading them, if not to please them; rhetoric is always associated here, in any case, with *what* is said, with the aim of having at least an impact on them through emotions. Rhetoric is the interpersonal use of language in everyday life. It may be conflictual, as in dialectic or argumentation, or it may bring people closer together, as in conversational situations when we wish to establish or emphasize a particular connection with them. It may also be intended to establish a certain distance between them and to indicate which distance is preferred by the speaker. With rhetoric, we can express, affirm, diminish, or increase the social distance between us and others, and make this distance known for professional or personal reasons, as we do when we like or dislike someone. That distance can vary, but for Aristotle this is not really what matters in rhetoric, for social links are already presupposed by the existing order of the City. The interesting question for him is not how we know that someone is persuaded or pleased, but how we can convey a determined belief by

---

[10] This may lie at the source of the distinction between persuasion and conviction. "You have persuaded me, but not convinced me" is a common saying meant to establish the difference between the speaker's uses of arguments and the negative response of the audience. I could be persuaded rationally and not be innerly convinced, for example in the case of belief in God. As an opponent to Pascal could have said, "*Je suis persuadé, mais pas convaincu*."

some reasoning when confronted with a plurality of solutions: "The subject of our deliberation (i.e. of the conclusion of our debates) is such as seems to present us with alternative possibilities."[11] If we have managed to make the other adopt the choice we favor, then we will have persuaded him or her. Aristotle sees the question when he should also integrate the distance it can represent as another important variable in rhetoric. The word *alternative* is another expression to denote *questions*, since questions, like A or not-A (e.g. "Are you coming tomorrow?"), display one alternative, just as the question "Who is coming tomorrow?" entails several ones. This is the root of the distinction between *elementary alternatives* (two opposite answers, one being true) and *complex alternatives* for which several answers are possible, as in the question, "what are you doing tomorrow?"

For Aristotle, dialectic is meant to refute one position and give arguments in favor of the other, while rhetoric seems more encompassing in that it also includes positive answers, forming texts or narratives and pleasant speeches without necessarily considering what the opposite view would be, i.e. by giving an array of arguments in favor of that position. In this sense, rhetoric is the positive side of refutation and also the condition of possibility of answering without contradicting. The interesting aspect of Aristotle's definition is that it does not restrict rhetoric to being the sole inverse of dialectic. As a matter of fact, Aristotle, without being explicit, allows for rhetoric to deal with questions as its subject matter. Nonetheless, he never offers a theory of questioning per se, one which is necessary for a complete view of rhetoric and he only refers himself to questioning in the last book of his *Topics* (Book VIII), where it is designed as a dialectical strategy to defeat the opponent. In other words, *problematology*[12]—or the study of questioning as the first and fundamental step and origin of philosophy—has not been adumbrated by Aristotle, in spite of many allusions to the notion of opposite viewpoints and of alternative positions. The basic reason for this "repression" of questioning, to use a Freudian term, is the legacy of Plato's view, which Aristotle never

---

[11] Aristotle, *Rhetoric*, 1357 a5.   [12] Meyer, *Of Problematology*.

fully renounced. When Aristotle realizes that there are other forms of arguments than apodictic ones, which are more flexible, less conclusive, and for which verisimilitude is enough and likelihood cannot be superseded in favor of certainty, he fails to analyze them as problematic, in the non-propositionalist conception of the term. Strong statements are apodictic truths, weak ones are rhetorical. How could rhetoric, then, deliver forms of propositionalist truth other than weak ones, if the ideal of propositionalism is apodictic truth and apodictic conclusions? Scientific syllogism is undoubtedly Aristotle's model, yet he cannot gloss over the reality and usage of those weaker forms of discourse in which probable conclusions also emerge, but without any scientific conclusiveness. Indeed, these represent the greater part of our reasonings in life. Paradoxically, the problematic, the questionable, though omnipresent in everyday life, remains unthought as such, as if rhetorical discourse were meant to save us from such a radical turn in thinking. Is rhetoric, then, merely a necessary handicap for reason, but still a handicap, by being less conclusive than logic, the template of rationality? But how can the existence and recognition of rhetoric as a valid way of inference and suggestion be accepted without giving room to the questionable which it is constantly addressing?

Let us then rehabilitate questioning. Problematology is the first philosophy that has taken radical questioning as its own object, even if radical questioning has been practiced by all major philosophers in the past. Problematology explicitly anchors thought in questioning and, as a consequence, thematizes the question–answer couple on which it is based. The basic unit of thinking is no longer a judgment or proposition but the *problematological difference, from which judgments only emerge to be considered as answers*. Why should questioning be viewed as the foundation of thought, that is, as its unique starting point? If we wish to offer an answer to that question, we must begin by raising the question of what is first (or fundamental). What could the latter be if not questioning itself? It is the only possible *answer* since any other answer would, as answer, presuppose *questioning*. Someone who would question this, for any reason whatsoever (reasons which are, in general, historically determined) and would disagree with our *answer*, would still be questioning, and he or she would thereby confirm precisely what he or she is denying. Philosophy was defined by Aristotle as the science of "the first principles."[13] If we adopt this definition of philosophy, we cannot but affirm that questioning is that very first principle. As a result, thinking derives from questioning by embodying it and is always embedded in it, in one form or another. Thinking is the way human beings articulate their answers to the problems that they have to face at each moment and that they express in the form of questions. Do we not first have to question, before arriving at an answer? In spite of the strength of this conclusion, most philosophers are reluctant to abandon propositionalism, even when faced with our times of radical questioning. This is probably because philosophers are, in this respect, like everyone else: they dislike what is problematic—problematic opinions, problematic viewpoints, and problematic norms and standards. Moreover, to render explicit the solution to problems is what counts most to philosophers; answers are their goal too and the questions, once solved, disappear from the field of view. As a consequence, is not the aim of questioning, in philosophy as elsewhere, to reach an answer? Why would questioning become its own object and supersede the propositionalist views of thought, language, and reason, even if propositions are in fact misconceived, being nonetheless answers but without questions? Today, however, things have changed: everything has become questionable. In public and in private life, in politics, in science, and in the humanities, even in our relationship to religion and God and, we could even say, in society in the largest sense, the problematic is everywhere, although it is still not always conceived of as such.

There are several reasons for the repression of questioning as the new foundation of thought, a repression which can be seen in the contemporary treatises on rhetoric. First, as stated earlier, people do not like what is problematic in their life; they would rather do away

---

[13] Aristotle, *Metaphysics*, I, 982 a4.

with it. Second, the whole tradition of philosophy has been centered on the model of science dominated by apodictic conclusions, where questions that are solved disappear, a model which, until Nietzsche, Marx, Freud, or Foucault and Derrida, was still widely accepted but came to be "deconstructed" because of its numerous internal contradictions, giving rise not to a new philosophy but limiting itself to the deconstruction of the older one. Deconstruction purports to bring to light the presuppositions of the old propositionalist model, without going beyond it, except in a "nihilistic" aspect. For Foucault, the traditional view of reason had to be seen as a form of power and domination. There is no room, however, for a new philosophically radical discourse in this enterprise. There is no will to construct something else instead; philosophy thereby became abandoned to emptiness, to the void of Nothingness (Heidegger), to the hidden "will to power" of those who cling to literal discourse as the only one deserving to be called truth-bearing or left open by radical deconstruction.

Third, the first principles proposed in the past have always been Being, God, the Subject (Descartes) or Consciousness (Locke) and not questioning, in spite of the fact that they all have been *given* as *answers*, even though those who justified them as answers were radical questioners, like Socrates or Descartes. How could they have ignored the fact that God, Consciousness, or subjectivity were actually *answers* to the question of what is considered to be first and foundational? They did so, however, because they were implicitly assuming from the very beginning that an answer is that which eliminates itself *as answer* when it eventually eliminates the question to which it is an answer. Being, God, and the subject could never have emerged as first *answers*, but rather as the first object of a first true proposition (without question), confirming the primacy of apodictic foundationalism, one which, in the eyes of propositionalist metaphysicians, excludes any alternative judgment. But this is an unquestioned conception of what an answer should be, even for our radical questioners of the past, a conception based on the repression of questions in the guise of solution. The awkward consequence of such a presupposition is that propositions seem, in the end, to come from nowhere, or, as in the case of deductions (whether scientific or not), from one another. The necessity of upholding the necessity of necessity as the norm of *logos* is in no way necessary and could hardly be proven without infinite regress. It is therefore highly questionable. If the very definition of truth is only propositional, questions disappear from thought, and when they do not, they are turned into some propositional modality.

Fourth, since the propositional model of thought seems to be well-adapted to the arrangement of results in science, this view has enormous appeal in philosophy, which aspires to be as fruitful and certain as science. Since Plato, philosophers have always been fascinated by the progressive and cumulative aspect of science, of which philosophy seems deprived. What is most characteristic of science is its apodicticity, and what is apodictic excludes alternatives; this even seems to be the aim for pursuing apodicity. But a paradox emerges in this attitude. The underlying problem here is to make all problems disappear. This "secret" foundation gives rise to an inconsistent view of propositionalism as composed of "answers" to a problem that cannot even be formulated since it is a problem. For such a model of thinking, a science of the problematic is a contradiction in itself. Since science actually works very efficiently, why should thought, in the largest sense of the word, renounce such a model and not struggle for the same efficiency? Last but not least, this repression of questioning in philosophy is to many a philosopher and rhetorician something reassuring with respect to their vested institutional practices and routines of research. Novelty often appears frightening. It is as though they had the deeply entrenched feeling of being deprived of their academic past, or fear the reproach that they might have been wrong during their career. In sum, most of us do not like what is problematic. We do prefer certainties, even if certainty sometimes leads us in the wrong direction, in life as in thought. And this probably explains the success and resilience of propositionalism, in spite of its drawbacks and flaws. By modeling itself on science, propositionalism has imposed itself as the true and ideal conception of thought in the larger sense. And this explains why Socratism, with its emphasis on questioning, disappeared once and for all in the bottle of hemlock that Socrates swallowed.

As for rhetoric, it is ambiguous from the propositionalist view of reason, since it plays on alternatives, on different possible answers, treating opposite viewpoints as if they all could be acceptable and as if questionable answers could be admitted. Rhetoric has always been seen as a by-product of reason, an offshoot of propositionalism in waiting. But the fact remains that, in rhetoric, one has A *and* not-A because real people oppose one another in simultaneously holding mutually contradictory propositions. If this were not the case, there would never be any debate. Even at the end of a debate, no party can be sure that he or she is *right* and has *the* true and only answer, but rather that he or she has merely reached a likely or a useful one. Maybe the opponent also has good arguments. For that reason, no one can definitively label the opposite answer as simply "false." This is also why we say that rhetoric deals with the problematic, and why the problematic is a positive step for thought, the first step necessary for reaching the solution, which, in a sense, already belongs to it. The problematic is not solely the expression of a contradictory position but, by expressing different viewpoints, is also the positive expression of distinct viewpoints, which may even be equally valid.

The Roman vision of rhetoric or the privileged status of the speaker

After Plato and the primacy of *pathos*, after Aristotle and the primacy of *logos*, Cicero offers the primacy of *ethos*. In the wake of Aristotle's treatise, the next great breakthrough in rhetoric was achieved by Roman rhetoricians. If the most innovative surviving voice is Cicero, the most synthetic is certainly Quintilian, a century later. After Quintilian, imperial power, and later Christianity, became less and less tolerant of open debate, the former for political reasons, the latter for dogmatic ones. The Roman contribution nonetheless remains essential to rhetoric. The basic feature of Roman rhetoric is the privileged role attributed to *ethos*, to the orator, in contrast to *logos* in Greek rhetoric.[14] Cicero, indeed, devotes an entire book to the role of the speaker, entitled *De Oratore*. What are the virtues of a good orator, if not the good itself? Virtue is the human capacity to enact and vindicate what is good for humanity. It is thus the ultimate argument. More specifically, the value of what is said depends on the value of who says it. The authority of the speaker is what counts and this authority is often political or, at least, social. *Ethos* thus became the metonymical name for the dominance of *ethics* and virtue in the definition of the persuasive. *Ethos* is identified with the speaker, what he *is*, what he claims to be and that in the name of which he asks to be trusted and followed. *Ethos* has to provide the credibility, the authority of the speaker; "We may apply *ethos* whenever he speaks of what is honorable and expedient[15] or of what ought or ought not to be done."[16]

In the Roman world, oratory is a social institution, as the title of Quintilian's synthetic work reminds us. This synthesis of rhetoric is based on the right or the opportunity to speak on a given matter in various codified circumstances. Such a right is socially defined and determines the rhetorical genre adopted. Roman society, in contrast to Classical Greece, is hierarchical and aristocratic. When someone speaks and what he speaks about depend on who he is, to say nothing of his political role and social position. This predefines the type of speech that is expected and considered as legitimate (i.e. convincing) by the audience. Authority is not only a matter of expertise, of technical skill or knowledge of the questions at stake, or even of humanistic virtue, but is directly linked to the role of the speaker in society and the

---

[14] The Greeks were led to reinvent the totality of *logos* when *mythos* and its religious explanation of the cosmos and the social world proved fictitious. They thus created metaphysics, logic, biology, physics, rhetoric, and so forth, to explain what happened in the world as well as in the mind. The Romans inherited this Greek world view. They did, however, add their own perspective to this way of thinking, with remarkable innovations in art (most notably in painting and in architecture) as well as in law.

[15] Expedient here means convenient, useful, appropriate, and opportune.

[16] Quintilian, *Institutes of Oratory* [also called *The Orator's Education*], tr. H. Butler (Cambridge, MA: Loeb Classical Library, Harvard University Press, 1921), 6, 2, 9–13. An excellent edition in one volume has recently appeared, translated by John Selby Watson, edited by Curtis Dozier and Lee Honeycutt, New York, 2015.

place he occupies in the social hierarchy: the speaker fulfils his *ethos* by displaying the virtues of his role. This makes a big difference to the way the arrangement of discourse is conceived, an arrangement (*dispositio*) which, to a large degree, is what Romans understand by rhetoric. For Quintilian, for instance, "rhetoric is the art of speaking well,"[17] an *ars bene dicendi*, and, as we all now know, because the way each one of us speaks depends on the convenience of speech, is often determined by his social background and education. Discourse does not begin democratically, as in Classical Greece, with the exposition of a question which poses an explicit problem, as Aristotle claimed,[18] but begins rather with an engaging answer, intended to render the audience attentive and receptive to the speaker's solution. In Roman rhetoric, interest in the question is not so much to be created or vindicated at the beginning of the speech, but more attention is given to the formal aspects of the answer, the ways in which it is expressed, as expected from this or that speaker. The exception, even for Aristotle, is the legal case, probably because court is already an institutional setting, even in democratic Greece. Hence, the fascination of Roman rhetoricians for legal rhetoric.

As we have said before, this fact raises the fundamental question of what the best arrangement of a speech should be, beginning with the *exordium*, where the question to be discussed is already considered by the audience to be relevant and interesting in the context in which it takes place. Given this difference between Greek rhetoric, on the one hand, which is based on the question to be solved, and Roman rhetoric, on the other hand, which starts from an *exordium* stressing the answers, we can now bring out the basic features of rhetorical discourse as they have been theorized by Roman rhetoric. The latter hinges on the speaker's ability to arrange his answers according to four basic criteria: in 1), we have the *inventio*, in which the speaker has to *find* the right answers in favor of his cause or those which are the most pleasant; in 2), we have the *dispositio* or the *arrangement* of answers according to the various arguments and counterarguments

---

[17] A famous definition is to be found in the *Institutes*, 2, 15, 38.
[18] Aristotle, *Rhetoric*, bk. III, ch. 13, 1414 a30.

which can be proposed during a debate, which must in any event end with a conclusion; in 3), the speaker must respect a certain style—this is what is called *elocutio* or the expression of speech; and to achieve this, 4), the speaker must utter his discourse (*actio*) by 5) using his memory (*memoria*). These 4) and 5) elements are sometimes conflated into one phase, which is simply called the speech utterance, in which the speaker garners all the arguments and the conclusions on a given question in the best order. *Invention* is by far the most important part of speech for the Romans, and that is why Cicero devoted a whole book to its analysis.[19]

Invention is used for the six parts of a discourse: the Introduction, Statement of Facts, Division, Proof, Refutation, and Conclusion. The Introduction is the beginning of the discourse, and by it the hearer's mind is prepared for attention. The *Narration* of Statement of Facts sets forth the events that have occurred or might have occurred. By means of the *Division* we make clear what matters are agreed upon and what are contested, and announce what points we intend to take up. Proof is the presentation of our arguments, together with their corroboration. *Refutation* is the destruction of our adversaries' arguments. The *Conclusion* is the end of the discourse, formed in accordance with the principles of the art.[20]

The aim of the speaker, according to Roman rhetoric, is to be approved or at least be recognized in his position, by being seen to embody the human or humanistic values associated with *Romanitas*, such as courage or determination, wisdom or experience, mastery of the subject or elegance (eloquence) of style.

In fact, three actions summarize the three goals of rhetoric:[21] *delectare, movere,* and *docere,* as Cicero put it in the *De Oratore.*[22] These aims

---

[19] Cicero, *De Inventione* [*On Invention*], tr. H. M. Hubbell (Cambridge, MA: Loeb Classical Library, Harvard University Press, 1949).
[20] *Rhetoric to Herennius,* tr. H. Caplan, bk. I, III, falsely attributed to Cicero (Cambridge, MA: Loeb Classical Library, Harvard University Press, 1954), p. 9.4.
[21] M. C. Clarke, *Rhetoric at Rome* (London: Routledge, 1996), p. 50. See also G. Kennedy, *The Art of Rhetoric in the Roman World* (Princeton: Princeton University Press, 1972), pp. 103–230.
[22] Cicero, *De Oratore,* II, 128 (Cambridge, MA: Loeb Classical Library, Harvard University Press, 1942). (English translation D. Sutton, *About the Speaker*).

were then taken up again in Quintilian's *Institutes*.[23] They represent the Latin equivalents of *ethos*, *logos*, and *pathos*. To *please*, to *teach*, to *move* constitute the basic and commanding triptych of Roman rhetoric. 1) To *please* is to present oneself as an adequate speaker, to fit the situation well and to exemplify the necessary personal virtues required to inspire credibility. It is expressed in features of discourse that are called *epideictic*, i.e. charming and pleasing, and capable of captivating an audience or, at least, of inducing it to listen with attention and receptivity to *what* is at stake in the speaker's speech. 2) To *prove* is the basis of reasoning; it requires argumentative skill, specific knowledge (for instance, of law), but also the mastery of philosophy in one's personal life as well as displaying it in one's speeches, in order to highlight the answers to be given to the essential issues of life, as the ultimate objects of debate. It is the moment of *narratio*, where questions ensue from one another, sometimes after answers have been made explicit. They may refer to alternatives which give rise to contradictory reasoning and the exposition of their solutions. They can also be presented as already solved by rhetorical narratives, with appropriate figures of speech that make up the type of style which is the most appropriate to the subject. Discourse must be topical, i.e. refer to the "right" questions or the relevant ones for the audience. 3) The third and last component of Roman rhetoric is the stirring of emotions: *movere*. It is what we expect from well-narrated stories; they move the feelings of the audience in the direction the speaker wants.

For the Romans, these three dimensions may be accentuated according to the particular circumstances, giving rise to a specific mode of speaking, but the three of them always mingle in variable proportions in any speech. As a result, it is not always easy to separate these components from one another. The pleasant aspects of discourse, for instance, can be very emotional too, according to the speaker's strategy.

---

[23] Quintilian, *Institutes*, 12.10.59 and 3.5.2.

What does the Aristotelian view of rhetoric have in common with its Roman counterpart?

At this stage in our historical reconstruction, it is interesting to recapitulate the points of divergence and convergence between Greek and Roman rhetoric. Both conceptions of rhetoric deal with the problematic in a particular way, by resolving it or by presenting its resolution with a certain degree of likelihood, usefulness, or pleasantness. If the Greeks after Aristotle emphasized *logos*, the question or subject matter, the Romans took *ethos* as their starting point. The value of the speaker and the values defended by him as well as the quality his reasoning do not, however, change the common goal, which is resolution. For Aristotle, speech is mostly divided into two parts—staging the problem and inventing its solution, even if, a few lines later in his *Rhetoric*, he appears to favor a more complex division.[24] For the Romans, the four parts of rhetorical speech are also supposed 1) to present the speaker as the right person (*ethos*), 2) to defend the particular issue at stake, as will be done later with arguments (*logos*), 3) before the audience (*pathos*) concludes accordingly that the answer given to the question is the right one (by being convincing or pleasant). The question which has been initially raised has disappeared *as a question* in the proposed conclusion. The speaker has had the advantage of mobilizing his own resources (*ethos*) by expressing through his speech (*logos*) what the audience is most likely to approve of, given its feelings on the matter (*ethos→logos→pathos*).

The long agony of rhetoric

Rhetoric has been definitely and decisively construed as *ethos*-centered, *logos*-centered, and *pathos*-centered with Cicero, Aristotle, and Plato respectively. These orientations will return throughout the whole history of rhetoric, with variations certainly, but without

---

[24] Aristotle, *Rhetoric*, bk. III, 1414 a30–1415 a15, but the discussion on the various parts of speech can be found up to 1420b.

altering the underlying rationale and structure of rhetoric as defined by these Founding Fathers.

Even if several authors have written on rhetoric in the Middle Ages,[25] such as Augustine, they have not added anything essential to the work of their predecessors. Their contribution belongs rather to the continuation of Ancient Rhetoric, while also beginning to stress that part of rhetoric devoted to the poetic amplification of language initiated by Longinus, in the third century AD, with his treatise, *On the Sublime*, where Longinus focuses on style and amplification in the use of the figures of rhetoric, seeing the latter as the template of rhetoric itself. As the new physics develops in the Renaissance, reasoning will progressively vanish from the discipline, just as open debate will desert European civilization in those times of religious confrontations. Dialectic as the narrative core of education was still practiced in university debates during the Middle Ages, as attested to by the contradictory discussions (*quodlibet*) of Aquinas in his *Summa Theologica*. But it was mainly used to confront Aristotle with the Holy Scriptures in order to bring out a synthesis of both. Apart from this ambition of philosophical or theological confrontation, rhetoric will weaken in each of its other goals, especially the civic ones and the scientific ones, abandoning them more and more to other disciplines, and losing more and more ground, when compared with theology (in which emotions became the expression of sins), or with metaphysics (in which amplification is the means of glorifying God). With time, rhetoric would shrivel, eventually reduced to a mere discursive tool of embellishment for courtiers or poets, who were averse to literal discourse for obvious reasons. Rhetoric has, in other words, emptied itself of its problem-solving features: "The apparent decline of rhetoric during the Middle Ages was reversed during the Renaissance, when rhetoric, mainly because of the rise of humanism, achieved an importance that is difficult to overestimate."[26]

---

[25] See J. Murphy, *Rhetoric in the Middle Ages* (Berkeley and Los Angeles: University of California Press, 1974).

[26] T. Conley, *Rhetoric in the European Tradition* (Chicago: University of Chicago Press, 1990), p. 109.

However, it was rhetoric *stricto sensu* rather than argumentation which increased in importance here, as the study of the techniques of resolution was increasingly left aside. Rhetoric as humanism was based on a new role for *ethos*, more or less focused on *ethics*, on the humanity of men as the ultimate source of value, rather than on *ethos* as the character and exemplary value of the speaker. This intellectual backdrop was reinforced by the appearance and spread of a new religion: Protestantism. Rhetoric became the language of preaching for or against Protestantism, in a period of intense religious rivalry and political violence. Dialectic, in spite of Peter Ramus' work (1555) on the subject, also lost its constitutive role of *inventio*, thereby benefitting analysis as it would later be formalized by Descartes (1637). The general trend in the evolution of rhetoric from the Renaissance to our present times is a restriction of rhetoric, as Genette calls it.[27] "Rhetoric restrained" is the keyword of that evolution because the remaining area for rhetoric came down to the study of the figures of speech, understood as ways of saying in a figurative and ornamental way what could or sometimes, as in poetry, could not be, said literally, or even translated literally.[28] In any case, from the seventeenth century onward, it was Dumarsais' famous book on *Tropes* (1730), followed a century later by Fontanier's *Traité général des figures du discours* (*General Treatise on the Figures of Speech*, 1827), which came to dominate the field. At the same time, traditional rhetoric became revitalized by religion, especially in the conflict between the Reformation and the Counter-Reformation. Rhetoric in England followed the movement, by focusing on the right criteria for persuasion, as expounded in Bishop Whately's *Elements of Rhetoric* (1828) for instance, and "continued to be backward-looking," as Conley puts it.[29] Whately wished to adapt Aristotelian rhetoric to the doctrinal necessities of persuasion of his own times, while Hugh

---

[27] G. Genette, "Rhetoric Restrained," in *Figures of Literary Discourse*, tr. A. Sheridan (Oxford: Blackwell, 1982), p. 103.
[28] Paul Ricoeur, *The Rule of Metaphor*, tr. R. Czerny, with K. McLaughlin and J. Costello (London: Routledge, 2003).
[29] Conley, *Rhetoric in the European Tradition*, p. 240.

Blair, a century earlier, had not innovated much either, when in his *Lectures on Rhetoric*, he focused on taste and style in order to bring to the fore the aesthetic aspect of rhetoric against the backdrop of its other features. As for Campbell's *Philosophy of Rhetoric*, it was meant to adapt rhetoric to the empiricist point of view, as developed by David Hume, in order to account for the empirical features of rhetoric, such as persuasion, by relying on the empirical characteristics of the mind such as those developed by Hume in his *Treatise of Human Nature*, such as feelings or probability.

The turning point in the curtailment of the rhetorical field is undoubtedly to be found in Descartes' scientific revolution. His four rules of method, expounded in his famous *Discourse on the Method*, is the official moment when rhetoric is consecrated as no longer argumentative, or inventive, and associated with the acquisition of knowledge, which Ramus called dialectic. What are these four rules, what do they say, and what is their relationship to rhetoric? If we look at them closely, they translate the four main parts of rhetorical discourse into the analytical language of mathematical problem-solving, definitively displacing into the domain of scientific method what rhetoric hoped it could contribute to knowledge by structuring argumentative speech.

First rule:
Never to accept anything as true if I did not have evident knowledge of its truth: that is, carefully to avoid precipitate conclusions and preconceptions, and to include nothing more in my judgments than what presented itself to my mind so clearly and so distinctly that I had no occasion to doubt it.[30]

What does Descartes propose here? He suggests that the only way to deal with a question is to discover (*inventio*) what can be established as out of the question. This will lead the mind to generate apodictic arguments, which by nature exclude opposite arguments, arguments which could have otherwise been held to be equally probable or, as

---

[30] Descartes, *The Philosophical Writings*, tr. J. Cottingham et al. (New York: Cambridge University Press), vol. 1, p. 120.

Descartes dubbed them, "doubtful." To sum up, the first rule can be paraphrased in the following way: *eradicate the question; exclude the alternatives (considered as doubtful propositions because one cannot really distinguish between the probable, which is sometimes true, from the false since they look the same); find the logical arguments, the right propositions that comply with the necessity of observing necessity in discourse, as science does, and more especially mathematics, where certainty is thereby guaranteed.* The first rule can be epitomized by saying that it is necessary to find a necessary initial proposition which will make the question disappear and command the entire chain of answers. What rhetoricians once called *inventio* is now transformed into Descartes' first rule for attaining true *knowledge* as defined by the propositionalist model of science.

Second rule:
To divide each of the difficulties I examined into as many parts as possible, and as might be required in order to resolve them better.[31]

This second rule of the method to acquire scientific knowledge is also clearly borrowed from rhetoric. In the *dispositio*, it is necessary to divide and expound all arguments one by one, arranging them according to the criterion of the *pro et contra*. This is no longer necessary here due to the rule of exclusion of alternatives stipulated by the first rule. What remains are the different propositions established as true and certain, and this becomes the basic rule of decomposition of complex truths into simple ones, also called, since the Greeks, *analysis*.

Third rule:
To direct my thoughts in an orderly manner, by beginning with the simplest and most easily known objects in order to ascend little by little, step by step, to knowledge of the most complex, and by supposing some order even among objects that have no natural order of precedence.[32]

---

[31] Descartes, *The Philosophical Writings*.
[32] Descartes, *The Philosophical Writings*.

In other words, after analysis comes synthesis, which was assimilated to *elocutio* in rhetoric and which puts back into orderly speech or coherent narrative what has been decomposed into various elements. One unravels the elements of the solution in order to express them in a coherent system of narrative resolution.

Fourth rule:
To make enumerations so complete, and reviews so comprehensive, that I could be sure of leaving nothing out.[33]

This last rule is only astonishing if we lose sight of the fact it is a transformed version of what rhetoricians once called *memoria*. In itself, it is useless when we practice science or mathematics. We follow an order of resolution, and when it is completed, it is over. Why go back on every step, to check that nothing has been left out, if the solution has been reached? But that is not the aim of this rule. The aim of this rule is to complete the transformation of dialectic into an analytic method of resolution, such as that found in the physical sciences, especially those which make use of mathematical equations. Borrowed from rhetoric, *memoria* undergoes an analytic treatment, the goal of which being to use what could have been creative in rhetoric if it had not, so to speak, been rhetoric. Dialectic once had that inventive power, but no longer.

What is left to rhetoric, if not solely the flowers of speech found in literary works and in figurative language in general? Argumentation has now been expelled from rhetoric and has been transformed into a new form: scientific discourse. An argument is now exclusively defined as a scientific reasoning or a demonstration, a piece of calculus or an experiment based on observed facts, used deductively or inductively in a chain of statements held to be theoretically sound for the purpose of explaining the phenomena.

After rhetoric has been reduced to style and its figures of speech, the main question was to know what remains of rhetoric. Would rhetoric regain its former territories once the influence exerted by

[33] Descartes, *The Philosophical Writings*.

Dumarsais and Fontanier, with their arbitrary and scholastic catalogs of figures, was exhausted? Rhetoric, as Aristotle understood it, i.e. as a combination of argumentation and figurative discourse, would experience a definite revival, when the focus of philosophy began to turn toward language. And this revolution in rhetoric was mainly due to Perelman's *New Rhetoric* and Toulmin's *Uses of Argument*, both published in 1958, despite other forms of renewal in approaches to rhetoric having also progressively emerged throughout the twentieth century by focusing more and more on language.

The revival of rhetoric in the twentieth century

The resurgence of rhetoric in the twentieth century responded to the same problem as its emergence in Greece and Rome, even if some authors have privileged the role of *ethos*, while others focused on *pathos*, and most of them on *logos*, in virtue of the increased importance of language in philosophical studies from Wittgenstein onwards. Rhetoric always develops under the pressure of history accelerating its pace. Old answers become problematic, coexisting with the new ones which are not, thus creating a possible confusion between old and new which necessitates a procedure to demarcate them (i.e. argumentation). Arguments are meant to justify the answers one is willing to accept as such, while rhetoric *stricto sensu* is a way of speaking of the problematic without going any further, as if it did not matter that the non-problematic had become questionable. Figurative language has a way of maintaining the old literal identities, thereby giving rise to fiction, while argumentative language fights to delineate areas of validity in spite of the losses in scope. The Greek classical world, the Italian Renaissance, and the world of the twentieth-century's intellectual revolutions have brought an acceleration of history, with its conflicts and debates, with its obsolescence of answers, especially ideological ones—this opposition between the old and the new being the main ingredient in any renewal of rhetoric.

Table 1 shows a broad classification of the main key names or movements of rhetoric in the twentieth century. Many other rhetoricians have

Table 1 The major theoreticians of rhetoric of the twentieth century

	Ethos (the weight is on the speaker)	Logos (the weight is on language)	Pathos (the weight is on the impact and the role of the audience)
Rhetoric as style, based on figures, aiming at education, edification, or pleasure	Dramatization (K. Burke, 1950)	Structuralist Rhetoric (Group Mu, 1970)	Rhetoric as the theory of misunderstanding (I. A. Richards, 1936). Theories of Evaluation as Metarhetoric (R. Weaver, H. Johnstone, L. Bitzer, C. Willard,... 1953–89)
Rhetoric as reasoning, as argumentation, or as the new dialectic	Speech-Act Theory (Austin 1962, Searle, 1969) and its pragma-dialectical extension (F. Van Eemeren and R. Grootendorst, 1984) The Theory of Communicative Action (J. Habermas, 1981)	The New Rhetoric (C. Perelman, 1958) The Modalization of Arguments (S. Toulmin, 1958) Theory of Argumentative Connectives (O. Ducrot, 1972) Informal Logic (A. Blair and R. Johnson, 1980, H. D. Walton, 1987)	Hermeneutics (H. G. Gadamer 1960) Reception Theory or the Reader as Audience (H. R. Jauss, 1972; W. Iser, 1976)

followed one or several of the schools of thought mentioned above in the pursuit of their own view of rhetoric. Even if they often diverge from these schools in one or several aspects, they do not really propose theories that are as new or innovative as those in the table. This is why a few words of explanation should be given on what each of these names represent for rhetoric. Doing so will enable us to see in what respect the authors mentioned in Table 1 brought something really new to rhetoric and in what sense they have been able to rejuvenate it after so many centuries of scholastic analysis of figures of speech. Nowadays, most rhetorical studies focus more on rhetoric than on its *modus operandi* and ought to be rather called *metarhetoric*. These studies bear, for instance, on the nature of evaluation, communication, validity or fallacy, inference or the nature of the audience, and so forth. Most of the key names are well known, such as Wayne Booth,[34] Christopher Tindale,[35] James Crosswhite,[36] or Stephen Yarbrough.[37]

a) I. A. Richards and the Philosophy of Rhetoric

Richards defines rhetoric as the "study of misunderstanding and its remedies."[38] By using the same words, each of us gives others the impression that the meaning to which these words refer is identical for everyone, whereas others may well have something different in mind. This can lead to the manipulation of minds when the process is intentional, but it can also be unintentional, resulting in impressions of undue consent and perfunctory agreement. Let us consider a few examples. Everyone is in favor of justice, freedom, and the like, but can anyone claim to understand these terms as everyone else does? Rhetoric emerges in the interstices of linguistic ambiguity which

---

[34] W. C. Booth, *The Rhetoric of Rhetoric* (Oxford: Blackwell, 2004).

[35] C. W. Tindale, *Acts of Arguing: A Rhetorical Model of Argument* (Albany: SUNY, 1999); *Rhetorical Argumentation: Principles of Theory and Practice* (Thousand Oaks, CA: Sage, 2004).

[36] J. Crosswhite, *The Rhetoric of Reason* (Madison: University of Wisconsin Press, 1996).

[37] S. Yarbrough, *After Rhetoric* (Carbondale, IL: Southern Illinois University Press, 1999).

[38] I. A. Richards, *Philosophy of Rhetoric* (Oxford: Oxford University Press, 1936), p. 3.

ensues from the use of a common and public language. Why do we have a *pathos*-centric view of rhetoric here? What makes language rhetorical is the absence or rather the impossibility of availing oneself of a completely univocal language. Each word, each sentence, let alone each group of sentences or text (or narrative), supply an abundance of possible readings and possible interpretations—even opposing ones—a fact which provides rhetoric with a play on ambiguity not only possible but unavoidable. The weight of this rhetoric is carried by the audience, which must unravel these multiple readings, discuss them, assess them in function of what it is itself ready or unwilling to accept. Above all, rhetorical ambiguity allows each one of us to draw conclusions according to one's values as an audience, and those conclusions are always influenced by accepted judgments and the feelings to which they give rise. Misunderstanding is fundamentally, then, an appeal to *pathos*, to disambiguation by the audience.

b) C. Perelman (and L. Olbrechts-Tyteca) and The New Rhetoric

Perelman's work is a landmark contribution to the study of rhetoric in the twentieth century.[39] With him, rhetoric undergoes a deep revolution and renewal, a fact which has made him probably the standard reference both on the continent and in the English-speaking world. His work may be put on equal footing with that of Cicero or Quintilian and will no doubt be read as such in the coming centuries.

---

[39] I have often heard and read comments on the role of Lucie Olbrechts-Tyteca in *The New Rhetoric*, in which Perelman is said to have minimized or even exploited her contribution to the Treatise. For someone like me, who knew them both closely for more than a decade, such a suspicion is nonsense. It is worth recalling that Perelman was hidden during the war and protected by Lucie Olbrechts and her husband who, being much older than he, treated him like the son they never had and this affectionate relationship prevailed until Perelman's premature death in 1984. I can testify that the friendship between Perelman and Olbrechts was a true and reciprocal one, without any question of rivalry or wish to exploit the other—indeed, quite the contrary. Their complicity and complementarity were remarkable. Perelman very often called on Olbrechts to discuss his papers, his books, his lectures and was always very grateful to receive her comments. As for their respective contribution to *The New Rhetoric*, I cannot add anything to the excellent analysis of D. Frank and M. Bolduc, 'Lucie Olbrechts-Tyteca's *New Rhetoric*', *Quarterly Journal of Speech*, vol. 96, no. 2, pp. 141–63.

I say this with all the more conviction since, despite having been his assistant for more than a decade and his successor to the Chair of Rhetoric for more than three decades thereafter, I do not share his view of rhetoric, which I find too propositionalist. Nevertheless, he was a generous thinker because, when I developed my own philosophy, *problematology*, he supported it with enthusiasm, accepting the fact that rhetoric dealt more with questions in debates than with theses.

The main originality of Perelman's "New Rhetoric" lies in his systematic approach to an extended conception of rationality based on non-logical arguments, which have a rationality of their own. He argued that the latter can deliver strong conclusions through a specific type of rationality which is neither experimental nor logical. These conclusions are nonetheless as *convincing* as any other type of inference. Argumentation is the method of reasoning best suited to the rationality required in dealing with human subject matters, particularly when, as is most often the case, it is impossible to demonstrate anything conclusive about such questions, as in ethics, for instance. This is also the reason why Perelman put so much emphasis on legal rhetoric and the role of the judge. Only law enables people to decide between alternative and conflictual views, since everyone usually wants to be "in his or her right" to act as he or she does, when ethical standpoints buttress their conflicts.

The questions dealt with by rhetoric are important, if not essential: they concern law, our way of life, religion, social conduct, and so forth, because we can only give arguments in the form of reasons when we have thoughts to believe in or motives to act upon. What is the rationality of such a practice of reason adapted to the situation, as Lloyd Bitzer would have called it?[40] The fact of being reasonable, that is to say, of being adequate to the circumstances, is much more important than being rational in the traditional sense of the term, which implies *one* and only one solution. Had Perelman lived longer, I think that he would surely have continued his theorization of rhetoric by linking it to a certain form of pragmatism.

---

[40] L. Bitzer, "The Rhetorical Situation," *Philosophy and Rhetoric*, vol. 1, pp. 1–14.

But Perelman's view of rhetoric has often been qualified as neo-Aristotelian because it is reasonable, if not rational, to provide arguments which are convincing due to the type of *logos* used. For Perelman, the speaker and the audience are reasonable insofar as they both submit themselves to the conclusions embodied in the arguments employed by either one. After Aristotle, Perelman conceives of rationality as a capacity of *logos*, and does not grant any role to our emotions, which we must control through reason, nor in the qualities of the speaker, ethical or not, which are only peripheral to the value (or validity) of the arguments themselves.

Perelman thus deliberately reduces rhetoric to argumentation, which he defines as "the study of the discursive techniques allowing us to induce or increase the mind's adherence to the theses presented for its assent."[41] What kind of *logos* enables the speaker to convince his audience? How will he proceed? The speaker has no room for choice, or rather, what he wants to say depends on the point to be stressed. He amplifies the validity of his point by finding *"liaisons"* (links) with what strengthens his thesis, and "dissociations" with what is opposed to it.[42] Even the figures of speech which he uses have an argumentative impact because they purport to emphasize, highlight, and illustrate *what* is at stake. This can lead to further arguments or even to judgments of value because the audience naturally repels what is contrary to its own values and adheres to what confirms them, sometimes simply by being in agreement with them. This is where people are said to be reasonable and comprehensible in their motives, and where the traditional concepts of rationality and apodictic conclusiveness are too exigent. Rationality as usually conceived of is hardly adequate when one wants to explain how and why people behave the way they do and believe in what they hold to be their values.

---

[41] C. Perelman and L. Olbrechts-Tyteca, *The New Rhetoric*, tr. J. Wilkinson and P. Weaver (Notre Dame, IN: University of Notre Dame Press, 1969).

[42] C. Perelman, *The Realm of Rhetoric* [1977] (Notre Dame, IN: University of Notre Dame Press, 1982), p. 49.

A central question is to be able to discover how many types of arguments we have at our disposal when we argue. The list seems infinite. Perelman decides that there are only three types:

We will examine three types of liaisons in the following chapters: quasi-logical arguments, arguments which are based on the structure of reality, and arguments which establish this structure.

Quasi-logical arguments are those which can be understood by way of comparison to logical, mathematical, formal thinking. However, a quasi-logical argument differs from formal deduction in that it always presupposes adherence to no formal theses which alone allow the application of the argument.

Arguments that are based on the structure of reality depend on liaisons which exist among the elements of reality. Belief in the existence of such objective structures can be conveyed to varied realities: relations of causality, or essences of which certain phenomena are only the manifestation. What is important is the existence of agreements which are not questioned and which the speaker uses to develop his argumentation.

Arguments which establish the structure of reality are those which, starting from a known specific case, allow the establishment of a precedent, model, or general rule, such as enable reasoning by model or example. It is in this same category that we will examine the different types of arguments by analogy which serve sometimes to structure an unknown reality and sometimes to take a position in regard to it.[43]

To this he adds the concept of universal audience. This is one of the trickiest notions in Perelman's *New Rhetoric*. Descartes, we saw, transforms the four main parts of discourse, as devised by rhetoric, into analytical sequences meant to ascertain truth by eliminating the process of its discovery. Perelman does the reverse, by supplementing analytical reason with a rhetorical equivalent which would be as rational but in the extended sense of the word to be given by rhetoric, in order to justify the validity of everyday and legal arguments. Universal audience is the rhetorical form of Reason, as understood by the classical philosophers, such as Descartes or Kant. When "rhetoricized" and confronted with a rhetorical debate, our mind is

---

[43] Perelman, *Realm of Rhetoric*, pp. 50–1.

rational in its own way. It aims at universal conclusions and targets a universal audience. The aim is to extend the domain of validity and act as if, as in Adam Smith's theory of moral sentiments, there is an external spectator who is an internal judge in every one of us. The universal audience is embodied in the universal appeal that is invoked in any debate, or any conclusion, whatever the effective and real audience that is addressed, itself often limited by its own interests. Perelman denies the reductive point of view which would consist in believing we only work on that limited audience. He believes that any audience does transcend itself towards the universal and hence can possibly review its own positions. In fact, we speak as if we were addressing ourselves to everyone and anyone at the same time. If we say, "Respect the flag because you must respect your country," this argument is not valid for you or me in particular, but for anyone who values his or her country.

There is nonetheless a weakness in this notion of universal audience. It lies in the assumption of its underlying omnipresence, whereas we *actually* address ourselves to particular people with their particular interests. The universal audience is like Durkheim's collective consciousness (or Kant's Transcendental Consciousness): it is affirmed as being in everyone's mind without being in any one in particular. When we address ourselves to some singularized audience, Perelman says, we would (or should?) regard it as if it could be *any* audience rather than being a particular one. Unfortunately, this is very rarely the case. If I want to convince my son to go to bed early so that he may be better prepared for school the following morning, I do not necessarily treat him as I would treat any other young man of his age whom I do not know. However, my attitude could be translated as if I actually did. In this case, I could probably have retreated behind some universal audience or judge approving me, simply because I would prefer to avoid giving my son the impression I am partial in my decisions. But with my son, I see him as someone very close, who must obey *me*, and consider him in his singularity, and maybe, as more susceptible to fatigue than others, who nonetheless would go to bed later. I could also, it is true, universalize my point of view by taking some hindsight and contend that any audience of that age should go to bed at a specific time, because attendance at school is at stake. I would not, then, consider my son as *my son* in particular but as a token of any schoolboy of his age. But who would see his child as being something other than his or her own child? Do we care as much about other children and their problem of bedtime? Do we really have a general rule in mind? Perhaps we should, but usually we do not.

This problem of the link between argumentation and the universalization of ethical principles has formed the core of Habermas' theory, but it does not belong to Perelman's objectives. He does not trust ethics to solve moral conflicts between human beings since too much *pathos* is at stake in it, in his opinion. That is why instead he put his trust in the law and why he analyzed legal reasoning and, in particular, the necessary role of the judge, who is always legally obliged to decide between two parties in conflict when they go to court. The judge is expected to act in a dispassionate way, as is legally required, by remaining external to the conflict in question. Perelman has one motto: lack of confidence in ethics, strong faith in legality and the judge.

c) *Habermas and the pragmatics of communication*

Habermas' view of rhetoric is also centered on argumentation, but his primary concern is with *ethics* and with what *ethos* is committed to by sole virtue of simply arguing with someone else, who is thereby endowed with the same rights to debate and express her opinions as the speaker. This is the basis of Habermas' foundation of universality. For him, arguments are speech-acts in the sense that the very fact of saying something to someone implies the mutual recognition of the same rights. As a consequence, the speaker is committed by the fact of argumentation to the implicit moral view of reciprocity, putting the speaker on an equal footing—a very anti-Roman view indeed. This is a consequence of communication. Speaking, when conceived as argumentation, is thus a *request*, a mode of asking others to recognize as mutual the conditions of validity, which are implied in the conditions of use of speech. This mutual recognition of each other's claim to validity in what one says is thereafter extended by Habermas to the social domain. This is the basis of a wider recognition of each other as equal partners in social and political discussions, leading to the possibility of a deliberative democracy such as those of the West today. This recognition of *ethos* as *ethos* is, for Habermas, the basis of *ethics*, i.e. of reciprocity as the transcendental condition of any possible communicative behavior, understood as establishing the conditions of shared universal aims. The foundation of ethics lies in the conditions of argumentation. The right to argue then becomes reciprocal and egalitarian; it expresses the universalization of the conditions of argumentation as leading to the mutual acceptance of one another, which thus becomes the basis of any possible universalization. If there is a possible consensus to be found between human beings on certain matters, it is based on the mutual acceptance of one another as having the same rights to speak and to respond, to object, to propound, and finally, to defend his or her own views. Argumentation enables social agents to recognize each other as equals through the validity claims embedded in arguments, and this can lead to ethical agreements on basic rights.[44] This is how Habermas links practical argumentation to political life.

What is striking in this view of rhetoric is the fact that it does not provide, properly speaking, a new understanding of rhetoric, but rather a view of the ethical role of rhetoric in communication. It is not even a conception of rhetoric in the larger sense but rather of argumentation. The weight placed on the universal audience by Perelman is here displaced onto the universal speaker. We could epitomize Habermas' claim with this formula: from universalization through *pathos* to the universalization of *ethos*. A new ethics was thought to follow from this shift based on a new foundation of ethics, the latter eventually leading to the foundation of the Kantian categorical imperative, which for Habermas remains the last word on ethics.

---

[44] J. Habermas, *Moral Consciousness and Communicative Action*, tr. C. Lenhardt and S. Weber Nicholsen (London: Polity Press, 1990), p. 48. See also Stephen White, "The Presuppositions of Argumentation," in *The Recent Work of Jürgen Habermas* (New York: Cambridge University Press, 1988), pp. 55–8.

Perelman's view, at least, was compatible with other forms of approaches to ethics, such as utilitarianism. But in the end, Habermas faces the same difficulty as Perelman: universal *ethos* is no clearer a notion than universal audience. What can universal *ethos* be, if we only address others as *individual* speakers? There is another difference between the two philosophers, however: Perelman admits conflict and opposition as essential features of argumentation, whereas Habermas holds the view that consensus is the ultimate goal of his "universal pragmatics," as he calls it. Argumentation should terminate in some agreement because it is already embedded in the same claims of speech. For Habermas, this conclusion must even lead to further generalization: if people argue, it is because they want to find what they necessarily have in common through and in spite of what divides them. Nor is there room for emotions in such exchanges.[45] Reason is the sole presupposition of reason, just like universal consensus. The final agreement aimed at is qualified as rational because it follows the very principles of universalization, which are seen to be the foundations for giving reasons when one embarks on a given argumentative process. *The ethos of argumentation is the recognition of any ethos*, and the reason why it is called *ethics* is given in the conditions of debate in social and political life. To lay bare a shared ethics, with its implicit principles, would then be the ultimate goal of any argumentation. My *ethos* is your *ethos*, and indeed should be any *ethos*. Misunderstandings about what is said can only be due to a lack of dialogue and to an untimely break in the question–answer sequence. It can also result from a (bad) will to impose a point of view without discussion, by sheer authority alone. Critical wisdom then becomes necessary if both parties sincerely aim at reaching some agreement and not simply for each to impose his or her own views on the other. Questions and answers help clarify the meanings of the words used so that misunderstanding can disappear and leave room for agreement. A democratic society, a pluralistic one, is then, for Habermas, necessarily an argumentative one.

---

[45] G. Myerson, *Rhetoric, Reason and Society* (London: Sage, 1994), p. 43.

There is another view of rhetoric, or rather of argumentation, which is even more ecumenical than that of Habermas, but in a different sense: the pragma-dialectical approach.

d) F. van Eemeren and R. Grootendorst's pragma-dialectical approach to argumentation

There is a difference between arguing with a view to establishing norms and imposing norms on argumentation. The former view, that of Habermas, is based on what he considers to be the necessary and inescapable presuppositions of argumentation as they present themselves in the argumentative process. The latter view, defended mainly by Frans van Eemeren and his successive co-authors, instead upholds a conception in which argumentation *should* follow certain norms and rules, short of being valid or adequate, even if most people *actually* bypass the majority of these norms and rules in order to be more efficient when persuading someone. Confrontation does not necessarily come to an end, to an agreement, but it nonetheless produces some understanding of the differences. The aim of argumentation—and not of course of rhetoric in the larger sense of the term, as we use it here—is agreement, sometimes, as in court, with a third partner who judges and decides, like a jury. If agreement brings out an answer to a given question, it does not generate consensus, a broader task which may be too much to ask from argumentation. Hence such curious sentences as: "The study of argumentation is a branch of—what we call—*normative pragmatics*. In the descriptive approach, which starts out from argumentative practice, the epistemic, moral, and practical challenges provided by 'real life' are often motivating occasions to get theorizing about argumentation off the ground. The normative approach sets out from considerations regarding the norms of reasonableness that good argumentation must satisfy."[46] According to these authors, argumentation ought to be normative because it is based on the goodwill of the protagonists, who are sincere in their desire "to resolve their differences

---

[46] F. van Eemeren and R. Grootendorst, *A Systematic Theory of Argumentation* (New York: Cambridge University Press, 2004), p. 10.

of opinion."⁴⁷ Regulations are thus necessary. "In my view," van Eemeren writes, "it is of vital importance that the practice of argumentative discourse contributes optimally to realizing the normative goal of resolving a difference of opinion."⁴⁸ But in many cases argumentation is not so consensual; there is an opposition, a contradiction, which often goes beyond argumentation. And the arguments resorted to, whether valid or not, are all fair game for that purpose, even fallacious ones if necessary. Imposing one's point of view is as important as merely expressing one's opinions as "better." But it is still argumentation. There is, after all, no doubt that the ideal situation in warfare is that all parties comply with the noblest rules of war, yet, as we know from history, very few wars have been waged with elegance and fair play.

According to these authors, then, what is argumentation? It is a game with very strict rules, which enable the speaker to play fairly, in order to gain the agreement as a goal. In argumentation, they contend, one never wishes to express oneself or show that one is better or the best; it is rather an intellectual battle in which the winner gains the agreement of an interlocutor who is supposed to surrender. Hence the following quandaries: why do people have to agree necessarily, when most of the time they do not, even after a sound argument? Is it a failure and, if so, what kind of a failure is it? Does it deserve reproach and moral condemnation, or is it only a pragma-dialectical rejection for not having strictly and fairly followed the rules (this is what they call a *fallacy in reasoning*)? For van Eemeren, what matters in argumentation is what we *should* do rather than what we *actually* do and this is the entire problem posed by such an approach. It is as if one were explain actual political life by resorting to the ideals of what politics should be. Were we debating in an ideal world, the ideal conditions of argumentation would never tell us how argumentation actually works, but would simply indicate how it ought to work, since in an ideal world harmony would eventually prevail. Their motto is

---

[47] van Eemeren and Grootendorst, *A Systematic Theory*, p. 135.
[48] F. van Eemeren, *Strategic Maneuvering in Argumentative Discourse* (Amsterdam: Benjamins, 2010), p. 266.

"be reasonable," as if reasonableness could be imposed either by discourse, due to its own rationality and presuppositions, or by a pre-established agreement on how the discussion should unfold. Is it not just as rational or reasonable to see the speaker's attitude as a way of expressing his own views without necessarily wanting to modify the audience's beliefs? These authors could reply that what we hope to achieve when we argue with someone is to reach some agreement. Otherwise, we would not debate with her. But is agreement the same thing as consensus, a consensus starting from the acceptance of rules preceding the debate itself? The idyllic goal of falling into each other's arms seems an excessive requirement heaved onto the shoulders of argumentation. Take the case of a law suit: we argue *against* the other to obtain victory, whether or not this victory is deserved.

This strategic maneuvering is, for van Eemeren, the beginning of rhetoric which, in contrast to argumentation, is a non-rational strategy put in place to win an argument. It begins when the ideal norms of a "right argumentation" fail to be respected in real life. One may be convinced by bad arguments, and the end result can be a false (or a good) agreement, even a harmful consensus, as in Nazi Germany. The ethical viewpoint should not be reduced to the fact of having reached *one* answer shared by the interlocutors, especially if not withstanding, all rules being respected, the final answer is not ethical in the common sense of the term. Did Hitler not convince a majority of the German people that the Jews were their enemies and had to be eliminated? Alongside active persuasion, one also has passive consent. We all know the result of Nazi argumentation: an answer accepted or tolerated by the majority of the German people inexorably led to the systematic destruction of the Jews, but it may doubted that, literally expressed as such, the German people would have given their approval to the extermination process which followed. What, then, was agreed upon when the Nazis *convinced* the German people? Is it really the goal of all arguments to overcome contradiction through agreement? Do they not often reinforce prejudices by stressing accepted viewpoints and values? Very often, as in court, A argues against B, but it is not to convince him or her, but to convince C, who is the judge. Let us go one question further. Can we ever fully convince anybody at all? This is really an important question, to which a major book, written by Marc Angenot, was devoted several years ago.[49] The answer is "no." This is because there are too many possible misunderstandings (and consequences) caused by a single argument, not to mention the hidden interests lurking behind it. These misunderstandings are repressed as if they did not exist nor count, so that they will serve as the implicit presuppositions to conduct a debate. According to Angenot, if we "argue," it is always at the surface, formally, so to speak, hence his conclusion that all argumentation is nothing but a *strategic behavior, like so much behavior in social life*. The core reasons for undertaking argumentation is often to dress our interests and emotions in an acceptable (and sometimes accepted) manner to all parties, who remain motivated by opposing goals, i.e. their *own* goals. The question posed by Angenot is whether agreement is itself something other than a rhetorical and perfunctory surrender. Are consent and agreement not mere illusions of rationality or reasonableness? And when "true" agreement or conviction obtains, does playing by the rules really guarantee that the result be ethical, by virtue of the very observance of these rules? Are we sure that starting with two opposing viewpoints and ending with one, in cases when this happens, is really in line with the process of ethics because of the ethics of the process?

In virtue of what has been said above, we can classify the pragma-dialectical approach to argumentation in the *ethos* column of our table of theories. *Logos*, embodied in the argumentative use of speech-act theory, is subject to a rule-oriented procedure rooted in *ethos*. *Logos* is then subordinated to the ideal goal of reaching one answer on which everybody *ought* to agree, eventually uniting the protagonists around the same belief.

But what can be the rules or "codes of conduct" for the argumentative *logos* to be able to decisively resolve divergences of opinion?

---

[49] Marc Angenot, *Dialogue de sourds. Traité de rhétorique antilogique* (Paris: Mille et une Nuits, 2008).

How must *logos* be effectively conceived of in order to reach any consensus about an issue? What are the ideal norms *logos* ought to comply with in order to be an ideal argumentation?

What are the rules, then, of argumentation as a fair game?

1) Discussants must not prevent each other from advancing standpoints or from calling standpoints into question.
2) Discussants who advance a standpoint must not refuse to defend this standpoint when requested to do so.
3) Attacks on standpoints must not bear on a standpoint that has not actually been put forward by the other party.
4) A standpoint must be defended only by arguments relevant to that standpoint.
5) Discussants may not falsely attribute unexpressed premises to the other party, nor disown responsibility for their own unexpressed premises.
6) Discussants may not falsely present something as an accepted starting point or falsely deny that something is an accepted starting point.
7) A standpoint may not be regarded as inclusively defended if the defense does not take place by means of an appropriate argument scheme that is correctly applied.
8) The reasoning in argumentation must be logically valid or must be capable of being made valid by making explicit one or more unexpressed premises.
9) Inconclusive defenses of standpoints may not lead to maintaining these standpoints, and conclusive defenses of standpoints may not lead to maintaining expressions of doubt concerning these standpoints.
10) Parties must not use any formulations that are insufficiently clear or confusingly ambiguous, and they must interpret the formulations of the other party's as carefully and accurately as possible.[50]

---

[50] These ten rules quoted here come from the two chapters on fallacies in F. van Eemeren, Rob Grootendorst, and F. Snoeck Henkemans, *Argumentation*, chs. 7 and 8

Rhetoric is here not only reduced to argumentation but to what argumentation *should* be, and validity here entails that reasoning be devoid of logical fallacy. In this way, negotiation, manipulation, concession in spite of opposition, rejection, *ad hominem* attacks on the interlocutor, or argumentation as the rationalization of the speaker's standpoint and prejudices, the appeal to the emotions, and so on, all seem to stay outside the boundaries of such a theory. Incidentally, we find a similar set of rules prescribed for the use of argumentation in a much older book on rhetoric, written by Josef Kopperschmidt. For this forerunner of the pragma-dialectical approach, the question was already one of knowing whether and how argumentation can be considered as fair game, so that at the end of the argument a winner emerges and the other parties readily accept not only having lost but concede to the opponent's conclusion (agreement). If a speaker wants to be persuasive, he must apply a set of minimal rules, rules which again most speakers and interlocutors do not always actually use. This is because doing so would limit their argumentative strategy and the various options at their disposal. It would impose too many constraints on the speaker's choices. The speaker aims to win the argument, not to be angelical or fair—unless, of course, it turns out to be more efficient to be so or at least to appear to be so.

For Kopperschmidt, there are not ten but seven rules to be adopted in an argument in order for it to be persuasive, if not also to be *ethical*.

1) The speaker must be convinced of everything he says, so that there is no manipulation.
2) The speech-act of persuasion can only succeed if the speaker is seriously interested in reaching an agreement with his interlocutor.
3) The speech-act of persuasion can only succeed if both interlocutors play the same game and respect the decision without influencing each other by other means than argumentation.

(London: Routledge, 2002), pp. 110-36, and can also be found in van Eemeren and Grootendorst, *A Systematic Theory*, pp. 190-6.

4) The speech-act of persuasion can only succeed if the speaker is capable (*fähig*) of discussing his interlocutor's arguments and of being possibly convinced by them (example: "Sarah is capable of hearing whatever arguments about what she has to do about her health, when discussing with her physician," but she may reject his advice or even his opinion. Hence rule 5).

5) The speech-act of persuasion can only succeed if the speaker is ready (*bereit*) to become convinced by his interlocutor's arguments (example: "... and Sarah is now ready to accept the fact that she has cancer and what she ought to do to fight the disease").

6) The speech-act of persuasion can only succeed if the speaker feels obliged to act according to his convictions.

7) The speech-act of persuasion can only succeed if the proposition debated is based on facts that allow for a debate between the communication partners.[51]

All of these rules, however artificial and variable in number, have a single goal: to transform a linguistic exchange into a persuasive one by means of prescription. Nevertheless, they cannot do so without recourse to a vicious circle. They introduce right from the start, a priori so to speak, a sincerity clause, a norm of goodwill for the final surrender, a pre-accepted (and convincing) norm of acceptance of arguments, based on the fact that the audience will only be moved by valid arguments, and more particularly, by leaving implicit beliefs, prejudices, and emotions outside the transaction. All these clauses are unrealistic because they are based on an a priori consensus between the protagonists concerning the necessity of defining the game's rules of play, without manipulation, emotion, foul play, and so on.

---

[51] J. Kopperschmidt, *Rhetorik* (Stuttgart: Kohlhammer, 1973), pp. 85–97.

e) From S. Toulmin's umbrella of logic to the informal logic movement

If logical *reasoning* is defined by its completeness—i.e. by the fact that all the necessary premises which entail one and only one conclusion are mentioned, thereby excluding any possible opposite conclusion (apodicticity)—in argumentation we have inferences in which upholding some premises may be as problematic as deriving a conclusion from them. Toulmin's problem is to account for both logic and argumentation within a single model, which would nonetheless also take their difference into account. With this purpose in mind, he establishes a unique model of all reasoning, underpinned by an implicit logic, in order to show that what is weakened, problematic, or absent in argumentation with respect to formal logic does not impede the attainment of reliable judgments. This general model of reasoning is now very well-known but can be briefly recalled (Figure 1).[52]

At first sight, this model may seem strange or unduly complicated. In fact, it embodies all possibilities of valid reasoning, from logic (which is argumentative, in a strong sense) to argumentation as we understand it today, in which conclusions are only likely and plausible without being necessarily true.

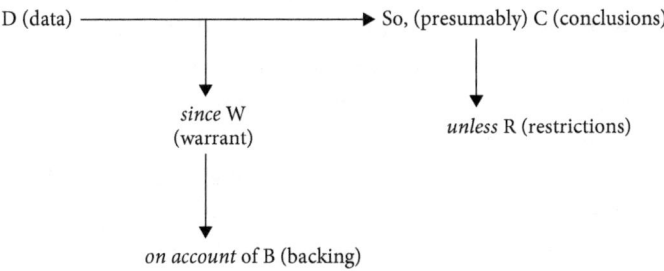

Figure 1 Toulmin's Model

---

[52] S. Toulmin, *The Uses of Argument* [1958], 2nd edn. (New York: Cambridge University Press, 2003), p. 97.

Let us illustrate this model by taking up Aristotle's example: "Socrates' face is red, so he is ill."

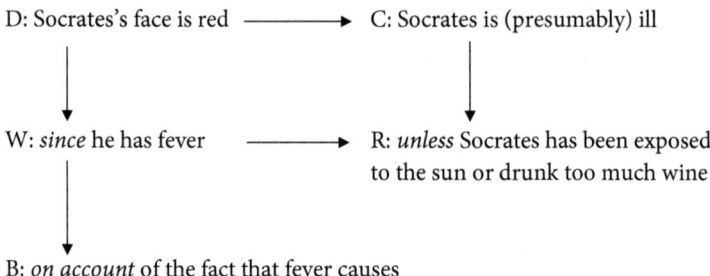

B: *on account* of the fact that fever causes people suffering from high temperature to have a red face

We cannot reasonably affirm that all men who have a red face are ill, since there are many other possible reasons for being red-faced, such as alcohol consumption or even mild exposure to the sun. Given all of these clauses W, B, and R, however, the conclusion he is ill ensues as "necessarily" as it would in a logical inference. If we fail to mention the possible restrictions for C and the factual premise W backed by B, the conclusion would merely be likely, if not unlikely. As we can see from this model, we can easily pass from an argumentative inference, in which the conclusions are presumably true, to a logical one, in which the constraints are stronger insofar as they are explicitly posed.

The striking feature of Toulmin's model is the absence of *ethos* and *pathos*, as if *logos* alone had and could fulfill all the tasks assigned to rhetoric, from persuasion to emotion (unless, of course, we accept to limit ourselves to a restricted vision of argumentation in which they can be dispensed with).

The "Informal Logic"[53] movement, initiated by Anthony Blair and Ralph Johnson, and pursued in a much enriched way by Douglas Walton,[54] is in the tradition of Toulmin's approach because it

---

[53] For a good synthesis, see Ralph Johnson, *Manifest Rationality* (London: Routledge, 2000).

[54] See mostly D. Walton, C. Reed, and F. Macagno, *Argumentation Schemes* (Cambridge: Cambridge University Press, 2008); D. Walton, *Informal Logic: A Pragmatic Approach* (New York: Cambridge University Press, 2008); or D. Walton,

provides a model of reasoning which is not, strictly speaking, logical. It is also the source of another movement of thought which brought the evaluation of arguments to the fore, the "critical thinking" movement, in which the cogency of an argument or the analysis of fallacies (which are criticized by comparison with the validity of formal arguments) are key features. The difficulty with "informal logic" is that correct thinking does not always contribute to the persuasiveness of an argument. A speaker does not always persuade his audience with correct arguments alone. Sometimes, speakers have to resort to "*good*" (or efficient) arguments, which may be logically incorrect but are nonetheless argumentatively powerful. The "Informal Logic" movement is the counterpart of the evaluation tendency, which has developed in American rhetoric, whose aim is to evaluate what a "right" argument should be, for any speaker as for any audience. The basic question, in the informal framework of argumentation, is of knowing how arguments, though not logical, should be construed and arranged to have nonetheless a validity of their own and avoid lapsing into fallacies. The difficulty with this view is that there are no general rules or principles which ought to be systematically applied to argumentation, since the latter is very often a *strategy* that resorts to logically invalid but good reasons, insofar as their result is concerned and obtains by convincing or by moving the audience.[55]

f) Kenneth Burke and American rhetoric

Two of the basic features of American rhetoric since Burke has been its non-systematic character and its versatility. The various conceptions of rhetoric we find in American rhetoric nonetheless have one point in common: they entertain a view of rhetoric based on *ethos*, i.e. on the dramatization of situations which are meant to educate and bolster the speaker's capacity to adapt himself in the New World. That is why

---

The Place of Emotions in Argument (University Park: Pennsylvania State University Press, 1987), in which the focus mainly targets *ad hominem* strategies.

[55] Objections gathered in Johnson's *Manifest Rationality*, p. 260.

rhetoric is "sermonic" (Weaver)[56] or "dramatizing" (Burke),[57] insofar as the situations involve each of us as speakers and interactive beings.

Burke's rhetoric has been considered one of the most important contributions to the field, even if it is unsystematic and too often jumbled in its presentation, leaving the reader bogged down by digressions. There are some interesting points, however. People are divided and are often in conflict. Rhetoric is what enables them to recapture some form of unity. Rhetoric as a process of dramatization and its resolution are ensured through symbolic action, for the most part through language. Influence on others is made possible by means of a crucial operation of identification: identification of the group, of its ideas, of the problems to be addressed, of the individual, as in the example of the presidential candidate who reminds the audience of his own origins or background. The identification of the scene, of the agents, of the act, of the purpose, of the agency of speech, form the basic "pentad" (i.e. five elements) of strategy present in the unfolding of rhetorical discourse, recalling Quintilian's famous questionnaire:[58] "Where? When? How? Who? By what means?" Burke is probably more original when he describes what he calls the "four master tropes" which are the most used rhetorical tools of identification.[59] *Metaphor* gives a perspective; *metonymy* a reductive viewpoint on the scene, with its object and its agents, by singularizing their basic features; *synecdoche* offers a general representation; and finally, *irony* enables the speaker and the audience to mark their distance in a dialectical way (and not in a confrontational manner, since the aim of rhetoric, its *ethos*, is to bring them closer together).

Metaphor, metonymy, synecdoche, and irony were already described as the basic tropes in Giambattista Vico's famous *New Science* (1720). For the Neapolitan thinker, they represent the elementary stages of

---

[56] Richard Weaver, *Language is Sermonic* (Baton Rouge: Louisiana State University Press, 1970).
[57] K. Burke, *A Grammar of Motives* (Oakland: University of California Press, 1969).
[58] Quintilian, *Institutes*, 5, 10. *Persona, factum, causa, locus, tempus, modis, facultas*.
[59] Burke, *Grammar of Motives*, pp. 503–17.

historical development: the time of metaphor is that of sensory images and epitomizes the age of gods; metonymy singles out prominent characteristics (qualities or attributes) and therefore epitomizes the age of heroes while also characterizing observation and empirical evidence; synecdoche as a figure of generalization prevails in the time of humanism and science, in which equality between men and universal scientific laws have emerged; as for the time of irony, it is the period of rhetoric, since it focuses on the distance which allows rhetoric to become conscious of itself as such. From metaphor to irony, we pass from identity to difference and even to opposition. In this sense, Vico's views have been recognized as a precursor of the Hegelian vision of history.[60] Dialectical division uses the spectrum of identity and difference to express and amplify the different human attitudes adopted by rhetoric to convey the multifariousness of social and psychological relationships, varying from identity to conflict. Rhetoric is always perspectivist. If Burke's conception has its source in Vico, it will find its continuation in the work of several American rhetoricians, such as Charles Willard: "The task of Argumentation is to identify and reconstruct the conditions of dissensual discourse. Its *epistemic interests* inhere in a concern for the social construction of knowledge, the judgmental, veridical and rhetorical method by which communities achieve confidence in beliefs. The point is to explain how groups sustain intellectual stability yet are able to change."[61] Tolerance for disagreement is based on the freedom guaranteed by society. In this respect, the *relationship to the other* is what counts. The influence the speaker purports to convey to the audience is the value of disagreement, of respect and tolerance, needed to establish a New World composed of immigrants coming from different cultural backgrounds. From this Henry Johnstone concludes that the aim of rhetoric is to justify the speaker's judgments,

---

[60] On this, see Hayden White, *Metahistory* (Baltimore, MD: Johns Hopkins University Press, 1975).

[61] Charles Arthur Willard, *A Theory of Argumentation* (Tuscaloosa: University of Alabama Press, 1989), p. 11.

often through recourse to a philosophical position.⁶² For Johnstone, rhetoric is "an art of evocation" rather than of persuasion: it is "a search for morale because we are demoralized by shabby thinking, by sophistry, by revolutions, by relativism, skepticism and many other tendencies."⁶³

g) The structuralist view of argumentation: the Group Mu and Oswald Ducrot's view of argumentative markers

In the 1970s, structuralism became the dominant approach to the humanities and the social sciences in Europe, before gaining wide currency in the English-speaking world. Its key figures included Lévi-Strauss, Derrida, Foucault, Barthes and, in rhetoric, the Group Mu. The latter was a group of six linguists and semioticians who developed an original conception of rhetoric at the University of Liège. They were not interested in argumentation as a mode of inference because they saw it as too restrictive an analysis of discourse, and in particular, of literary discourse, their main concern. Structuralism was based on Ferdinand de Saussure's linguistic system, viewed in terms of differences and oppositions which could be used to characterize any human question dealt with in the humanities and social sciences, as though language were an autonomous, self-sufficient entity—structures are supposed to be independent of history—in which both speakers and audience play a minimal role (if indeed they play any role at all). In other words, speakers and audiences are subject only to the constraints imposed by the natural or internal structure of language.

If rhetoric's aim is seen as the clarification of literary discourse as the paradigm of figurative speech, it is no wonder that rhetoric should be defined as "the knowledge of the techniques of language characteristic of literature."⁶⁴ Can we still distinguish rhetoric from poetics?

---

⁶² Henry Johnstone, Jr., *Validity and Rhetoric in Philosophical Argument* (University Park, PA: Dialogue Press of Man & World, 1978).
⁶³ Johnstone, *Validity and Rhetoric*, p. 76.
⁶⁴ Group Mu, *A General Rhetoric* [1970], tr. P. Burnell and E. Slotkin (Baltimore, MD: Johns Hopkins University Press, 1981), p. 19.

The basic figure of speech, for the Group Mu, is no longer metaphor, as it was for Aristotle, but the synecdoche, since concepts are considered inclusive classes of other concepts.[65] In spite of these limitations, the Group Mu has restored the relevance of the four main operators in rhetoric, already underlined by Aristotle in the *Topics*[66] and in the *Rhetoric*[67] which are meant to encompass all the possible responses, from complete approval to utmost rejection of a given answer. Those four operators range from identity to difference (opposition): you can approve of a judgment without restriction (=), modify it (±), add another judgment (+), or contradict (−). You can proceed *ad rem*, by only laying stress on the sole answer, or also *ad hominem*, by approving or attacking (disapproving, rejecting) the interlocutor, or both. Generally, approval and rejection are terms that should be reserved for *ad hominem rhetoric*; behaviors are not propositional, in as much as the terms "agreement" or "contradiction" usually are. The Group Mu calls these four operators (or operations): substitution or repetition (or permutation); addition; suppression-addition as modification, and suppression.

The structuralist view of language was later applied to argumentation in the work of Jean-Claude Anscombre and Oswald Ducrot.[68] Their basic idea is that language has an argumentative impact by virtue of markers (also called *argumentative connectors*) such as "not," "but," or "even." If I ask someone "Do you want to go for a walk?" and get the answer "The weather is nice today, *but* it's not very warm," my interlocutor means "no" and I understand this answer perfectly well, even if it has not been expressed literally as such. Why is this the case? The reason is the following: if my interlocutor had wanted to go for a walk with me, she would not have considered the alternative by insisting finally on the negative reason. She would have merely said "yes." But my interlocutor did not want to upset me by

---

[65] Group Mu, *Rhétorique de la poésie* (Paris: Le Seuil, 1990), p. 54.
[66] Aristotle, *Topics*, 161a 1.   [67] Aristotle, *Rhetoric*, 1402a 30.
[68] J. C. Anscombre and O. Ducrot, *L'argumentation dans la langue* (Brussels: Mardaga, 1983).

brutally rejecting my proposition so, instead, she expressed something like: "A is a good reason to do W, but not-A is a stronger reason not to do it, and this is why, after confronting the two options, I suggest that not-W is the right answer because it relies on a stronger argument, not-A." Implicitly, we observe that even in this theory questions as alternatives are the object of argumentation. This fact is stressed by the argumentative marker "but": it means "even if there is a good reason to go in one direction, there is a better one to go in the opposite."[69] When you have "A, *but* B," the pragmatic fact of uttering "*but something*" indicates that B is the argument that really counts and overrides the preceding one, that A is merely a concession to the consideration of the question submitted to you by some speaker. If my interlocutor had wanted to accept my invitation, she would have said A only, but the very fact that she does add "*but B*" implies I should infer that the answer is negative. Hence, B is the reason, the premise for the implicit conclusion and answer that my invitation has been rejected.

Sometimes connectives purport to strengthen the conclusion, as in the following example: "He is intelligent and even very kind." By that, the speaker wants to strengthen the good opinion the interlocutor may have of the person. One can use a different marker such as "moreover" or "besides": the daughter who endeavors to give a positive idea of her boyfriend to her parents because that relationship is viewed as highly problematic by them, might say something like: "John is very kind, and besides, he's also very intelligent." Each time, according to Ducrot, argumentation is meant to put a cursor on a sort of scale of strength, at the end of which would be situated some implicit conclusion. In the above example, the daughter places the cursor farther along the scale of positive conclusivity (or if there was a minimizing effect, farther back), thereby amplifying the conclusion

---

[69] We can illustrate this remark nearly indefinitely with examples: "Your boyfriend is clever *but not very nice*" stresses the overall negative character of my daughter's boyfriend, as a good argument for her to leave him before more serious problems arise, for instance.

that John is a nice boy (or minimizing John's positive *ethos*, as in the following example: "John is not very clever, and what's more, he failed his exams last year").

In this view of argumentation, it is more appropriate to speak of alternatives or underlying questions, of which those alternatives are the propositional expression. Argumentative connectives or markers are meant to articulate or take up some question raised through an answer which refers back to it. Another example clearly highlights this: "I really must go to New York for business, and *incidentally*, I will (*even*) see some old friends while I'm there." By connecting the first statement to the second with the expression "*incidentally*" (or with the use of *even*), I clearly stress the good reasons I have to go to New York. I add another reason which bolsters that decision against any further questioning, which could have arisen on the basis of the first argument alone. We also find arguments which have a selecting function in contrast to the literal reading which leaves the alternative intact. These ways of speaking are used to orient the audience toward one specific answer which is absent from the literal expression that offers two readings. When someone says, "He is not as tall as his sister," one could logically reply that 1) he could be taller, or 2) that he could be less tall than she is. Yet everyone understands right away that the speaker means "he is smaller," because the lack of tallness is what is *in question* in this negative statement and not the opposite term of the alternative. The same applies in the contrary argument. Had I said, "He is not as small as his sister," I could also have logically concluded that he was smaller, but, argumentatively speaking, this possibility is excluded. I shall then usually conclude that he is taller than she is because the question is whether he is smaller or not.

While our language contains many such connectives, it would be a mistake to reduce argumentation to their presence alone. Ducrot's analyses are in many cases illuminating about the way we suggest conclusions and inferences in our natural language using these connectives. The latter are present when the question at stake has to be taken up in some way in the answer. But many arguments do not contain argumentative markers. When a lecturer says at the end of a talk, "It's one o'clock," he is suggesting that the time of his speech is over and that it is time for lunch. This is because in many European societies, it is a *topos* to have lunch at 1 p.m. There is, however, no connective present in this utterance.

h) Hermeneutics and reception theory

Rhetoricians, when confronted with a text, have two questions in mind in interpreting that text: what is in question in the text itself and how do we discover it through our own questioning? This suggests a more fundamental query: are the questions raised by a text to be found in the text alone, as Hans-Georg Gadamer claims,[70] or do they come from the reader, as the Reception School affirms,[71] most notably in the work of Hans-Robert Jauss?[72] If all the questions raised by the text were in the text, the novelty of history would be impossible. All possible questions would already be embedded in the text, irrespective of the questions that the future might bring. The history of possible readings would only have to unfold itself one reading after another through time, according to some kind of Hegelian, pre-established finality.

The opposite conception, affirmed by Reception Theory, is as absurd as the Hermeneutical Theory sustained by Gadamer, because if all the questions raised by a particular text had their origin in the answers defended by successive readers throughout history, every new answer would be relative to the reader and the text would merely be a pretext for relative and arbitrary interpretations, without the constraints and limitations put by the text in the answers it gives rise to, among the different interpretations.

---

[70] H. G. Gadamer, *Truth and Method* [1960], tr. J. Weinsheimer (London: Continuum, 2004).

[71] On this, see R. Warning, *Rezeptionsästhetik* (Munich: Fink Verlag, 1994).

[72] H. R. Jauss, *Aesthetische Erfahrung und literarische Hermeneutik* (Frankfurt: Suhrkamp, 1991); and W. Iser, *The Act of Reading* (Baltimore, MD: Johns Hopkins University Press, 1980).

The solution lies in the combination of both views: the reader asks questions that are history-dependent, but which must be answered in light of what the text says. Questions emanate from the text and are taken up by historically conditioned readers, who very often perceive these questions differently. Those various readers are themselves questioners. Reading and interpretation thus represent a dialogical or dialectical process.

Non-Western rhetoric

Marx used the terms of the "Asiatic Modes of Production" to describe societies in which basic structures and ideologies have changed only very gradually. The same comparison applies in the case of rhetoric: imperial structures seldom favor rhetoric as argumentation. In China[73] as well as in India, nonetheless, there have been isolated moments of dialectics or sophistic.[74] But for the most part, rhetoric has served other purposes than those developed in the Western world, where it has reflected the movements of history. While democracy allows for controversy, empires seldom do. Metaphorical language is specific to literature in the Western world, but it is not *the* characteristic of language itself, as is the case with many Far Eastern languages. The meeting of rhetoric and argumentation in one single discipline we now call Rhetoric is typical of the Greek legacy in Western culture and in many ways as a legacy it is unique. However, epic poetry (sometimes accompanied by dance extolling it) can also be found in many cultures such as India or China.[75] As a rhetorical means of amplifying and sublimating the values of some

---

[73] In China, Anne Cheng observes the emergence of argumentation (*bian*) at the time of Mo-Zi as characteristic of a discussion of authority and the rejection of arguments in its favor (*Histoire de la pensée chinoise* (Paris: Le Seuil, 1997), p. 90).

[74] D. Knechtges and E. Vance, *Rhetoric and the Discourses of Power in Court Culture* (Seattle: University of Washington Press, 2005); J. P. Reding, *Les fondements philosophiques de la rhétorique chez les sophistes grecs et les sophists chinois* (Berne: Peter Lang, 1985).

[75] George Kennedy, *Comparative Rhetoric: An Historical and Cross-Cultural Introduction* (New York: Oxford University Press, 1998).

historical moment, however, it has been fully theorized as rhetoric only in Western philosophy. Everywhere and at different times, rhetoric has been the language of the courtier, reinforcing the power in place, or the voice of the community, amplifying the supposed current social virtues.

Conclusion: toward a problematological conception of rhetoric

Rhetoric in the twentieth century has experienced a tremendous renewal. All the forms of rhetoric encountered above, concentrated on either *ethos*, *pathos*, or *logos*, place the weight of emphasis on only one of these components, at times neglecting the other two but always putting them at a subordinate level. What can be seen at the close of this chapter on the history of rhetoric is that this subordination has always been the case. There have always been three kinds of rhetoric: one founded on *ethos*, largely Roman in origin; one giving preeminence to *logos,* as indeed most are, due to Aristotle; and one focusing on *pathos*, as in Plato, forming a cluster of rhetorical approaches meant to focus on the role of the audience and its emotions. The impact of a rhetorical relationship is charm, influence, persuasion (i.e. agreement), which depend on the fact that the audience is convinced, pleased, or manipulated. All these conceptions are, of course, defendable but they fail to integrate the other two types of approach.

Problematology is the theory of rhetoric which integrates these three aspects into one synthetic conception by putting all three components on the same footing in its analysis of the rhetorical relationship.[76] This requires a new foundational link which questioning provides.

Problematology has accomplished a Copernican revolution in rhetoric, by emphasizing the role of questions in language, in debates, as well as in the expressive discourse of rhetoric *stricto sensu*. It grants

---

[76] For a recent synthesis of problematology in all its aspects, see Nick Turnbull, *Michel Meyer's Problematology* (London: Bloomsbury Publishing, 2014).

equal importance to the speaker, the audience, and the medium they use to relate to each other. Rhetoric is specific insofar as it is a negotiation between speakers and the audience through language, visual or spoken. This enables the speaker to propound an answer to a question, either raised by the audience or being of some concern to it, which will, whether divisive or not, express the distance between them, as a kind of measuring rod. In social life, rhetoric is used to modify this distance, let alone to make known how it is felt.

It is now time to tackle the different elements—questions and answers, *ethos, pathos, logos*, the negotiation of distance—contained in our definition of rhetoric, in order to see how rhetoric works. By integrating these components into one single view, we shall be able to provide a general theory of rhetoric and argumentation.

2

The question-view of *logos*

Questions as the objects of discourse

People who speak and write always do so with a question in mind. Their discourse should be viewed as an answer (or cluster of answers) they consider to be true (or that they want their interlocutor to believe in) and adequate or relevant to the situation in which a given problem arises, and to which they are responding, or who simply have their interest aroused by this answer. In their eyes, the answer not only matters to them but also to their audience, which is in this sense "interested." This is why the speaker communicates what he thinks in terms of answers, even if his speech or text does not explicitly refer to itself as an answer. If the underlying question has not been explicitly raised before by the audience, the first step is to convey an interest in the problem dealt with. Rhetorical discourse often begins by piquing such interest, by capturing or, if necessary, by captivating the audience, even if that particular audience has not thought about that question before. Another way of proceeding, for the speaker, is to begin by explicitly formulating the question he has in mind if he expects to get the answer from his interlocutor. In all cases, however, the question–answer difference is the core of discourse, speech, and language. Questioning covers all our intellectual processes, from perception to discourse, because we perceive and categorize reality in terms of the problems we face and must solve, in order to move among others, physically, psychologically, and socially. This is why science, too, is a questioning process. It begins with questions and ends up with answers, answers which turn out to be provisional solutions.

What is Rhetoric? First edition. Michel Meyer
© Michel Meyer 2017. First published 2017 by Oxford University Press

As for perception, it is evoked in a famous passage in Sartre's *Being and Nothingness*. Sartre describes Pierre entering a café in search of Paul. Since he cannot find him in the crowd, there is no positive answer to the question he came to solve. He then says to himself, "Paul is *not* there." This sentence is not an avowal that nothingness would exist as such, but is simply an answer, if a negative one, to the question he had in mind: "Is Paul there or not?" Perception, like any other mental activity, is rooted in questions. This is why in the case of perception, what is irrelevant to the question (the people who are not Paul) remains in the background, leaving persons and objects in a cloud of perceptual indifferentiation, while our mind focuses on what or whom we are looking for. This is the basis of current work in visual rhetoric.[1] Images are more persuasive because they are shortcuts, i.e. they present in a condensed or immediate way what Perelman calls a presence, rendering the image more emotional than a text because the message conveyed is directly presented. At the same time, perception is just one among many other intellectual activities upon which questioning bestows a structure. In perception there is always what is in and what is out of the question, if only implicitly. As a result, we must envisage a specific label for the difference between both, and this amounts to characterizing the distinction between question and answer, whatever the context and the modalities of their appearance. Let us call this difference the *problematological difference*. The success of this difference hinges on the necessity of avoiding confusion and amalgamation of the problems we encounter with a range of answers, because sometimes, by merely speaking of our problems, we may have the feeling that we already have their solution. Even in psychoanalysis, where it is useful to render the patient's problems explicit, such an attitude is not sufficient for psychological recovery because it only makes the subject conscious of his or her problems without solving them; it should rather render him or her sufficiently aware of these problems to pursue the analysis. In science too, the adequate

---

[1] Ch. Hill and M. Helmers, *Visual Rhetoric* (Mahwah, NJ: Lawrence Erlbaum, 2004).

expression of the problem is certainly the first moment of its *resolution*, as a necessary step to the discovery of its *solution*.

Without the presence of an (implicit) question, people would not speak or write, a fortiori when the question is explicit. This explains why, if someone to whom we speak asks what we mean, we usually refer ourselves to *what is in question* in what we say (or write) and produce some equivalent answer. When asked about the meaning of a whole discourse, we often respond by speaking of "what is *in question*" in *what* we said. Interpretation relates the answer qua answer to its corresponding question. When this is not possible, the meaning of our discourse remains *in question* because we cannot avail ourselves of an answer pinpointing precisely what the problem was.

I am reminded of a peculiar situation in which a woman who I did not know approached me one day. She began to speak about what I suspected was her dog: "You know, Mirza is ill." I was surprised because I knew neither the woman nor her dog and was indeed astonished by the incongruity of the situation. Why was this woman addressing herself to me? In fact, although I understood the words she used, I could not figure out what problem she had. Her discourse remained problematic because I could not figure out *which problem* was hers and, more importantly, why she thought I could do something about it. The communicative transaction was thus bound to remain problematic and incomplete. Was she expecting help from me or was she waiting for a compassionate response about her poor dog? Or did she want to speak with someone (or anyone) about her problems, in a simple case of loneliness? I could not answer these questions because everything was questionable about her behavior and I had no answers available even with regard to the question she was framing.

We often experience a similar feeling when we visit a foreign country, where we know only a few words in the language spoken. When we reply by using these few words, people often begin to make long speeches in reply, as if the few words uttered were a sure sign that we were able to entertain a full conversation and understand everything that could be said in that language. The truth of the matter is that, in such situations, we cannot figure out what is in question in the speech of others; what they are saying remains completely opaque. In sum, if you do not see what is in question, you cannot understand what is said since what is said is an answer to an underlying question. By contrast, we can define a good orator as someone who masters what he talks about, because he "knows the question."

Questions, when problematic, initiate debates and controversies and, when they are less problematic, serve to trigger rejoinders and formal agreement about that question. A low level of problematicity for a given question usually leads to more conventional and even friendly discussion, with the indirect effect of diminishing the distance between the protagonists. Or it is more conflictual and divisive because the level of problematicity is high. Highly problematic questions cannot but lead to conflict and opposition because they have to be solved rather than rhetorically eliminated. Hence the search for an agreement or, at least, a settlement. If a mayor of a town, for instance, asks if he or she should invite extractive firms to come to the town to frack the soil with the aim of finding new sources of energy, the discussion may turn out to be strongly confrontational, in spite of the significant amounts of money at stake.

Logos *as the expression of the problematological difference*

At least since Aristotle, the role of *logos* in rhetoric has always been central. But *logos* is also an ambivalent concept since it is both the locus of the enthymeme or inference, and a tool used by speakers to produce pleasant speech. The latter is characteristic of literary rhetoric through style and form. Literature can also use realistic language, in addition to figurative language. In either case, a rhetoric based on the figures of style is also found (even if only to a lesser degree) in everyday language and, as Perelman notes, it can also be employed in argumentative strategies. It is necessary then to put some order and structure to the nature of figurative language, in literary rhetoric, and to the different ways in which figures of speech share the field of rhetoric with the basic operators of argumentation. The unity of argumentation and rhetoric *stricto sensu* requires that the same basic operators be at work, giving rise either to figures or to arguments.

Let us go back, then, to the most elementary principle of language use we have already identified: people speak, write, or even paint and sculpt because they have a question or a problem in mind. They either propose the answer to this question to a given audience or they ask this audience to bring out the answer themselves, provided that the question expresses a shared concern between the protagonists or has been made so in the opening address. Explicit language always relates to a question, even if it does not appear to do so. This explains why empirically oriented analyses of language have failed—from Frege, Russell, and Wittgenstein, to Searle and Austin—to develop a question-view of language of the type we are attempting here. These thinkers were dominated by propositionalism, hence their obsession with reducing the meaning of sentences to truth-values. They could not see language as the embodiment and the implementation of the question–answer dualism since they conceived even questions as ways of asserting something, as only "answers" do. Questioning, like negation, was seen simply as a matter of propositional modality. In their world, we deal with statements because what matters is the truth-value of such statements and only assertive judgments have truth-value, whether in isolation or in inferential chains. The sole concession these philosophers of language would have accepted would have been to integrate questioning into the broad category of speech-acts. In this view, question-raising would become a mode of intentionality, one which is referred back, in the last analysis, to a subjectivity generally situated outside of language or indexicalized by language.

The problem here is that linguistic exchanges, or even continuous monologues, cannot be reduced to a mere sequence of propositions related to one another simply on the basis of their inferred or observed truth. Nor can they be reduced to a mere chain of logical links, as though propositions emerged by themselves in response to the sole requirement of expressing something true, independently of the problems which gave rise to their utterance, and as if what they answered to were irrelevant. Nonetheless, the role of context as a set of problems to be faced cannot but appear as relevant to the production of these utterances. One must supersede the limited task taken by philosophers of language of only analyzing propositions as bearers of truth-values and seeing their links as merely logical, as if the problems underlying the use of language were merely chronological and counted for nothing. The reason for such a situation is that the context helps us understand why sentences purport to convey something other than their truth-value or their inferential value embodied in the link between interconnected truth-values. If I say, for instance, "It's cold outside," whether this is true or not, the reason why I utter such a phrase at a given moment cannot be fully explained by appealing to speech-act theory alone, nor to any current empiricist view of language, even one which is based on the "language of sensation" which only describes how we use language to record the impact of sensible qualities in speech.[2] If I say something like "It's cold outside," this is not because I want to show my keen sense of observation but because there is a problem with the weather (for example, because I have to choose my clothes before going out) to which my statement is an answer. This answer is intended to provoke, by its impact, by the questions it raises, some response in the audience. At the outset, I have a *question* in mind ("Should we go out all the same?" or "Should we get our coats?" etc.). The difficulty with the usual examples we find in textbooks of analytic philosophy is that they neglect this dimension of question-relatedness. Russell's famous example, "Is the present King of France not bald?" echoes an unrealistic question that nobody would actually raise.[3] Why would anyone ever utter such a sentence if the speaker had no particular question in mind? The sentence is nonetheless analyzed for itself. As a result, once on the table, the only debate that can ensue is whether this proposition is true, false, metaphorical or nonsensical. Most of all, this sentence does not respond to any problem raised by any real

---

[2] As in J. L. Austin, *Sense and Sensibilia* (Oxford: Oxford University Press, 1962), or as in phenomenology more generally.
[3] B. Russell, "On Denoting," *Mind*, vol. 14, no. 56, 1905, pp. 479–94.

locutor; it appears, rather, as the illustration of a philosophical question nobody asks in real life. Hence the lack of solution as to its real meaning ("Is it an absurd or false sentence?"). The question which should be addressed to the locutor who utters "Is the present King of France bald?" is why, indeed, he is even raising such a question, since there is no present King of France. What does he mean when he asks this question?

When we say something in normal circumstances, i.e. not in textbooks, which are detached from any actual context of utterance, we always raise, at the same time, a question. Every language user knows this de facto, in contradiction with what most philosophers of language have upheld for many decades. To deepen this approach to language, let us consider some additional examples.

Discourse as the answer to an implicit question

If someone addresses his boss by telling him, "You're an honest man," it is most likely that the addressee will feel somehow in question, as if the question of his honesty had been raised or, worse still, was a legitimate concern. If taken literally, however, this statement is in itself a compliment, formally speaking. Nonetheless, anyone confronted with such a sentence would rightfully feel that it is really no compliment; quite the contrary, indeed. The reason is that this statement, like any other, is perceived and received as an *answer*. As such, it raises the question of the question which is presupposed in the address, i.e. the question which is at stake. Hence the question to which that statement is viewed as the answer is: "Are you honest (or not)?" The fact that such a question has been raised in the first place implies that it makes sense to ask it, otherwise why would the locutor bother to say it in the first place? The questioning implied in the speaker's attitude explains why the interlocutor rightfully feels in question. Such an attitude is certainly not advisable, particularly if one wants to keep one's job. Let us now imagine the effect that the same utterance would have during a televised political debate during a presidential campaign. One of the two debaters casually mentions "my opponent is an honest man." Such a statement would have a disquieting and insidious effect on the audience, since it implies that this very question, i.e. the question of the honesty of the competitor, is somehow relevant. It would unavoidably raise doubts about that opponent's honesty, as if the question merited further investigation while at the same time claiming that the right answer is that he or she is honest, since this is what has literally been affirmed. To speak, then, is to offer an answer, but an answer to a question that the audience is itself asked to take on, by virtue of the fact that no answer can be envisaged without considering the question to which it is an answer and which is raised by this simple fact. Agreement or acceptance here would mean that the audience accepts the answer given without further questioning, confirming the answer for what it is: a true answer to a question that is thereby solved.

The same reasoning applies to negative statements. If I say, "John is not lying," this statement is received as an answer. But to what question? Is John then a liar? If I say that he is not, this proves that the question makes sense, otherwise why would I have said this, even if only to deny it? Let us consider a further example. If I say to a friend who hopes to see me soon, "Yes, I'll come tomorrow," she is more or less assured that I shall actually come tomorrow. But if I affirm something apparently stronger, such as "yes, I'll definitely be there tomorrow," which expresses the fact that raising some doubt makes sense (given my usual habits), my interlocutor will certainly have doubts about my presence, for the simple reason that I have literally raised a doubt that is supposed to be irrelevant to my very statement.

The same operation in which questioning is always the underlying structure of understanding can be seen in Freud's famous analysis of denial (*Verneinung* or negation). How does problematology allow us to explain this fact that a statement can mean exactly the contrary of what it affirms? If I say to someone "I have nothing against you," by this she will understand "I have something against you." Rhetoricians have known this figure of speech since the Romans, under the name *praeteritio*, but Freud uses this figure of speech to explain how strong desires, however repressed, reappear at the surface of the mind in the form of a negation which he calls *denial*.[4] In rhetoric, we also use minimization to respond to a speaker when a high level of problematicity implies a high potential for aggressivity. What matters here, rather, is understanding how that figure of denial or *praeteritio* works, and more specifically how we can account for the inference from such a statement to the opposite one as being its true meaning. The only valid way to reason in this matter is to recognize that we here face an *answer* which corresponds to a question *which we simultaneously* (i.e. *through negation*) *declare as not being raised* (e.g. the question of my hostility toward my interlocutor). If you had explicitly asked me, "do you have anything against me?", the fact of having responded "no" ought to have been sufficient to put an end to the story, by literally suppressing the suspicion literally raised. This is quite an unambiguous answer and it brings the original query to an immediate conclusion. But if this question has never been explicitly asked, and if I say, without apparent reason, "I have nothing against you," I implicitly raise the question of my hostility towards you at the same time as I deny that it is relevant. As it is contradictory to uphold these two claims simultaneously with the same answer, the proposition "I have nothing against you" destroys itself and proves a self-defeating utterance. Which answer remains, then, once the question has been raised if the answer I originally proposed disappears? Only the opposite answer can then impose itself, namely that I have something against you. This is the way we all understand such a denial.

These examples show that a statement, a proposition, is actually an *answer* (*apokrisis* in Greek, hence the word *apocritical*) and should always be considered as one. Such an answer always refers, in turn, to a question, whether raised or solved. This fact confirms that language has a dual nature: answers are apocritical as answers but also problematological in that they refer to questions, namely the questions they raise as well as those they answer, i.e. those we answer when we

---

[4] S. Freud, "Negation" [1925], in *Metapsychology*, Standard Edition, vol. 11 (London: Penguin Books).

speak or write. This feature of language is worth noting, since it can be found in even the most banal examples of language use. This can be observed by taking the example of an elementary assertion in which questioning seems totally absent and apparently out of place. No allusion, no reference to any question can apparently be found by clinging to the mere formal surface of the statement, although, as I shall show, questions are part of its "underlying structure." For example: "Napoleon lost at Waterloo." Such an assertion is elementary since it has one subject and only one predicate. No question is expressed there. Assertions with such elementary structures are extremely common. No trace of a question appears or seems necessary to understand these sentences. But can we really be so sure of that? Philosophers and linguists alike seem convinced about this, but how do we actually proceed when we understand such a sentence and its terms? In order to reach this understanding, we have to know, among other things, and even if only approximately, *who* Napoleon is, *where* Waterloo is, *what* happened there, *when* it happened, and *what* a battle is. All these referential terms are nothing but interrogatives, used to indicate that the corresponding questions have been taken up and answered. The terms, nouns and attributes, are made for that. The Greeks, incidentally, called such interrogatives *categories*, probably because the terms employed in Greek to express categories are all interrogatives, something we tend to lose sight of in our modern conception of categories.[5] *Who* is Napoleon for a given speaker or audience? This term refers to a cluster of answers, indeterminate in number and known in variable ways by each individual, even if there is a common cluster of shared knowledge which is necessary for us to communicate with one another about Napoleon. These answers all bear on questions of *who* Napoleon was, *where* he went, and *what* he did at another moment (or *when*), and so on. The word "*Napoleon*" has the virtue of recapitulating all these implicit

---

[5] Aristotle. *Categories*. See especially Charles Kahn, "Questions and Categories," in *Questions* (ed. H. Hiz, Dordrecht, Reidel, 1978), p. 227. It was William of Ockham (1288–1347) who first underlined this fact.

answers without having to mention them, if not explicitly raised by the interlocutor. It is like a reservoir of knowledge from which communication must draw. So Napoléon is the man *who* made the 18 Brumaire, *who* won the campaign of Italy, as well as the man *who* had an affair with Désirée Clary, *who* eventually married Josephine (and so forth). Each term, *Napoléon, Waterloo, lose*, etc., is a shorthand summary of multiple answers, which do not need to be recalled or which are partially known. The terms of language cover a whole range of questions which are no longer raised, and these terms synthesize the whole gamut of answers to those questions referred to by the interrogatives *"who," "what," "where,"* which, used affirmatively through assertive propositions, draw out the indeterminate arrays of answers conditioning the linguistic exchange. Language presupposes that its protagonists avail themselves of a minimal number of common answers for which each linguistic term is a summary, a digest, or a memory. The terms of language are meant to economize on the answers to be given. For example, when we use the term "London," we avoid having to specify a cluster of possible aspects of places or itineraries, although we are still able to understand what we mean by the term "London" and to convey it successfully to others. Luckily, terms spare us from having to specify all those answers and this, indeed, is precisely their role. These questions—*where, when, why*, etc.—do not reappear in our exchanges unless there is a problem in the understanding of the message. Terms condense a sequence of solved questions, which, though having disappeared in these terms, can be revived if the terms used prove to pose a problem for the audience.

How did philosophers and logicians, such as Frege, the first to be interested in meaning as a logical identity between equivalent statements, treat these concrete realities of language? They negated these realities and erased the role played by questioning in the determination of meaning in real contexts, preferring to focus, as in science, on *reference* rather than on answerhood when dealing with terms and propositions. Reference, in propositionalism, is the object of the terms we use; it is *"what"* is denoted by these terms and, when we deal with propositions, it is their truth-value. Two propositions which have the same truth-value are thus equivalent for Frege.[6] Only their *sense*, i.e. the thought attached to them, makes a difference in interpretation. On the basis of Frege's views, for example, "Napoleon lost at Waterloo" is interchangeable with "the man *who* made the 18 Brumaire coup d'état is the one *who* lost at Waterloo" because each term and each statement have the same reference, so that we can always substitute one for the other while at the same time transforming either statement into the following: "Josephine's husband lost at Waterloo," without altering its truth-value and thus its meaning. But such an equivalence is completely unimportant in rhetoric, as it is in real life, because it is based on merely formal grounds. What is in question is the battle of Waterloo and who lost it, not Napoleon's marital status, even if it could give rise to an equivalent statement with respect to meaning. The questions we raise in saying "Napoleon lost at Waterloo" aim at an underlying significant fact of Napoleon's reign, marking its end or alluding to what usually happens to dictators engaged in endless military conquests. One could also be interested in the question about Waterloo or about who lost that battle and not in the fact that the defeated Emperor was married, or not, and to whom. The fact that Napoleon was Josephine's husband is completely irrelevant to the question concerning the battle of Waterloo and its meaning, restricted or extended, even if both expressions happen to refer to the same person and even if the same truth-values are preserved when one statement is substituted for the other.

As a result, the terms we use in our language are nothing but the epitome of diverse answers that are repressed as such, i.e. which are uttered without reference to any of these solved questions, even if we know it is the case and that it matters to understand these terms. In fact, *what* is in question is what we mean by "reference": *what*, *who*, *when*, and so forth, have a referential function because they are the designators of the objects of discourse and give it its content. The question–answer complex has disappeared in the process, but the

---

[6] G. Frege, "On Sense and Reference," in *Translations from the Philosophical Writings*, ed. P. Geach and M. Black (Oxford: Blackwell, 1970), pp. 56–78.

"*what*" nonetheless remains, if only in relative clauses. The term which condenses and integrates all variable (I do not say "subjective") knowledge is a kind of summary of these answers. They enable us to use the term "*Napoleon*" in a relevant way without further explanation from the beginning. They are present in the name "*Napoleon*" but they nonetheless remain somewhat presupposed in the multiple uses of the term "*Napoleon*": he is the man *who* . . . just as Waterloo is the place *where* and so we could regress back indefinitely along the chain of questions, if necessary (*what* is the 18 Brumaire? A coup. *What* is a coup? And so forth). Terms, in sum, are economical. They provide us with points of reference in our conversation with others, others who also have a presupposed level of common knowledge, which cannot be rendered explicit in every act of communication. In order to communicate efficiently, we need to resort to terms which allow us to economize and spare us the requirement of giving a long list of clarifications, even if the protagonists of the linguistic exchange do not avail themselves of exactly the *same* answers. These interlocutors nonetheless possess enough of these answers to understand each other and communicate *about* what is in question at the moment of their encounter without too many misunderstandings (otherwise, a dialogue between them would take place to clarify *what* is said) and to know *what* is in question with enough precision to be able to proceed further. They would then ask questions which would be revivified thanks to *wh*-interrogatives: "*who* was Napoleon?", "*what* did he do?", "*why* did he do it?", and so on, giving rise to answers mentioning *what* is in question through interrogative clauses.

Why are answers usually composed of a subject and a predicate?

This difference between the known and the unknown, however formal, is the source of the difference between terms usually called the *subject* and the *predicate*. In order to answer what is in question, the speaker must make the difference between question and answer recognizable. In order to achieve this, he relies on something which is "out of the question" and specifies what needs to be solved or is already solved. Answers usually contain both as an explicit difference. Let us consider once again a very elementary question: "What time is it?" Here, you are asking about the time, and you know enough about it (though not everything, otherwise there would be no question) to correctly use the term "time." You have, so to speak, an "idea" of *what* time is, even if you raise a question about it. You indicate what is problematic about it, through your use of the *"what."* As for the answer, it expresses the problematic *as being solved* and as a result, the expression of the answer combines both the questionable and the answer which concerns it. Hence the necessity of uniting a subject, which is usually out of the question, and a predicate, which indicates what you have asked and solved about this subject. "It's one o'clock" therefore stipulates what the question may have been or actually was, and what answer has been given to it. The difference between the two terms, i.e. the subject and the predicate, has no other origin than the requirement to express what is in question *as* no longer posing any question, by indicating that it has been solved.

Attributes allow us to specify questions (and are therefore found in answers), and the *what, where, when, why, who*, etc. designate what is in question in that particular question, i.e. what the particular question was. Without this approach to predication, one risks getting lost in desultory or haphazard explanations about the complementarity of the subject and the predicate, all the more unsatisfactory in that they fail to explain why we need *two* different terms to express what eventually refers to one identical fact or state of affairs; hence, the copula linking them, which sometimes reflects their identity (e.g. "Napoleon *is* the Emperor of the French"). A proposition is structurally an answer because, as an answer, it expresses the problematological difference by referentially stipulating that what is in *question* is treated as being *solved* (since it is an *answer*). One then has a term for *"what"* the statement is about and another for what question was asked and which is now solved, a distinction embodied in the difference between subject terms and predicate terms. Answers, however, do not appear as answers but as referring to *what* is said. To the question, "What do you mean by that?", we are always able to substitute the question, "but what is it all about?" to say "what is in question in all this?" Terms, clusters of terms, and texts all raise questions about *what* they say and therefore mean. When someone addresses someone else, the question is always, "What is the question behind *what* you say or to *which* you answer by saying it?" In the *ad hominem* version of this process, we have "why do *you* raise such a question?" or even "why do *you* question me?", as if, in the last analysis, it is the other person who is to be questioned. Would there be any ethics, morals, or even politics, if the other was not a question for us, as we are one for the others (Hobbes)? And is not rhetoric the expression and modalization of these various possible encounters with others?

What are the most basic principles of *logos* and why?

The ultimate principles of thought and *logos* have always been considered an enigma. Aristotle contends that the principle of non-contradiction is the supreme principle of language and thought.[7] To deny such a principle (i.e. to contradict its validity) is to presuppose it, he argues, because to deny it while at the same time resorting to it by contradicting it is logically inconsistent. Is Aristotle convincing here? One cannot presuppose the value of consistency precisely when the latter is at stake without falling into a vicious circle. After all, the denial may be self-defeating, but does this really matter to the hypothetical opponent if he does not care about consistency? If one is against this principle, one is certainly inconsistent, but does this really matter? One only thereby proves that to be consistently inconsistent is inconsistent (and also consistent, since it is the basis of the initial claim). In other words, Aristotle has not succeeded in proving the absolute primacy and foundational feature of non-contradiction with

---

[7] Aristotle, *Metaphysics* 4 (or Γ), 3, 1005b 32.

regard to the other principles, any more than he has proved why thought and language *must* rely on the three principles of non-contradiction, identity, and sufficient reason (to which the principle of excluded middle is also sometimes added as a consequence). Why are these *three* principles foundational with respect to *logos* and why are *those three* essential to, if not constitutive of, human thought? The difficulty here is that each principle relies on the other two and is dependent on them for its own validity, without any one dominating over the others. The principle of reason should come first, since it claims that thought requires principles, but what then would be the reason (or principle) of such a principle? As for the principle of identity, it stipulates that A cannot be other than itself, but such a claim is another way of affirming the principle of non-contradiction. The latter bases its claim on the fact that there is a reason for A not to be non-A at the same time, which is that A would in this case lose its identity. As a consequence, each of these principles implicitly refers to the others and requires them to be valid. In fact, we are in the presence of three self-evident principles which regulate thought in general but which are without real foundation, a foundation which itself, by definition, would require more originary principles to justify its own foundation, in turn.

Has philosophy or science been mistaken all these centuries in assuming these three basic regulatory principles to be preeminent, even if they scarcely seem to appeal to anything more than intuition or common sense? We feel that we must be consistent, that what is the case must be identical with itself, and that reason has the purpose of justifying what we say and what is the case in general. Should we go further, however, if it seems that we can scarcely succeed in doing so?

Perhaps, in the end, there is a good reason why we cannot succeed: a fallacious conception of reason, language, and thought underlies this impossibility. Propositionalism is successful because it deals with answers without questions. The aim of our questions, in most cases, is not to reflect or focus on these questions but to arrive at conclusions and solutions which enable us to get rid of these questions. By limiting ourselves to the mere consideration of efficiency and expediency, however, we are glossing over what is most essential to thought, namely its innermost workings and its real foundation. What counts, in philosophy especially, is not merely *having* results, but also understanding the process which leads to these results. In other words: "no solution without question," to loosely paraphrase a famous slogan of American history.

Problematology is better suited to provide a solution to the "enigma of the three principles" because, instead of reading these in a propositionalist way, as has always been done, it reformulates them as the source and embodiment of problematological differentiation in language and thought. There are three basic principles of *logos* because there is one requirement for answers, one for questions, and one for their differentiation conceived of as a passage from question to answer, reasoning being the source of this passage.[8]

A) The *principle of non-contradiction* can be considered the principle of answerhood. What makes an answer an answer? The most obvious and indisputable answer is that an answer is *not* a question, i.e. an alternative, A or not A. As a consequence, then, an answer must express one of the above and have the form A *or* not-A. It is therefore impossible for an answer to be both A and not-A with regard to the same question because it is only the question itself that can embody both. This is why debates and contradictory views defended by different protagonists in a dialogue or a controversy are possible: they are each *questioners*. Strictly speaking, the principle of non-contradiction merely stipulates that an answer is not a question, and where there is a contradiction, there can be no answer. Problematological difference is then the underlying imperative of language and thought in general.

---

[8] The principle of excluded middle states that an alternative must have at least two possible answers, a third one being excluded: "yes" or "no" are here potential answers, with "maybe something else" being excluded because it would leave the question totally open or unsolved.

B) The *principle of identity* is a principle that regulates more specifically the chain of questioning. *What* is in a question is something which must remain identical throughout its various expressions and sub-questions. The propositionalist reading specifies only that A is A and cannot be anything but A. This definition excludes questioning per se, as though identity were a self-evident requirement. What a problem is remains *what* it is in spite of the various displacements that may express it in different questions, each being a different version or reformulation (according to the results obtained) of the initial problem. Greimas has called this phenomenon *isotopia*, but it was already emphasized by Aristotle, when he wrote the *Topics*.[9] Topics also have the function of providing unity to discourse and dialogue.

C) The *principle of reason*, when understood as a mere ontological principle, stipulates that nothing is without reason, not even this very statement. What then could be the reason of such a principle? Once again, we are plunged into an infinite regression, a vicious circle, or what is rightfully called a *question-begging* process.[10] Perhaps we should restrict ourselves to a propositionalist reading: every judgment has a reason which is itself another judgment, or each thing has a reason to be what it is. But what is the reason of the first reason, if there is such a reason, since what is *first* cannot have something anterior to it? The problematological reading of the principle of reason is better suited here because it highlights the process of reasoning itself, without leading to such deadlocks. It can be formulated as

---

[9] A. Greimas, *Stuctural Semantics*, tr. R. Schleifer (Lincoln: University of Nebraska Press, 1983).

[10] For many, such as Carnap or Collingwood, metaphysics is the study of this embarrassment. Is there a first reason or cause which is itself without reason or cause, a *causa sui*? According to the principle of reason, such a cause would be contradictory. There is thus no first cause and the universe has always existed, without beginning and without reason. In the Critique of Pure Reason (A426/B454), Kant shows that these two positions are equally valid but are ultimately undecidable, hence the solution, which consists in maintaining that the principle of reason is a principle which links answers and questions, and justifies this relationship as a difference that is always to be applied and respected.

follows: there is no answer without a question that is the reason for this answer. The principle of reason characterizes answering as a dynamic process rooted in questioning. The problematological difference hinges on problematological *differentiation*. Such an account does not fall into circularity, nor does it need any other principle to justify it.[11]

[11] Is not the problematological difference, with questioning as its embodiment, the new foundational principle? If we ask what is first, the only answer we can give is that it is questioning itself, and if we call this into question, we still confirm our first answer, since we are questioning. Therefore, there is no other answer to what is first than questioning itself. Any other *answer* would presuppose *questioning*, since it would already be an *answer*.

3
Rhetoric and argumentation: the unity of the field

In what sense are questions the subject-matter of rhetoric?

Without the possibility of alternative answers, or even of more than one answer to a given question, rhetoric would be inconceivable. If it sufficed to answer questions in an unequivocal manner, there would be no rhetoric. If someone asks "what time is it?" and I give her the exact answer, there is no discussion; the dialogue stops and the question disappears through its resolution (i.e. the act of giving the answer). For rhetoric to emerge, an alternative must remain possible or another must arise in the folds of the literal answer, or because of this literal answer. This is due to the fact that the real question at stake lies elsewhere and is not literally the one that is posed. There is another question underlying or implied in the first question which gives it its sense and is understood by all the protagonists as implicit or, as linguists sometimes say, is "implicated" in the first question as the real one to be answered. Reaching it appears as the true goal of the linguistic exchange.

As a discipline, rhetoric includes argumentation as well as rhetoric *stricto sensu*. The latter involves the suggestion of devices which relate the explicit to the implicit through the use of figures. Argumentation, on the other hand, provides answers through reasons and arguments, which are often literal inferences. But there would be no rhetoric in the two areas of the discipline without the existence of alternatives, i.e. without questions. Such questions are the basic subject matter of any use of rhetoric, whether argumentative or not. They are, quite simply, dealt with in a different manner in rhetoric *stricto sensu* and in argumentation. Rhetoric always begins with a question to which it suggests that some other question (other than the corresponding literal one) is at stake. Rhetorical discourse suggests, implies, implicates, or "implicitates" another answer (i.e. leads a reader, viewer, or any audience in general, to "jump" to an implicit or implied conclusion). Rhetoric is a suggestion, by inference or by figurative language, that something other should be inferred or apprehended. In argumentation the suggestion of a conclusion is made through inference, based on reasons, arguments, or even linguistic markers, which induce that conclusion. If I say, for example, at the end of a seminar, that "it's one o'clock," the question of time is brought to the fore because of what we generally do at one o'clock, namely have lunch.[1]

The general formula, which epitomizes the specific nature of rhetoric, is then the following:

(1) $\quad a_1 \rightarrow q_1 \bullet q_2$

This is probably the most fundamental rhetorical formula because it underlies the unity of both rhetoric *stricto sensu* and argumentation while also explaining how rhetoric works as a specific process.

As already mentioned, there would be no rhetoric in the sole utterance of a proposition like "It is one o'clock" if someone had merely asked, "What time is it?" The interlocutor would have simply replied, "It is one o'clock" and that would be that; the question would have vanished once answered. But if the locutor says, "It's one o'clock," *although no one has asked the question*, it must be because he has another question in mind. The question to which a_1 literally answers cannot be a question q_1 that no one has raised. The literal

---

[1] We call such an association of ideas a *topos* or a commonplace. A *topos* often serves as one of the premises of inference in rhetoric because it is left implicit. It does not have to be made explicit due to the fact it is common and shared knowledge, or a common or shared answer (that is, an answer to a question thereby solved and known by the protagonists).

answer is then figurative for another answer, namely a_2, which corresponds to the meaning of a_1 in these circumstances. Briefly put, the rhetorical aspect of a_1 implies that another answer is sought, namely a_2, because q_1 amounts to raising q_2; q_1 is not really at stake here, having not been explicitly raised. A_2 is what the speaker wants to convey or suggest to his audience with a_1. Hence, a_1 refers (we use the symbol of the arrow to express this relationship of "reference to something": →) back to q_1 which, in its turn, refers back to q_2, to which a_2 is the answer. But how can we have access to the answer "a_2" from "$a_1 \to q_1 \bullet q_2$"? Without *topoi* or shared knowledge about such a link, this task is impossible.

As a result, there are two possible readings of the formal link between a_1 and a_2: one is argumentative, the other is what we call rhetorical in a strict sense because it is a figurative or non-literal reading of "a_1." In principle, one can choose either, and it is this equivalence between those two readings that renders the foundation of rhetoric *stricto sensu* and argumentation equivalent. Some examples will enable us to verify this. If I say "It's one o'clock" to suggest "It's time to have lunch," I can say either:

2) "It's one o'clock, *therefore* let's have lunch" (argumentative reading)

or

3) "It's one o'clock, let's have lunch" (rhetorical reading: to say A is to say B: we could even affirm "Well, it's time to have lunch," without saying "It's one o'clock").

We can therefore write:

4) "a_1" → "a_2" or, if one prefers, "a_1" = "a_2"

To say "a_1" refers (→) to saying "a_2," even though we do not say "a_2." We can conclude our seminar by simply saying, "It's one o'clock," without further ado, to suggest that the lecture is over because it is lunch time. "It's one o'clock" can be seen as an implicit *argument* for having lunch, or it can be merely understood as a way of figuring out, of saying (without, sometimes, saying it explicitly) that it is time to go to lunch. Therefore, "a_1" = "a_2" can mean $a_1 \rightarrow a_2$ or $a_1 = a_2$. In the first case, the rhetoric of the utterance is argumentative (the arrow "$\rightarrow$" then indicates an inference) and in the second, the utterance "a_1" is a way of indicating something other which is figuratively identical with a_1. Rhetoric in general, whether argumentative or not, consists in suggesting that what is evoked is that $a_1 = a_2$ or that $a_1 \rightarrow a_2$.

Of course, the choice of an argumentative reading or of a rhetorical one *stricto sensu* is based on the context, namely on the level of problematicity at stake. If the link between the time at which our seminar ends and lunch time is not clear in the mind of our students—i.e. if for them it is more problematic, due to a language barrier, for instance—the argumentative strategy will be more suitable. It anticipates possible explicit questions by dealing with them explicitly. Rhetoric is thus an economical means of avoiding explicitly providing a new literal solution by merely suggesting this solution, raising the question to the audience of what the literal final answer is.

Let us examine the implications of the equivalence between rhetoric *stricto sensu* and argumentation more closely. The fact of having a_1 as an answer implies a_2 as well. This is its reason or its argument. If I say "it's cold outside, *then* put your coat on," this statement is similar in structure to the following argument: "It's one o'clock, *then* let's have lunch." This is the argumentative reading of the link between a_1 and a_2.

The other reading is based on the figurative aspect of language and is more strictly rhetorical. It is no longer based on the inference of some conclusion, but covers the expression of the fact that saying a_1 (the quotation marks mean here "to say," hence "a_1") is presented as equivalent to saying a_2, unveiling some inherent meaning to a_1, an identity hidden in its literality, and thereby superseding and transforming the initial assertion into another one. To say a_1 is to say a_2 (or to figure it out) because a_1 refers also to q_2, to which a_2 is the answer. Saying something is here suggesting something else:

"$a_1 \rightarrow q_1 \bullet q_2$, then a_2" can mean either $a_1 \rightarrow a_2$, or $a_1 = a_2$.

To say "It's one o'clock" means "let's go to lunch," "a_1" is equivalent to "a_2." If it is one o'clock, *then* it is time to have lunch. I treat these two forms as equivalent, as if they expressed some identity, because saying a_1 is to say a_2, which implies that a_1 is a_2, not literally, of course, but figuratively. This is where "$a_1 \rightarrow q_1 \bullet q_2$," implying a_2, grants the two assertions a figurative identity. This is the "essence" of rhetoric *stricto sensu*: its purpose is to work on the figurative in order to provide an answer which, while being more or less questionable, is nonetheless treated and received *as an answer*. In my previous example, "It is cold outside," I am merely saying that it is necessary to cover up well to face the cold weather. In conclusion, then, with

1) $a_1 \rightarrow q_1 \bullet q_2$,

we have then two readings: an argumentative one

5) $a_1 \rightarrow a_2$

and a strictly rhetorical one

6) $a_1 = a_2$

A rhetorical expression can be expressed through the language of argument or implication,[2] or through the language of figurative speech, which amplifies, minimizes, or identifies some literal translation of what has been uttered.

The fact of saying without having explicitly raised the question q_1, which would have stopped the process with a_1, delimits the rhetorical fact in its largest sense: rhetoric begins when someone uttering A means or implies B. What is the relationship between this affirmation and our definition of rhetoric as the negotiation of distance between individuals on a given question? In fact, when B is figured out by A, the aim of A is to suggest some underlying question that A enables to solve as B. The real question at stake between the

---

[2] Even via a *modus pollens*: a_1, $a_1 \rightarrow a_2$, therefore a_2. If the first fact is known, we can leave it in the implicit and just say at one o'clock, "Let's have lunch now."

protagonists is the object of negotiation, as well as their distance, which can be very small as in conventional and everyday discussions.

In order to achieve this, there must be a *topos* linking the two questions q_1 and q_2. The *topos* enables the speaker to invent, discover, or make known that, when he says A, he implies B, let alone implicitly, as a conclusion or as a suggested reading of what is in question.

In rhetoric, there is always a question to which one answers with a "good" reason (a_1 leading to a_2 or which suggests it by inference) through some figure of style (a_1 is figuratively a_2). From conclusion to decision, there is also a good reason: namely, to put a coat on or to go to the restaurant.

These two readings of $a_1 \rightarrow q_1 \bullet q_2$, the argumentative and the figurative, can each be used preferentially with respect to each other, even if they are, from a rhetorical point of view, equivalent. To return to our first example, the speaker can say:

(5') "It's one o'clock, *therefore* let's have lunch."

But he can also express himself rhetorically and affirm, without implication:

(6') "It's one o'clock, let's have lunch," as if to say what time it is, meant the same as saying that the seminar participants should have lunch. In the above examples, we can always render 1) by 5) or 6), hence, once developed, by (5') and (6').

This law, "$a_1 \rightarrow q_1 \bullet q_2$," is the law of the unity of rhetoric. It leaves room either for rhetoric *stricto sensu*, as a figurative way of speaking, or for argumentation, as a way of implying a conclusion that the audience (or any speaker, for that matter) can infer through an argument.

But rhetoric in the larger sense is more than the laying out of a choice between rhetoric and argumentation. Rhetoric is a way of supplying an answer when the initial questions cannot be fully, scientifically, logically, or empirically decided once and for all. It is not because "a_1" $\rightarrow$ "a_2" that $a_1 \rightarrow a_2$. The quotation marks indicate a possible gap between words and things, reasons and causes, identity of speech and identity in the state of affairs of reality. Rhetoric fills the gap and it acts as if, in doing so, reality itself ceased to be problematic and answers could be arrived at. If Socrates has a red face, we have an argument that enables us to conclude that he has fever, but the color of his face is not the cause of fever. We nonetheless act as if we could infer some intrinsic link between the two, in light of the fact that Socrates does not drink and does not expose himself to the sun. The same reasoning applies to the figurative language of rhetoric *stricto sensu*. We act as if "It's one o'clock" were equivalent to "It's time for lunch" because to say one is to say the other, whereas both states of affairs are in fact distinct. This raises the question of what we mean when we utter either phrase. Here it is the underlying question which enables us to establish a relationship of identity. In fact, "It's one o'clock" might very well lead to other statements and to different behavior. When we say "a_1" = "a_2," the question is: what is the relationship between what is said in a_1 and what is said in a_2? Is this relationship a cause, an effect, a mere reason for uttering a statement, or is it a figure of speech, since we are only presenting "a_1" = "a_2" as $a_1 = a_2$, and "a_1" → "a_2" as $a_1 \to a_2$? Rhetoric spares the audience from having to pursue such an inquiry by postulating the answer. The audience succeeds in doing so by appealing to a *topos* or various *topoi*,[3] which enable it to establish the link between a_1 and a_2, based on the real underlying question, "What do we usually do at one o'clock?", which evokes various answers as *topoi*.

The two basic principles of rhetorical strategy

Rhetoric being the negotiation of distance between individuals on a given question, the speaker can adopt different yet equivalent strategies. He can play on the question: this is the *ad rem* strategy and he may argue in favor of one answer against another, for instance. He can also work on the distance between himself and his audience, to diminish this distance, increase it, or simply to reaffirm it, as a way of

---

[3] See M. Meyer, "What is the Use of *Topics* in Rhetoric?" *Revue Internationale de Philosophie*, vol. 4, 2014, pp. 447–62.

expressing his difference, i.e. his status, through signs, clothes, gestures, or postures, and so forth. He can also opt for a more radical *ad hominem* strategy which can be direct opposition or any mark of rejection, leading in any case to an increased distance from the other, by explicitly putting her into question. The basic principle underlying the speaker's various strategies in this regard is given by the *principle of adherence* we all have experienced in our personal life. This principle stipulates that there is equivalence, from a rhetorical point of view, between an *ad rem* argument and an *ad hominem* argument, one often being the substitute for the other, i.e. when one "lacks" good arguments to win the case. The reason for this equivalence is that we feel personally in question whenever we experience some disagreement or disapproval of what we think or do, sometimes even of our personal tastes. It is as if we were rejected as a person. Knowing this, opponents often shift from an argument about the question itself to an argument aimed at the speaker or at the audience, leading to a wider gap between them. In some ways, we are what we think, choose, and say. But a speaker can also directly react to the distance itself, especially if the question is highly problematic. The inverse is also true, of course, and the passage to the *ad hominem* strategy can bring the parties closer to each other (e.g. "You and I are both experts on this subject, so you know as well as I do that . . . is the case," and so forth).

The *law of distance* runs as follows: distance L increases when E (the *ethos* or speaker) and P (the *pathos* or the audience) become increasingly separated due to the increasing level of problematicity of the question motivating their exchange. $L = E - P$ and as a consequence $\Delta L = \Delta (E - P)$, with E standing for *ethos* and P for *pathos*.[4] The more a question is divisive, and thus conflictual, the greater the distance. Friends, lovers, or spouses who cease to get along usually put distance between themselves in order to avoid seeing each other. The effect of distance is always to diminish the emotional impact of the conflict, thus enabling the protagonists to be more "reasonable" or at

---

[4] Δ = distance.

least, less passionate in their choices. The resolution that everyday life does not succeed in bringing about, when the conflict is too intense or without resolution, the court, for example, may succeed in bringing about. A legal trial increases distance by playing on the formality and the decorum of the court.

Questions, too, have an effect on distance. The more divisive they are, the greater the distance between audience and speaker widens. The level of problematicity of a question increases that distance. The speaker can always pass from the level of the *ad rem* treatment of a question to the level of the *ad hominem*, especially when the distance is short, and when playing on the emotional aspects of the questions is easier to mobilize. The *ad hominem* is intended as a substitute for the *ad rem* to the extent that, when the speaker runs short of arguments, he usually displaces his attack onto the interlocutor. He can also do the reverse and begin to accommodate his audience by humor and flattery in order to gain its approval more easily, before he comes to grips with the question itself. This explains why people who are very much opposed on a given issue often wind up attacking their opponents on other questions, or personally, i.e. for lack of *ad rem* or objective arguments. The statement, "But you, you were in power when salaries were supposed to go up, and you didn't do anything," is a familiar reproach heard from many contemporary politicians who fall short of objective arguments when they have to defend themselves for instance, on their economic policy. When we cannot find the right arguments or good reasons, we generally resort to personal attacks, which have a greater destabilizing impact because it is people themselves who are put in question.

The principle of adherence explains why there is a rhetorical equivalence between the *ad rem* type of arguments and the *ad hominem* type. It covers a phenomenon that is known to everyone by their own personal experience. When people disagree on an opinion they hold, they often feel rejected or more fragile in their life choices; at the very least, they feel called into question in what they are, do, or like. In some way, a negative view on answers, on a lifestyle, or on basic tastes is transferred onto those who hold that view, who then feel associated with the negative features initially reproached to one of their opinions or choices. This explains why human beings need the approval of others and cannot stand the least disagreement on some of the minutest questions, or even about their tastes, as if their whole life were at stake in the latter. But an *ad hominem* strategy can also be used to diminish the distance. We feel more at ease when our shopkeeper strikes up a conversation with us, by speaking about the weather or our family, as if she were interested in these topics, even though we are fully aware that she does not care. In general, these amenities, which belong to politeness, enable us to entertain easy and pacified relationships with most people and purport to moderate the possible negative impact of distance because human encounters always put us somewhat in question in various ways. This phenomenon recalls the famous Hobbesian alternative "violence or ethics," or the Schmittian couple "friend or enemy." We adhere in what we say; we "are" to some degree what we uphold and are always implied and implicated to a certain extent (determined by our sensitivity) as human and social beings in the choices we make in holding the ideas and discourses we do.

Rhetoric or argumentation?

Having shown that rhetoric and argumentation share the same structure, namely $a_1 \rightarrow q_1 \bullet q_2$, which can lead to either as a strategy of persuasion, the question now is: why should we adopt a rhetorical rather than an argumentative interpretation of this fundamental law? When is rhetoric a better strategy than argumentation, and when is the opposite more suitable? In order to answer these questions, let us return to the definitions of rhetoric *stricto sensu* and argumentation as the two types of rhetorical processes in which questions are dealt with in specific ways, i.e. as distinct from science and formal logic. Argumentation is rooted in divisive and conflictual questions that are explicitly raised. To use a metaphor, we could say that these questions are "on the table" and lead to an open debate, with explicit alternatives represented in the opposition of the protagonists. They represent the "yes or no" response to a given answer, but also a chain of opposing answers to some initial problem which divides them. The best example of contradictory debate can be found in court because here it is formalized by legal procedures. Legal reasoning has always been the model of argumentation (Perelman) because, when an argument does not lead to agreement, it is incumbent upon the judge to rule on who is right and who is wrong. Indeed, this is even a legal requirement prescribed by the law since the Napoleonic codes of civil law.

Rhetoric *stricto sensu* operates in a different manner. Questions are less problematic and can be handled directly by offering answers that abolish (or repress) the underlying questions at stake. This solution is, of course, a purely formal one, since it does not suffice to present a question as solved in order to actually solve it, even if a solution would make it vanish. Hence the need for amplification or minimization: these are the usual means by which we resort to eloquence (or elegance), to style, and to figures of speech, amplifying what is supposed to be good and ignoring or minimizing what is deemed to be bad, as in funeral orations where the orator is supposed to gloss over what is negative about the deceased. Due to the fact that the speaker does not have to justify his answers, the audience can be charmed and manipulated by the speaker, in contrast to argumentation, in which only answers that are justified are allowed as such. The pleasantness of discourse is in itself the basic feature which can provide the illusion of offering the right solution in the situation to be confronted. Questions which are "under the table," so to speak, are necessarily those that are not very problematic. They are better handled rhetorically, by "swallowing" the questions in the presented solution. It is a way of burying them so that appeals to the right emotions and elevated eloquence of style are best suited for the speaker to handle those questions.

At a short interpersonal distance, you can have rhetoric or argumentation, just as both can also be used at wide distance. The basic effect that distance brings to rhetoric at large is the modulation or modalization of the emotional aspect, habitually present when distance is short. When oil was spilled along the Alaskan coast, the inhabitants had a strong emotional response despite those responsible being initially unknown to them. Here emotions of anger made it as if the distance between the parties had suddenly collapsed in the damages caused to them. It was also clear that distance and above all the high level of problematicity created by the damage caused by the oil spill also led to an argumentative counter-attack in court. In contrast, a dispute with my son about the right time to go to bed is emotional from beginning to end because the personal link between us is very strong and the distance is highly reduced: he is my son and I cannot treat him like anybody else with whom I might have a problem. But if I want to be obeyed, and since he does not want to comply with my order, I must offer good arguments to convince him to be "reasonable," for example, by invoking the attention and the concentration needed to get good school grades. But at the same time, I become more formal by adopting a more distant role, that of the father figure.

We can now establish a synthetic view of what is going on in rhetoric and argumentation (Figure 2). A few words about advertising, which mingles all of these strategies, will illustrate these differences and render more concrete the reasons for adopting either strategy embodied in rhetoric *stricto sensu* or argumentation.

In argumentation as in rhetoric *stricto sensu* some other question than the one deriving literally from speech is at stake; this question gives to speech its true meaning. More specifically, rhetoric as

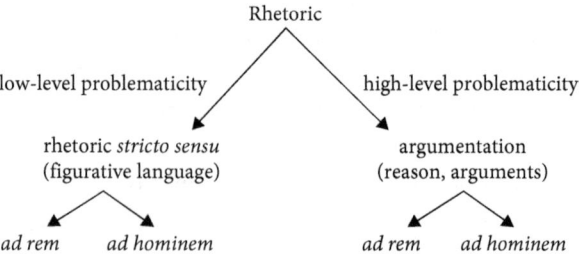

Figure 2 Diagram of rhetorical strategies

figurative language produces answers that are formulated as if the underlying question no longer arose. In order to achieve such a goal, eloquence (or elegance) and style are absolutely necessary. Sometimes figurative language serves an everyday goal and sometimes it aims at creating an aesthetic effect. The objective remains the same, however: to give the audience the impression that nothing is problematic or that something has ceased to be problematic, that some question has disappeared because it has been dealt with successfully, and that the solution is now obvious, thereby leading to the conviction that no further problem arises with respect to this question. Amplification (+) of the resolutionary aspects of the answers is then equivalent to minimization (−) of what is questionable. These are the two most current strategies employed in rhetoric in everyday conversation. Rhetoric, then, smoothes the problematic aspects which are always attached to social encounters, just as funeral orators have to solve the problem of presenting the deceased's life as devoid of any problem, as if he or she had only ever exhibited excellent personal qualities. The most interesting case, however, seems to be advertising.

Our first example is provided by advertisements for Chanel N°5. Here, the advertiser is confronted with an almost insurmountable difficulty, that of translating a fragrance into a visual commercial. How can this be achieved? The advertiser in fact follows the same strategy we have described. He treats the problem as being solved, but he radicalizes this solution. Let us focus on the famous TV spots on Chanel N°5. Such ads are based on the idea that, with Chanel N°5, all one's problems disappear. It is a magical solution because in real life, unfortunately, this is not possible, no matter how expensive the perfume. The ad will consequently stage the solution as a fairy tale, in which most problematic aspects of life can be overlooked or superseded thanks to Chanel N°5. The central feature of the commercial is Little Red Riding Hood. What is her problem? In this case, the answer is simple: to escape the wolves. Thanks to the power of Chanel N°5, it has become reality. She succeeds in taming the wolves and, instead of eating her, they all leave together to conquer Paris, symbolized in the TV spot by a door opening onto a golden Eiffel Tower which awaits them, with the wolves adopting the role of Little Red Riding Hood's bodyguards. This famous commercial has been seen on screens across the world for many years, but others have also been made that follow the same idea: with Chanel N°5, there are no problems anymore; all problems simply disappear.[5] The miracle accomplished by or through Chanel N°5 is a miracle only because the rhetoric of these commercials is the quintessence of rhetoric *stricto sensu*.

Many commercials do, however, have a different structure, which is argumentative rather than rhetorical when the initial problem is explicitly stated. Different brands of soap for washing machines, for instance, are directly compared with one another on TV or in newspapers, and the question explicitly put forward is that of their efficiency: which soap is best? The answer or argument for the "right" answer is buttressed by comparative advertisements. We also find mixed types of commercials for the same product, argumentative in some campaigns, rhetorical in others. Car brands, for instance, can be praised for the particular problems they solve, with numerous (comparative) arguments in favor of their technical advantages, such as speed or fuel consumption, but they can also be extolled as a source of higher status or because they increase the pleasure of driving, i.e. provoking the desire to extend the journey by taking nice little side roads which lead the driver to forget all the other problems of his life while driving the car advertised. Renault, for instance, built a whole advertising campaign on the pleasure offered by the comfort of their cars, which enables drivers to forget all of his or her other problems.

If we adopt the questioning view of rhetoric, the first sentence of Aristotle's *Rhetoric* becomes quite clear. Rhetoric and argumentation are the two possible, complementary ways of dealing with a question: either we confront it head on and give arguments pro and contra, or we offer an elegant answer in the guise of a solution. When we are

---

[5] There is another famous ad for Chanel N°5 in which the celebrated actress Carole Bouquet makes an orchestra rise from the ocean. This too is magic and is meant to show that real problems vanish when you are wearing that particular perfume.

confronted with a question that has no single literal answer or which is not even asked, a plurality of standpoints on that question is possible, referring to other questions which are the ones really at stake. Some answers are more likely than others and rhetoric is a means of finding or highlighting the "right" ones, by presenting them as more convincing or more pleasant, a discovery which is made possible by taking into account the problems of the audience, whether these problems are emotional or not.

How does the speaker induce the audience to lean towards the correct choice? He can proceed in two ways. Either he starts from the question itself, taking it as the starting point of his "speech" and giving arguments in favor of one of the two terms of the alternative. Or, a second solution, the speaker can address the question by directly focusing on the *answer* he has in mind, swallowing, abolishing, "repressing" the question, as if the sheer fact of suppressing the question in this manner were enough to bring about the right solution. Since the fact of providing an answer to an abolished question is not enough to convince or justify the validity of any answer, the only way to make such answers acceptable is to enhance the style by an adequate figurative language, usually tinged with the best eloquence possible. Is this not the way we have understood rhetoric *stricto sensu* thus far?

By way of conclusion, then, argumentation relies on explicit problems as its starting point. These problems are "on the table," so to speak. As for rhetoric *stricto sensu*, it relies on addressing an issue through the answers which may be given (without explicitly treating them as a source of alternative viewpoints). Rhetoric deals with questions "under the table," with what the speaker deems to be an unproblematic "solution," whereas argumentation puts the question "on the table" because he cannot escape from the opposed viewpoints, very often because of the high level of problematicity of the question.

Rhetoric and logic: two views of inference

Since Aristotle, reasoning has been considered less through the lens of the rhetoric vs argumentation couple than through the logic–rhetoric opposition. The difference between the latter two lies in the fact that logic excludes alternatives, while rhetoric does not. As a result, rhetoric is less conclusive, and attaches to alternatives certain probabilities of truth or occurrence. "The subjects of our deliberation," says Aristotle, "are such as seemed to present us with alternative possibilities (...). There are few facts of the 'necessary' type that can form the basis of rhetorical syllogisms."[6]

Hence the basic question of rhetoric since Aristotle: what is the specificity of rhetorical inference, i.e. of the enthymeme? In an enthymeme, it appears that some judgments remain implicit, either the conclusion or a premise. The premises concerned are usually either obvious truths or highly questionable ones, hence the advantage of leaving them implicit. If I transform "Socrates' face is red, thus he has fever" into a logical syllogism, I would have to add, "men with a red face have fever" in order to be able to deduce, necessarily, that Socrates has fever. The problem is that the implicit premise "those who have a red face have fever" does not make sense, given the number of other reasons to have a red face. People can stay too long in the sun or drink too much alcohol and thereby become red-faced. As a general premise, then, the unmentioned premises are either too numerous to name or else false, which means that they are likely to be true under certain circumstances which cannot be fully present in the premises (Socrates never drinks, nor goes into the sun). As for the conclusion, it has more impact if the audience draws it by itself. But in logic, the specification of all premises is absolutely necessary if one wants the conclusion to also be necessary. This indeed is the only guarantee of the validity of the conclusion, which in its turn must also be stipulated.

Is the difference between logical inference and rhetorical inference only dependent, then, on psychological variables or on a wish to manipulate what is affirmed at the beginning, while logical inference needs to be complete to be more "perfect" and thereby conform to the model of science? I do not think that the reasons explaining the

[6] Aristotle, *Rhetoric*, 1357a 3–25.

differences between these options hinge upon such factors. Logical inference is neither "stronger" nor indeed preferable to argumentative inference. It is a different mode of reasoning, adopted to different problems and circumstances. Logical reasoning is stronger with regard to logical validity (but it is circular to say so) because it brings out the necessity of the conclusion (usually called *apodicticity* by logicians), but in another sense the conclusion is less strong because the premises already "say it all." Rhetorical inference relies on selected and multiple *topoi* and judgments, bringing as new (because the conclusion is not implicitly contained in the premises) a contextual conclusion, and rendering it, in some ways, unexpected and controversial. Logical conclusions have been considered, among others by John Stuart Mill, as already contained in their premises.[7] The purpose of logical inference is simply to unfold what is already implicitly known. If I say, "All men are mortal" and "Socrates is a man," the conclusion that he is mortal is not only logical and true, it is also unsurprising. But it fails to explain the circumstances of his death. In contrast, if I affirm that Socrates shocked the notables of the city state and that he delegitimized them with his accusatory speeches, so that they wanted to get rid of him before he could influence the youth in the "wrong" direction, Socrates' condemnation (and suicide) is not necessarily implied in the premises, even though these premises help us to understand why it happened. As such, this inference brings something new, which is not contained in the initial description and which establishes a probable causal link between the two events, namely Socrates' subversive behavior and the strong response it provoked.

The real question, then, is how we can account for the differences between logical inference and rhetorical inference without presupposing that the latter is a weak form of the former, as is often claimed by logicians. The logical model of inference is better suited to expound the results of chains of propositions related conclusively, if not apodictically. The difference between the two types of inference

---

[7] J. S. Mill, *A System of Logic* [1843] (New York: Cambridge University Press, 2012).

bears on their formal features, which explains why logical reasoning is apodictic, and indeed has to be so, while everyday reasoning is rhetorical, being predicated upon circumstances and the nature of the interpersonal relationships on which rhetoric relies. Nonetheless, there is an underlying factor common to both: questioning, however different the manner in which questions are dealt with by either approach. Logic excludes any questions by positing their answers as premises of its inference, whereas rhetoric leaves these questions open by leaving implicit what would preclude those questions from arising.

Let us return to some examples. Suppose I am taking a stroll with a friend in the forest. Suddenly, ahead of us in the distance I see what looks like snakes curled up on themselves. These snakes could simply be a tangle of ropes, but this is only one possibility, the least dangerous one. I warn my friend to be careful since there is a potential danger ahead: "snakes are venomous." Two things may happen: my friend may stop walking entirely or she may ignore my warning and go on walking as if I had said nothing. What do these two alternative responses imply? Either she does not believe there are snakes ahead (since they are just ropes), or she does not believe that these snakes are dangerous. It amounts to *questioning* either my contention *about the subject* or questioning my claim *about the predicate*. These two questions are the only ones possible, and indeed they may give rise to a debate between us. Logical inference evacuates a priori these questions by answering them in the form of explicit premises. So if my friend replies, "No problem, let's keep going," I know that both either have been answered negatively in her mind and that we do not share the same answer concerning the situation (we do not face snakes or these snakes are not dangerous). A debate is possible since these two questions remain possible, and this is where rhetoric begins. In logical inference, this cannot happen because such questions on the subject or the predicate are eliminated at the outset by virtue of having their answers posited a priori as premises. This is why logical syllogisms often have two premises: one to exclude any question on the subject and another to avoid a priori any possible question on the predicate. As a result, the impossibility of an alternative is transferred to the conclusion, which is what renders it out of the question (i.e. apodictic). This, indeed, is the definition of what logicians call apodicticity: a judgment is apodictic if the opposite judgment is impossible. This is also the definition of logical validity. Logical inferences are apodictic. We now know why rhetorical inferences are not, since they generate conclusions which remain more or less problematic, or at least, potentially debatable.

The basic difference between a logical inference in which all premises are formulated and a rhetorical inference, in which they are not, is the fact that, by specifying all questions as answered in the premises, there is no room for further questioning, at the end as at the outset. In a rhetorical inference questions are left open and the debate can reappear, least of all because the conclusion is, as a result, only likely. Argumentation is a questioning process allowed for by the absence of the premises which would have prevented these questions from arising. If I say, "Socrates is mortal because he is human," I can ask why this is the case, but it would be nonsensical to do so if I add the premise "All humans are mortal" right from the beginning. This is because the question is itself answered in this very statement and this renders the conclusion "logically valid," i.e. necessarily true. Logic avoids questioning, whereas rhetoric reveals it. This is why logic has often been considered a stronger form of reasoning in one sense (no room is left for another conclusion) and a weak one in another sense (because no space is left for more flexible ways of reasoning by appealing to various other premises and answers). To transform a rhetorical inference into a logical one is therefore quite easy: I exclude any question on the subject ("Socrates is a man") and on the predicate ("All men are mortal") by giving the answer in both cases; this necessarily implies the truth of the conclusion ("Socrates is mortal"). The reason why we do not proceed in this way in everyday life and the reason why rhetoric is so useful is because the possible questions implied by any speech always remain quite numerous. Who would say that all snakes are venomous or exclude the possibility that ropes might indeed turn out to be snakes? The circumstances of observation are necessary to decipher the facts, and questions can arise at any point along the way. In logical reasoning, we would have to exclude the possibility that not all snakes are dangerous by affirming the first premise, "All snakes are dangerous," and by sticking to the fact that we are approaching snakes and not ropes. Logic, in this case, would be of no help. This is why we usually face two questions when we say "snakes are venomous": one on the subject (ropes or snakes?) and one on the predicate. By precaution, if not by ignorance, we should try to avoid walking on whatever it is that lies ahead of us. The same reasoning applies to Aristotle's example. This is because "all people who have a red face have fever" is false as a universal statement because only those who do not drink or do not go into the sun are referred to here. If you stroll around in the sun and have a red face, you are not necessarily ill. You could say, as Toulmin's model suggested, that "people who have a red face, who do not go into the sun and do not drink alcohol, have fever," but no one expresses him or herself in such a way in real life. This is why such statements are usually left unspecified. It would be too long and too "uneconomical" to put all premises on the table, even were they not false. We simply say, "He has a red face, he must be feverish" to suggest that we should check his temperature to see if he is ill. The question of the color of Socrates' face is raised to settle the "debate," to give an argument in favor of one answer to the question, "is he ill or not?"

Rhetorical inference is thus a questioning process and the questions it raises often remain at the end of the process, except in the case of law, where the judge has an obligation to resolve outstanding issues. The questioner relies on non-problematic opinions, which are often left implicit even if they are shared (*topoi*) by the interlocutors, who use them as a springboard to propound a non-problematic opinion formulated in such a way as to render it acceptable.

Ethos, pathos, and *logos* as present in rhetoric and argumentation

We saw earlier that the rhetoricians of the past, like those of the present, have more or less explicitly focused on one of the three components of the rhetorical relationship and, in doing so, subordinated the other two. But in all cases, the aim was to account for rhetoric in terms of the relationship between the three in general, whatever the priority given to one of the three. As discussed in Chapter 1, Plato focused on the role of the audience or *pathos*. Aristotle gave pre-eminence to *logos*, style, and enthymeme—even if he had recourse to each of these three elements to explain different kinds of rhetoric, such as legal rhetoric (*ethos*), epideictic rhetoric, or everyday conversation based on the use of pleasant discourse (*logos*), and deliberative discourse as found in politics (*pathos*). As for Cicero, he stressed the foundational mission of *ethos* by rooting true rhetoric in the role and virtues of the speaker. In my view, these three components, however important their role in each of these three currents of thought should instead be put on an equal footing. Rhetoric is as much grounded in *ethos* as it is in *pathos* and *logos*. This is what makes the rhetorical transaction distinct from all other intersubjective relationships. No synthesis of all the currents that contribute to the diversity of rhetoric is possible unless we accept the idea that *ethos*, *pathos*, and *logos* are each of equal importance. In order to develop such an integrated view, however, we need an operator of synthesis to articulate them. We need to study the role of each of these three components in turn and through the lens of the question-view of language and thought. For Aristotle, who granted supremacy to *logos*, *ethos*, and *pathos* nonetheless played a significant if subordinate role, yet these three elements remain unrelated in his work because he did not conceptualize rhetoric in terms of questioning.

Ethos, for problematology, is the person who addresses a question with an answer or who brings this question to the attention of the audience. His ability to do so can hinge upon his moral virtues, his expertise, or simply on his knowledge-oriented (or personal) authority to raise and deal with certain questions, whether universal or particular. As for *pathos*, its difference is here problematological: *pathos* is a questioning agency, acting within a certain distance. It represents other individuals who must be taken into account in social and political life. It is not necessarily more of an authority than *ethos*.

Pathos is simply another person, who has her own emotions and viewpoints which affect the problems she has, in a particular way. As for *logos*, it embodies the expression of the difference between question and answer, marking it explicitly and implicitly (i.e. contextually) so that interlocutors can recognize themselves as questioners or respondents, each in turn insofar as they recognize what is in question (or who is in question) and what is out of the question.

4

The common operators in figures and arguments

The main classes of arguments and their operators: identity, similarity, inference,[1] and contradiction

How many types of arguments and of audiences are there and on what basis can their nature and number be established? The answer to these questions is that they can be deduced from the four basic operations of responses for calling into question the speaker's position. When we argue about words or things, we always adopt a position on the answers given to us or which we give to the audience. First of all, we must be sure that words keep their meaning and have their identity confirmed by our responses. Semantic controversies, discussion of what we really mean, the interpretation we give of what is in question, all this belongs to a strategy of the explication of answers. The second type of argument (±) is given by modification of the answer, which requalifies or adds nuances to the initial answer. It is a way of preserving it as an answer. The third type of behavior is to add new answers, either to buttress the initial answer with clarifications or to offer a new and different line of thought, implying other statements which may eventually lead to the abandonment of the initial answer. We are thus very close to the contradiction of the latter. This explains why all our possible arguments can be ranged according to

---

[1] Inference can express a consequence as a different statement reinforcing the initial statement or leading to its rejection (−).

the operations =, ±, +, and −. The operation + is generally associated with inference, since an inference is a relationship between different statements. Let us consider the argument of precedent in law: it is a form of =, of identical norms implying identical treatment. To take the example of an *ad hominem* argument such as "If you don't do this, you'll be punished," this, surely, is not a logically valid inference. But nonetheless it highlights perfectly the qualification of the action in terms of cause and effect (inferred by the audience). All arguments met in everyday life, if not also in the sciences, rely on identity, difference, and contradiction, provided that difference can mean requalification or addition, the latter leading to the reinforcement or to the negation of the initial position. All this is true for *ad hominem* structures (e.g. approval, rejection) and for the corresponding *ad rem* ones (agreement, contradiction).

By virtue of the correspondence between figures and arguments, we should not be surprised if the four operations regulating argumentation also allow us to qualify the main types of figures of speech. From identity to opposition, we have known since the Group Mu that this was the case.

The nature of the question and the way we handle it depends on its level of problematicity. More or less implicit, more or less in need of being expressed as problematic, varying levels of problematicity give rise to different types of figures, from figures of sound to tropes and figures of thought, where the question at stake is explicit. But this does not prove that they bring out answers that are deemed adequate: hence the four possible responses given by the audience, from agreement to disagreement, from identity to opposition, passing by way of similarity and the addition of an answer, before confronting the case of negation and opposition. Considered separately, figures must be considered to be the voice of the problematic when put on a scale of problematicity, whereas for the four operations providing the answers about the speaker, answers express the level of acceptance and deviation, thereby "measuring" the acceptance of what the speaker propounds. The fact that a speaker utters answers normally implies, with respect to pre-existing answers, a possible level of deviation from sheer approval. This is why the four basic operations of rhetoric can also be found in all the figures, i.e. in the figures of thought but also in those of sound, grammar, or meaning.

How many audiences and how many types of answers are possible?

This question may seem surprising because many people feel that there is an infinite number of answers and audiences. A closer look reveals that the range of possibilities of answers, and therefore of audiences, is in fact limited to a small number: =, +, ±, and −. Each of these four possible responses characterizes the four possible classes of audiences. These audiences reply by questioning more or less the answer (*ad rem*) given by the speaker or by questioning the speaker himself (*ad hominem*). There are only four ways of reacting to a speaker: you approve, you disapprove, and in between, you may modify his answer (and qualify or re-qualify it, by playing on words and their definition, for example) or you may simply add another answer. Authors have characterized these four types of response or operations in more or less the same way, by resorting to different terminologies, calling them *identity, similarity, difference,* and *opposition*,[2] or, if we follow the terms used by the Group Mu, *suppression-addition*,[3] *permutation, addition,* and *suppression*. These four types of response are intended to epitomize the classical operations just described, but they also add to the latter an emphasis on "deviation" with respect to literal language:[4] they are designated by repetition (phonetic, syntactic, and semantical), even if other words are employed which create a form of identity, requalification of the initial answer as a substitute, addition (of a new syllable, of a word, of a sentence, or of a group of sentences), and negation.[5] But as such they fail to integrate the figures of thought, which literally express a

---

[2] We could also label the four operators "identity," "difference," "inference," and "opposition" since a similarity nonetheless implies a minimal difference.

[3] This operation allows for maintaining identity across different terms. This concept of suppression-addition is not used, as I propose here, to specify the operation ±. This is why the vision of the Group Mu blurs the real issue to some degree.

[4] See J. Cohen, *La structure du langage poétique* (Paris: Flammarion, 1975), where he develops the concept of the figurative as a gap or a deviation from the literal.

[5] That is why, I suppose, Group Mu prefers to speak of suppression-addition in this case.

problem, even if the latter is "rhetoricized" in a form which leads the audience to consider it as tackled by the speaker. In the figures of thought there is no formal deviation with respect to literal language, but figures of thought are still figures, even though some theoreticians uphold the contrary view that they belong to argumentation. The rhetoric of textual meaning as an inference from a narrative is also left completely to the side. The classification of figures of speech, which has been tailor-made for literature and poetics, neglects the "rhetorical" side of the operators, in the sense that these four operations bear on the effect that an answer has on the audience and express possible responses to what is problematic. The ambiguity of a repetition is obvious: it can be something other than a synonymy (=)[6] and can also give a new outlook on the question (+), and qualify it (±) in another way, as in a definition which would resort to new elements (i.e. in order to avoid or win the debate and put any contradiction to one side, as in the debates on Islam and terror in which advocates of Islam deny that their religion, according to the definition they give, has anything to do with violence).

If the Roman authors and later, in the twentieth century, the Group Mu have relied on these four operations to explain the various rhetorical figures as well as the various types of arguments, these same operations were already singled out by Cicero:

> As to the actual form of the speech, its employment resembles that of weapons: it can be put to practical use, for threatening and attacking, as it were, but it can also be employed just like that, for the sake of giving delight. For instance, the doubling of a word is at one time forceful, at another time charming; the same can be said for repeating a word in a slightly altered, modified form, frequent repetition of the same word at the beginning of clauses, and return to the same word at the end of successive clauses, and also when one word repeatedly clashes with a certain other; adjunction; use of progressively stronger expressions; use of the same word several times in

---

[6] Perelman often used the example of *un sou est un sou* (a penny is a penny), a truth which no one can object to, but which suggests its opposite: namely, that even if a penny is not much, it is nonetheless the beginning of wealth. The equivalent English expression is "Look after the pennies, and the pounds will look after themselves."

different meanings; repetition of a word that was used earlier; and words that end in the same way or have the same case endings, or phrases that have the same length or resemble each other. There are also the figures of gradual development; inversion; elegant transposition of words; antithesis; asyndeton; avoidance of a subject; self-criticism; exclamation; minimizing; using the same words in several cases; relating what is derived from several individual things mentioned to each of them individually; appending a reason to a proposition; and also adding a reason to each separate statement; deferment; and again another kind of indecision; an unexpected turn; enumeration of points; another kind of self-correction; local distribution; running on; breaking off; imagery; answering one's own question; metonymy; the use of synonyms in successive clauses; effective order; reference; digression; and periphrasis.[7]

This is also a patchwork, even a hodgepodge, of most of the figures of language, including the tropes and the figures of thought, in which each of the four types of operations is present. Aristotle had also adumbrated these four operations when he characterized the various types of objections or replies brought out by an audience:

Objections, as appears in the *Topics*, may be raised in four ways—either by directly attacking your opponent's own statement or by putting forward another statement like it, or by putting forward a statement contrary to it, or by quoting previous decisions.[8]

What does Aristotle mean here by "previous decisions"? These are the previously accepted answers. These judgments were called *topoi*. A problem remains, however: what is the use of figures if they mean something which can already be said or found in our common, literal language? Is rhetoric, in this sense, merely ornamental?[9] When language means more or something other than the literal meaning, there

---

[7] Cicero, *De Oratore* 3, 206–7.   [8] Aristotle, *Rhetoric*, 1402a 35.
[9] Perelman and Olbrechts-Tyteca, *The New Rhetoric*, §41, p. 169: "We consider a figure to be argumentative, if it brings about a change of perspective, and its use seems normal in relation to this new situation. If, on the other hand, the speech does not bring about the adherence of the hearer to this argumentative form, the figure will be considered an embellishment, a figure of style."

is either some "supplement" (Derrida)[10] or a totally new meaning is adduced (Ricoeur).[11] In both cases, we are faced with a *figure* of speech or style. The problem with both authors is that their position is restricted to the analysis of tropes, because tropes do not allow for any literal reading ("Richard is a lion" is a demand for such a reading, but one which is literally an impossibility, since it stipulates that Richard is human and not-human). Usually, however, figures of speech demand a literal reading that does, or does not, pre-exist the utterance of the figure, but the fact that the audience has to discover this meaning does not render the figurative use of language redundant. The true meaning of the figure is to be inferred, discovered, or even rediscovered as an answer to a question raised by the figure to the audience or the reader. There can be multiple readings or various versions of that answer, with additions and concessions, but the aim of these figures is mainly to raise a question in the mind of the audience by dealing, often indirectly, with particular questions, namely those that have been treated in the speaker's answers.

Let us now synthesize what we know about each of those four operations.

a) =: this operator covers a wide range of forms of identities and is used in the rhetoric *ad rem* as well as in the rhetoric *ad hominem*, in which it is the marker of approval, of rejoinder, of agreement with the speaker. The most well-known forms are repetition, as in the rhymes of versification, and definition (when the latter is *not* meant to requalify the speaker's answer with different words, sometimes with new meanings, in which case it would instead *add* something to what he says). Usually, identity and definition are made explicit in order to render the speaker's meaning more precise, especially in the case of a defense. In other words, definition expands the speaker's initial answer, even if only through approving silence or a nodding gesture. In *ad hominem* terms, identity is a reply which confirms, whether

---

[10] J. Derrida, *Of Grammatology*, tr. G. Spivak (Baltimore, MD: Johns Hopkins University Press, 1976).

[11] Ricoeur, *The Rule of Metaphor*.

explicitly or implicitly, the speaker's position. A positive reference to oneself, to what a speaker is, is still based on identity. Let us also not overlook the fact that *silence* is quite ambiguous, since it can mean approval as well as disapproval. This explains why no speaker likes to be confronted with a silent interlocutor. Identity in general can be found in all the forms of figurative speech: in the figures of sound, we can have repetition ("Ah! Ah!" instead of "Ah!") as well as in figures of construction ("Yes! Yes! Yes!"). Shakespeare provided us with a famous instance of this phenomenon of identity of sound (homonymy) as a source of ambiguity in the first sentences of *Julius Caesar*: "But what trade art thou? Answer me directly. / A trade, Sir, that I hope I may use with a safe conscience, which is indeed, Sir, a mender of bad soles." The phonetic play on words is the following: *Soles = Souls*.[12]

b) ±: the above example, drawn from Shakespeare, illustrates the fact that operations of suppression and substitution combined are both variants of modification because, in the end, the initial answer is modified and apparently redefined by that substitution of new words, sounds, or sentences, which are meant to requalify the speaker's answer. The aim is to offer clarifications or to correct an answer, in order to reformulate it more adequately given the real question that the audience deems itself to be dealing with. This operation can be completed phonetically as in Caesar's "*Veni, vidi, vici*," a *paronomasis* (similarity of sounds, but difference in meaning) in which Caesar qualifies his strength and his ability as a general, amplifying what is in question as being solved, thanks to repetition in the strength of the verbs. Caesar's words as to their content can be seen as a narrative gradation.[13]

Permutation, for the Group Mu, is one of the ways of (re)qualifying a phrase. It is a figure of construction but it can also be seen as a figure of thought. The following chiasmus, for example, "I empty my glass

---

[12] Shakespeare, *Julius Caesar* I, 1.
[13] If, on the other hand, one prefers to stress the fact there is a lack of connection between the three words, this is called an *asyndeton*, also intended to reinforce some initial statement, which is requalified. It is then often seen as a mere repetition.

when it is full, and I make it full when it is empty" (Raoul Ponchon) adds a new answer, even if only through phonetic means (*Avida Dollar* for *Salvador Dali*, is a well-known anagram created by André Breton to stress Dali's cupidity).

c) +: Permutation and repetition can be compounded ("error, terror, terror, error"). What is significant in this operation is the fact that we can certainly modify a word or an expression to add some new perception of what is in question, or not at all as in the case of synonymy. In contrast, the operator ± modifies and requalifies what is in question by leading the audience to another perspective on that same question: who knew better than Breton that Salvador Dali loved money so much? In general, permutation is a figure of construction of words, syllables, and verses and is often used in poetry. Due to the ambiguity of their classification—since even repetition adds something, rhetoric being defined as a deviation that adds an answer to some pre-existing literal answer—it is preferable to abandon the Group Mu's classifications and return instead to our four rhetorical operators, with which we can insist, specify (modify), add a new positive or negative answer, and even attack it as contradictory or false. This applies to isolated statements, texts, and even to images.

d) −: suppression, negation, ellipsis, syllepse, apocope ("photo" for photography), irony, contradiction, denial, but also inversion, leading to chiasm (parallelism) and antithesis (as a figure of thought).

The lists of figures, of sounds, of words, of sentences, and of thought are highly variable.[14] As Roland Barthes wrote: "There can of course be no question of giving a list of the 'ornaments' acknowledged by the ancient rhetoric under the general names of 'figures':

---

[14] H. Lausberg's multifarious classification in the *Handbuch der Literarischen Rhetorik* (Munich: Steiner Verlag, 1960) (in English, *Handbook of Literary Rhetoric*, Leiden: Brill, 1998) provides a catalog which is no more "rational" or convincing than that found in Fontanier's *Les figures du discours* [1830] (Paris: Flammarion, 1977). The most useful synthesis of all the visions of the figures is to be found in Bice Mortara Garavelli, *Manuale di Retorica* (Milan: Bompiani, 1997). See also R. Lanham, *A Handlist of Rhetorical Terms* (Los Angeles: University of California Press, 1991) and A. Quinn, *Figures of Speech* [1982] (London: Routledge, 2010).

Table 2 Table of the basic correspondences between trope, figures of thought, and arguments

	R_1	R_2	A_1	A_2
		Rhetoric	Argumentation	
	Tropes	*Figures of thought*	*Topoi or topics*	*Arguments*
Audiences (or the different types of possible answers about a previous answer)				
= agreement (approval)	metaphor	identity, image, expressions of proximity and agreement, allegory, hypotyposis	quality ("What is X?"), definition of people and statements values ("It is better to do this than that"), non-problematic judgments of value as implicit premises or warrants	analogy, a fortiori conclusion, etc., approval, agreement, assertion
modification ± +/− ("yes, but...") −/+ ("no, but...")	metonymy	personification, narratives about a given question that give rise to sub-questions, but also restriction and amplification or minimization	commonplaces or shared judgments on a given question, deemed as a way of solving it, qualification ("It was not murder but self-defense")	qualification of the premises, selection of facts and values that identify the question in order to find the arguments
Addition + (*ad rem* implication of the audience) ("yes... then...")	synecdoche	generalization resorting to laws or general principles but also exemplification as a sign of such laws	Quantity (e.g. the snakes are venomous for *all* snakes are venomous), number, order, ("The more X, the more Y" or "the less X, the more Y") hierarchies and ordering of values	inference, causal links
Suppression − (explicit or implicit disapproval of the audience and of arguments)	irony	denial, opposition, antithesis, paradox, rejection, partial agreement or disagreement	difference as contrast (not as addition or qualification)	contradiction, negative judgment of the interlocutor, opposition, rejection, disapproval

dictionaries of rhetoric exist," but the *principles* underlying them are now established.[15] They present a recurrent structure of the same operations, extending, as we shall later see, to arguments and not just to figures. Figures of speech are meant to reflect the high or low level of problematicity of the *questions* raised by the speaker, while the four operations, in their various forms, are meant to express the reactions or possible *answers* about the speaker (*ad hominem*) or his speech (*ad rem*).

In the last analysis, we can see that the basic operators discussed above are common to all rhetoric and argumentation and give rise to the most elementary forms of figurative speech and to the four essential argumentative structures. Moreover, these operators are the source of the usual complex figures of style and of the full spectrum of arguments.

Figures and arguments are diversified on account of the four basic operators which underpin them as the source of answers. A metaphor,[16] for instance, is a condensed analogy[17] and relies on the operation of identity. The same reasoning applies to the rest of the most basic figures and arguments, as shown in Table 2. As for argumentation, properly speaking, all arguments are based on identity, difference, inference (or causality), or contradiction with respect to what is said or to admitted opinions which are the object of debates.

---

[15] R. Barthes "The Old Rhetoric," in *The Semiotic Challenge*, tr. R. Howard (Berkeley: University of California Press, 1994), p. 87.
[16] E.g. old age is the dusk of life.
[17] Old age is to life what dusk is to a whole day.

5

The argumentative structures

The four basic rhetorical operators and the origin of the major classes of arguments

The basic operations or operators of rhetoric, then, are identity (=), similarity (±), inference (+) and opposition (−). The parameter of variation, its cursor, is the difference which increases with respect to the initial statement. These operations give rise to the figures of style from which all other figures can be derived, often enclosed in scholastic classifications. They nonetheless remain offshoots of these four operators, however complex or complexified the list of figures may become. The same is true of argumentation. This is because these operators are basic and common to both rhetoric *stricto sensu* and to argumentation.

These four operators constitute the only possible ways of responding to previously given answers whose content is more or less problematic. In terms of the audience, we can agree or disagree, and in between we may modify the initial answer (or requalify it) or add a new answer which amplifies the original or adds a new point of view bordering on opposition. In qualifying a given answer, we can amplify it or minimize it according to its potential problematicity with respect to the audience from which an agreement is sought. Belonging to the *ad hominem* level of responses, we may have the reinforcement of the point of view, the contradiction of that point of view, and in between various expressions of harmony (such as empathy or sympathy, or concession) or of approval. The operator of identity usually bears on *who* or *what* the speaker is; the operator of similarity bears on the sharing of attributes (e.g. "You and I are both specialists, and...."); the operator of difference (e.g. "you are not very much aware of....")

enables the respondent to differentiate herself from the speaker and draw different implications; and finally, opposition to the speaker and even contradiction of him enables the respondent to play upon maximal distance by invoking different values embodied in various *topoi*.

How are the four basic operators of rhetoric used in argumentation and how do they give rise to the four major classes of argument? In a nutshell, arguments too fall into four broad categories: arguments from identity (such as analogy, recourse to precedent, etc.); from difference through the modification of some initial belief or opinion; from inference or causality, based on the consideration of causes or consequences (e.g. "If you do not do this, you will be punished"); and from opposition and contradiction. These four categories are =, ±, +, and −. Definition, redefinition, or qualification (as required by legal procedure: an act of killing may be qualified as murder or as an act of self-defense, in which case it is not punished) are ambivalent because they can add a new viewpoint on a given question or simply render it explicit or more precise in other terms. Authority and trustworthiness are essential to the audience's acceptance of arguments; even when these arguments are perfectly valid, they are not self-sustaining if there is some suspicion attached to the speaker. Douglas Walton would certainly categorize our four basic operators as *argumentation-schemes*: "Argumentation schemes are forms of arguments (structures of inference) that represent structures of common types of arguments used in everyday discourse as well as in special contexts like those of legal argumentation and scientific argumentation."[1] Instead of *schemes*, I prefer to speak of *ethos*-structures, just as the desire to please or to create fear belongs to *pathos*-structures. My concern for the moment, however, is with the *logos*-structures of argumentation.

As discussed in Chapter 1, Perelman did not distinguish the *ad rem* and the *ad hominem* procedures in his threefold classification of arguments: quasi-logical arguments (tautology, contradiction, and so forth), arguments based on the structure of reality such as causality

---

[1] See Walton et al., *Argumentation Schemes*, p. 7.

and inference in general, and those establishing the structure of reality, such as induction or analogy. *Arguments based on the structure of reality* can have an *ad hominem* bearing such as threats ("if you do not eat your soup, you won't have any dessert"), or any consideration of consequences. Personification also belongs to this class, in that the act and its author are taken as a causal relation. Other interactions between persons and acts pertain to the inference of coexistence. In the same manner, a fortiori arguments are part of causal arguments, such as those based on quantity, degree, and order. As for the third class of arguments, according to Perelman, those "establishing the structure of reality," they are nothing but inductive arguments, based on examples, analogy, illustration, model, perfection, and so on, which we already find in Aristotle's *Rhetoric* when he speaks of induction (*epagoge*).[2] In Perelman's view, these three major argumentation schemes seem so sweeping that, as in the various theories of figures, their underlying rationality does not appear very clear in spite of the fact that they are Aristotelian in spirit, at least those referring to reality. The formalism of quasi-logical arguments is also drawn from Aristotle's view of topics and dialectic.

As we have seen, then, the real process of argumentation is based on the four operations mentioned above, which give rise to four basic forms of arguments, whatever the subsequent differentiation, just as is the case for the figures of speech.

The four main classes of arguments

Figure 3 shows the argumentative responses. We can now compare the various forms of explicit agreement, ranging from complete agreement to the lack of agreement or total disagreement. Let us begin with explicit approval, symbolized by the sign =, which designates various forms of identity, such as giving a definition, a reformulation, or a repetition of an initial statement. If the agreement with a given answer is the case, so too is the rejection of the opposite

---

[2] Perelman and Olbrechts-Tyteca, *The New Rhetoric*, p. 350.

134 THE ARGUMENTATIVE STRUCTURES

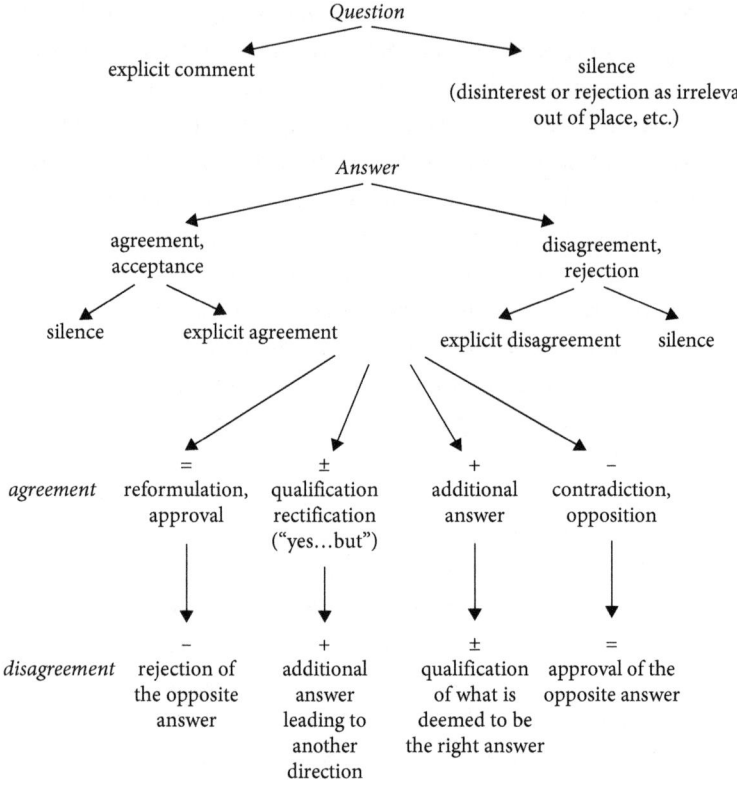

Figure 3 The argumentative responses

answer, i.e. the disagreement is null (−). As a corollary, if there is no agreement at all (−) then this implies the disapproval (=) of the opposite answer, as the last vertical arrow shows. The same reasoning here applies for intermediate stages. Requalification (±)—modification of the terms employed when there is agreement—corresponds to a minimal disagreement, expressed through an additional statement ("yes...but"). Finally, in terms of disagreement, an additional answer expressing agreement corresponds to a redefinition of what is not accepted. This explains the four vertical arrows linking the various stages on the line of agreement with their corresponding stages of disagreement. When the latter increases, the former decreases, and vice versa. In the end, all possible explicit responses to a speaker's address amount to the four possible operations, =, ±, +, and − applied to agreement as well as to disagreement.

The structure of an argument is meant to express an answer bearing on another answer which is deemed inadequate, wrong, or false, with respect to the original question that the initial answer was meant to solve. This structure can formalize the rejection or the acceptance of the answer offered, just as much as it can requalify it, with any purpose, or can add to it, again to *reinforce* it or even to *suggest* its abandonment or its blunt rejection.

A certain level of problematicity of the initial question gives rise to a modification of the distance between those struggling with that problem. This renders the debate or the exchange all the more emotional insofar as the distance between the individuals is short. This explains why a basic function of law, and of trials in general, is to increase or create distance between the protagonists via the court's ceremonial procedures.

Rhetoric associates in a narrative sequence (*dispositio*) statements on a given (though underlying) question embedded in this narrative: to say "q_1" is to say "q_2" because q_1, which was never explicitly raised, has as a consequence the raising of q_2, which its answer is intended to solve (via premises called *topics* or accepted facts and opinions, social or educational). To say, "It's one o'clock" is to say "Let's have lunch." This equivalence relies on a social *topos* associating lunch with that time of day. The two utterances "a_1" and "a_2" are rhetorically equivalent as utterances (not as statements) and argumentatively speaking, one is an argument for the other, since the fact "it's one o'clock" is a good argument to have lunch: "$a_1 \rightarrow q_1 \bullet q_2$" is the formal structure of any rhetorical argument. But the real question behind the arrow of implication is to know how far the audience can extend its application as an inferential structure. Is "to say A is to say B" grounded in the fact that A and B are causally linked? Does the inference of utterances constitute a causal link between the events themselves? The audience is constantly asked to answer that question, even by making as if, as in tropes, the solution could be the trope itself. This is the role of rhetorical argumentation; to bring this question to the fore for the purpose of judgment as well as for action. To say that snakes are venomous when there seem to be snakes on the path ahead is to suggest the question of whether snakes rather than ropes are the objects lying in the distance and whether they are dangerous or not. The fear following such a warning should incite the interlocutor to conclude and act accordingly. The sight of apparent "ropes" is nonetheless a reason to ask oneself whether they are real ropes or not and to alter one's itinerary, while, on the other hand, the warning that "Snakes are venomous" could be a good argument for minimizing the risks. There is a link between A and B "saying A is saying B." Although B and A are distinct realities, the statement about them suggests an unstipulated relationship between them. It is *because* snakes are venomous that we decide to walk away from the pathway. This is a good argument, "$a_1 \to q_1 \bullet q_2$, therefore a_2," even if the *cause* for being careful is the presence of snakes, which are probably dangerous.

How the basic logical connectives may have arisen from the rhetorical operators

An interesting point deserves to be made here. Is it not possible that the origin of the logical connectives could be these four argumentative operators? Let us see first how the *basic* operators constitutive of any argument can be turned into logical forms (Table 3).

Table 3 How logical arguments are generated on the basis of the operations of discourse

=: p	Identity, definition, quasi-logical arguments, analogy
±: $p \vee q$	Requalification, modifying definition, values, hierarchies
+: 1) $- p \vee q = p \to q$ or	Addition, new answer, if there is a link with the initial answer p, causality
2) $p \bullet q$	Narrative succession; argumentatively must be read as: "p and (even) q, i.e. as a reinforcement"
−: $- p$	Opposition, contradiction, defense

Two operations deserve special attention here: ± and +. When we deal with arguments, what is at stake are two different logical connections. From ± derives $p \vee q$, that is "p or q." The operator ± can be expressed by the logical connective $\vee$ because if p raises some doubt and requires clarification, the fact of saying q as an alternative way of rendering p suffices to render it acceptable. P has merely been expressed differently.

As for the operator +, it gives rise to another argument which, when put in perspective, can be interpreted as an inference. Even if p is rejected (or considered false), the fact of adding an answer, q, to the initial one, p, renders it a sort of validation because it links the two, as in the inference $p \rightarrow q$. In fact, the consequences are a way of judging p. We could even put forward an audacious hypothesis as to the origin of the logical connective of implication, symbolized by the arrow. Could the origin of such connectives be found in rhetoric? The main logical connectives might have originated in the *practice* of argumentation, since logic is a form of argumentation in which there are no interlocutors. Logic is a context-free concept and is certainly not dependent on any pragmatic use. To go back to the meaning of the operator +, the speaker adds q to p because he pragmatically implies that there is some link between the fact of saying p and the fact of concluding with q because he considers that from p, he can move to q, i.e. he can infer q. P is the condition for saying q, even if p is false.

For the operator +, we can also develop a second interpretation of the particular reasoning at stake. The interlocutor may add a statement to the speaker's initial one without intending to reinforce it, but simply to expand it: $p \bullet q$ (p and q) may have the structure of a narrative in which the consistency of the whole is provided by addition. Reinforcement is one of the usual goals of the operator +: p and *even* q. For instance, "John is clever, indeed very clever" could be a way for a daughter to justify the choice of her boyfriend to skeptical parents. In the first reading, the interlocutor rather than the speaker is generally the one who adds q to p in order to stress the relevance and validity of p by singling out an additional reason to adhere to p, namely q, because it is a well-known consequence of p. We have

$p \to q$: if p is true, as I want you to admit it is, then q is true, and we know that q is the case. This, then, is an additional reason to believe p as well and we can say that q is true because of p, even though I do not intend to go back to the question of whether p is true or false, and it can therefore be false, since q is the leading argument *in fine* ($p = 0$ or *1*). This argumentative way of understanding the operation of implication probably explains why $p \to q = -p \vee q$, as we know from our logic textbooks. This equivalence renders explicit the fact that even if p is contested, or considered to be false, or has to be rejected, the inference would remain valid on the sole basis of the additional statement q, based on the fact that it has been produced as a consequence of p, thereby reinforcing it (if it is not even a substitute for it). It is the true consequence q which renders p "acceptable," even though p could be *0* or *1*. $P \to q$ would be true even if p were false, because it is the role of q as an *additional statement* to win the *whole* argument. The speaker asks the interlocutor to reconsider her judgment on p on the basis of the additional answer q which renders $p \to q$ valid (for p, supposed to be *0*). P and q bear on a given question, and even if p is rejected by the interlocutor, the speaker's initial standpoint would remain valid because q would be considered as a valid argument ensuing from p.

Those four basic operators of argumentation have been conceptualized in terms of logic, but in argumentation they also are grounded in *ethos* or *pathos*. They have an effect and respond to some intention, whatever their logical structure. If I say, "You have to believe me, since, as a medical doctor, I am an expert on this question," this is an *ethos*-scheme, whereas if I say "You should avoid the snakes on the path ahead, they are venomous," it is a *pathos*-scheme (fear or prudence is the effect sought). In all these cases, the argument is $p \to q$, i.e. an inference: even if I am wrong, or even if you were not afraid, you ought to believe me (in the first example, you ought to take your medication, since I am a doctor, while in the latter example, you had better modify your path if you do not want to be bitten by snakes). This is why it is redundant to resort to more detailed catalogues of argument schemes, in which one would find many *ethos*-structures, such as the appeal to expert opinions, or to the trust of the speaker involving his authority, as well as *pathos*-structures, such as the mobilization of fear, hope, interest, and other emotions or feelings.

From the *ad rem* to the *ad hominem* or the adherence effect

There is a *principle of adherence* at work in rhetoric which enables the speaker to pass from the *ad rem* to the *ad hominem* when someone attacks or rejects our answers. In such a case, we feel in question as if our whole person were at stake. We do not like to be contradicted or disapproved of. This explains why, in argumentation, we move so easily from the *ad rem* to the *ad hominem*, especially when we are short of arguments with which to oppose those of our interlocutor. A politician, for example, who would say "we should do this because it is essential to the welfare of the country" is very often criticized in an *ad hominem* way, especially if the measure put forth is a good one of which everyone should approve. If his opponent does not succeed in contesting the argument, she will easily move to the *ad hominem* level: "Why didn't you do it, then, when you were in power?" The *ad hominem* is a substitute which compensates for a lack of argument on the matter itself. Such a strategy is possible because of the *principle of adherence*: in a way, we are *in* what we say, our answers corresponding to what we are, hence the emotions we feel when our discourse is accepted or rejected.

An argument is an inference based on the authority or expertise of a speaker (*ethos*) that leads to a conclusion, inferred, modified, qualified, or rejected by an audience (*pathos*). *Pathos* is molded by the opinions, emotions, or passions of the audience, its strength depending on the *distance* between individuals, i.e. between *ethos* and *pathos*. An argument is thus a reason for accepting or drawing the conclusion stipulated, suggested, or established by the speaker as a way of deciding between alternatives forming the question at the core of the encounter. Argumentation begins when there is a strong commitment to decide a question which presents a high degree of problematicity for the individuals confronted with that question. The degree of problematicity of the question is the "measure" of the distance between the individuals. However far apart they are, they become closer when the problem they are confronted with leads to strong emotional reactions concerning the way questions are treated and by whom, the principle of adherence here allowing for *ad hominem* responses. A good example is the vast oil slicks which poured into the Gulf of Mexico in 2010 and triggered huge public demonstrations of hostility against the British Petroleum company. In a way, the damage caused abolished the ideal distance between the inhabitants and the oil company, leading to a court settlement of the conflict created by this unwilling shortening of distance.

6

The elements of rhetoric *stricto sensu*: the figures of speech

The figures of style as the tools of rhetoric *stricto sensu*

Elegance of style and eloquence in general stem from the capacity to organize discourse using the most adequate figures. By "most adequate," I mean the figures of speech which can deal with the underlying questions in such a way that they already seem solved. This is a way of figuring out what is at stake and at the same time, at least in the mind of the speaker, of making an impact on the audience which allows for these answers to be passed off as such. It is now time to take a closer look at these figures, to see how they function and, more specifically, to see how they make up what we usually call "figurative language."

Since Quintilian and the anonymous author of the *Rhetoric to Herennius*, rhetoricians have produced many distinct catalogs of stylistic figures, each more complex than the last, to the point that they have become highly scholastic and arbitrary. From Aristotle to Burke, the number of figures has changed constantly and the rationality behind the choice of individual figures has become more than questionable. For Aristotle, each figure, irrespective of its role and structure, is a specific way of rendering things by using terms other than the essential ones, i.e. the terms belonging to their essence, and which as a result imply features full of imagery, so that each type of figure of style is for Aristotle a metaphor. Hence, it is Aristotle's idea that a figure of speech is based on similarity and resemblance between two areas in which the figure brings correspondences to the fore.

The use of the word "figure" or image is intended to underline the projective effect of metaphor as the translation of something into something else by virtue of common properties. But Roman authors restricted the use of metaphors to condensed analogies and introduced an array of additional figures into rhetoric, since metaphors were restricted to "simile" and images of likeness. The question we have raised above, however, still applies. Is there rationality behind this extension and do all such catalogues of rhetorical figures have an underlying rationale? Obscure Greek and Latin names have been used to designate the proliferating figures in these catalogs, such as *enallage, prosthesis, zeugma, metaplasm,* and so forth. This has only blurred the question of unity and utility of figurative speech, even for the specialist of rhetoric. Instead, rhetoricians should clarify the purpose and the specificity of figures of speech in literature and in everyday language. In any case, the general intent behind these figures is to provide the speaker with numerous ways of conveying an answer to a question which has not been directly raised or solved as it would have been under these conditions. They thus represent the various devices used to present discourse as answering, indirectly, underlying questions, by simply suggesting or presupposing what is in question in the answer. Stylistic figures often ask the audience to take the final step themselves, by drawing an implicit conclusion suggested or implied in the very form of the linguistic figures used by the speaker or the writer. The aim of the speaker here is essentially to make an impact on the audience, to please it, to move it, or even to convey information about something.

Why, then, does figurative language have a greater impact on the audience than plain, literal language? This is probably the most interesting problem behind the use of non-literal language. Several answers have been given to this question and each is far from conclusive. The usual one is that the audience, by inferring the conclusion that has only been suggested or left implicit, will have more confidence in the answer because it has inferred it itself. An audience's imagination is also mobilized when a conclusion is left open, giving more weight to figures of speech and to figurative language in the larger sense. In any case, when language means more or something other than literal meaning, there is either some additional meaning which emerges from the text and is implied in its literal meaning or the reader privileges a totally new meaning which takes the place of the original literal meaning.[1] In both cases, we are faced with a *figure* of speech or style.

Figures have always been defined as "a deviation in sense or language from the ordinary simple form," as if ordinary language were not efficient enough to convey the meaning that the speaker had in mind.[2] Embellishment seems to be the key word here. It aims at fulfilling the function of *delectatio* ascribed to rhetoric by the Romans, as if a well-constructed speech in everyday language were insufficient or inadequate in this respect. For Cicero, too, figures or *schemes* "give brilliance to oratory,"[3] "for the sake of giving delight."[4] But Cicero also adduces another reason for using figurative language. Figures are intended to lay stress on a given point, highlighting *what is in question*. Figures attract attention to a given question in the argument that is essential for the inference to be made successfully. Figures emphasize the presence of a feature which should be noticed by the audience. Perelman theorized this argumentative view of figures two thousand years later:

From antiquity, and probably from the moment man first reflected on language, one has noticed certain modes of expression which are different from the ordinary, and they generally have been studied in the treatises on rhetoric: hence their name, *rhetorical figures*. Because of the tendency of rhetoricians to restrict their study to problems of style and expression,

---

[1] This recalls the opposing positions of Derrida and Ricoeur on the notion of the "supplement," referred to in ch. 4, notes 9 and 10.
[2] Quintilian, *Institutes*, 9.1.11.   [3] Cicero, *De oratore*, 3, 208.
[4] Cicero, *De oratore*, 3, 206.

rhetorical figures increasingly came to be regarded as mere ornaments that made the style artificial and ornate.[5]

As a consequence, a figure should instead be seen as argumentative when "it brings about a change in perspective and its use seems normal in relation to this new situation."[6] A figure creates a feeling of presence and reality, not in spite of the unusual form but *because* of it. Figurative language is preferred to plain, natural language because it is more economical and more striking when one wants to draw an audience's attention to a given feature or point in question.

Most of the time, however, figurative language does not have an argumentative function, even if it does so in the circumstances which Perelman clarifies. As for its aesthetic function, it has often been missed, especially by classical authors, such as Cicero or Quintilian, who viewed figures of speech as a pleasant kind of discourse meant to embellish plain language, even if figures sometimes filled semantic gaps by creating a second meaning distinct from the primary one (*catachresis*). Figures of speech, however, have constituted the style of literary works as much as they have been the basis of oratory. The important point here is to go beyond the plurality of figures and their catalogs, in order to recover the foundation of figurative language in its largest sense. Is figurative language an implication, a derivation, or a deviation of some literal truth from natural language, as though it were somehow unnatural? Is it another way of putting forth an argument in order to produce a greater impact through some increased visibility of the point in question? The view which has prevailed is that figurative language is a deviation from ordinary language.[7] But does this axiom really help to provide a key for a rational, structured, and inclusive "catalog" of figures?

---

[5] C. Perelman and L. Olbrechts-Tyteca, *The New Rhetoric*, tr. J. Wilkinson and P. Weaver (Notre Dame, IN: University of Notre Dame Press, 1969), Treatise, §41, p. 167.

[6] Perelman and Olbrechts-Tyteca, *The New Rhetoric*, Treatise, §41, p. 169.

[7] Cohen, *La structure du langage poétique*.

Unfortunately, tropes like metaphors, metonymies, or synecdoches (Group Mu) have been favored by those in search of unity, but they have failed to provide a general and unified view, probably because only a conception based on questioning can offer an underlying sense of unity and rationality. Indeed, only a questioning view can do full justice to the functioning of figures, however complexified and differentiated from one another they later become, when all the subtleties and nuances are deemed to matter. The fact of considering any figure of speech as a deviation from normal usage is nothing but a way of describing a semantic difference. But this would in no way explain why and when it would be better to proceed with figures and indicate why they are structured the way they are. Sometimes, as with tropes, there is nothing from which deviation could later be said to occur. This is probably due to the fact that the circumstances for such deviation are multiple (from creating new words to amplifying or minimizing opinions, for instance, without speaking of literary usages). Nonetheless, these circumstances have an obvious common denominator which has failed to be perceived so far. *Rhetoric* stricto sensu, i.e. *figures, is intended to deal with the problematic in an indirect way*, via the answers upheld and put forth. Figures offer a (new) point of view on what is problematic by or through the answer offered. They can highlight, stress, minimize, represent, or help to better identify some feature of what is in question. Figures have the specific purpose of treating the problematic *according to the level of problematicity* it embodies. They express a given level of problematicity insofar as the speaker has to take that level into account, since he wants to find the "right" answer or scheme that will enable him to deal with it *as if* the problem raised was solved.

In order to account for a unified and rational view of the figures of style, let us return to the traditional division between the *figures of words* and the *figures of thought* that we find in classical works of rhetoric, such as Cicero's *De Oratore* and Quintilian's *Institutes*. For the latter, "Most writers in fact, so far as I know, have agreed that there are two classes of Figures: those of *dianoia*, that is thought or mind or ideas (all these terms are used) and those of *lexis*, that is words or diction or Elocution or speech or style."[8] As for Aristotle, he did not specifically entertain a theory of figures. This is because he reduced all figures to metaphors, since he considered any figure as an image, or a *mimesis*, of something based on the features of something else and transferable to the initial thing (metaphor originally means "transference" in Greek) for which the figure is meant to be a conceptual or realistic mirror, even if the result is sometimes to keep the problematic open in order to better solicit the reader.[9]

This reminds us that rhetoric always gains momentum when the gap between words and things becomes wider because history itself is in a process of acceleration: old answers mingle with new ones, giving rise to possible confusion between the problematic and the non-problematic, if not to potential manipulation through advocating the former as if it belonged to the latter. Since this confusion enables the speaker to manipulate the audience (Plato's argument), it is necessary to give oneself a criterion or a procedure of decision (Aristotle). This is the goal of argumentation. Reasons or arguments enable speakers to stress what count as answers to the questions they raise and to affirm as false the opposite. Figures save us from having to make such a choice, while also allowing us to avoid accusations of manipulation. Figurative language enables us to leap directly from the problematic to some form of answer, given the fact that this answer does not have to be taken literally.

The four classes of figures

The *figures of words* encompass the figures of sound, the figures of construction or grammar, and the figures of meaning or *tropes*. Most classical rhetoricians had difficulty explaining the respective roles of figures in general through lack of an overarching principle, and

---

[8] Quintilian, *Institutes*, 9.13.17 (tr. p. 19).
[9] Cf. G. Kennedy's note on Aristotle's Third Book of the *Rhetoric*, devoted to style, p. 222 of his translation (*Aristotle, on Rhetoric: A Theory of Civic Discourse* (New York and Oxford: Oxford University Press, 1991)).

THE ELEMENTS OF RHETORIC STRICTO SENSU   147

because of that they face the same difficulty when they have to explain their subdivision into two classes, with three types in one and one type in the last class, the *figures of thought*. Figures of thought seem to exemplify "ideas" that are raised but which cannot be treated by "swallowing" them in a non-problematic discourse. These figures have often been said to be more useful in argumentation than in rhetoric properly speaking, for example, denial (or *praeteritio*), hypothesis, rhetorical questions (i.e. questions to which the answer is already known by the speaker and the audience, such as "Who is not in favor of justice?" answer: "Nobody, of course"), minimization or amplification, opposition, retraction, exemplification, partial agreement (concession), and so forth. Figures of thought appear as strategies. But is not rhetorical speech, like argumentation, already a strategy in itself? The catalog of figures has always been somewhat arbitrary, at least since Cicero. The lists of these figures of thought have been manifold, just like the lists of figures of speech, often designated with barbaric Greek names which render them even more obscure to the common reader. Let us summarize, then, what is commonly accepted about figures (Figure 4).

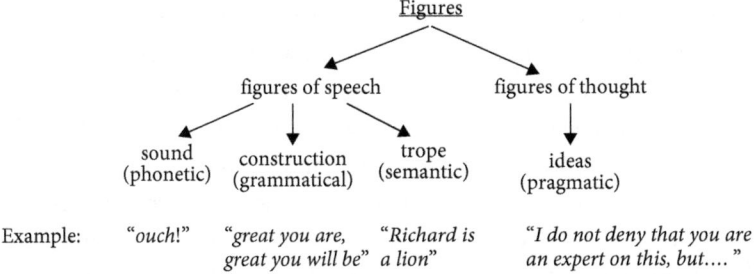

Figure 4 The basic catalog of figures

1) The *figures of sound* evoke the speaker's problem in an entirely unproblematic way for the audience. If I hear someone say "Ouch!" I know unequivocally that she is in pain.

2) The *figures of construction* (also called figures of translation or arrangement) are based on the inversion and modification of the

correct way, according to conventional grammar, in which speech is constructed. In the example "great you are, great you will be," the grammatical structure is distorted, since the adjective is put at the beginning of the phrase. Figures of construction reveal a greater level of problematicity in the question raised than figures of sound, in order to draw an increased focus on that question. In this example, the greatness of the person is more problematic than it sounds, and thus needs to be emphasized grammatically. The use of this figure purports to amplify greatness of the person mentioned by inverting the normal structure of the phrase.

3) *Tropes* are sentences or words that cannot be read literally. As a result, they do not stipulate what they really mean—one has to infer it. Very often, they cannot be reduced either to an equivalent literal answer that would render the trope superfluous, being then a mere ornament of some underlying and available literal truth that would somehow pre-exist it for all protagonists; although, with time, as Ricoeur says, metaphors become worn out. But when this is not the case, tropes—or rather metaphors—remain enigmatic, as Aristotle already noted.[10] For him, metaphor was the epitome of all figurativity, since a figure is always an image of something expressed in terms of some other thing, even if it is by virtue of some similarity between properties, which can give either a deformed or more accurate image of the initial thing or event. Tropes, then, have a specific nature and a specific function: to raise a question in the mind of the receiver through the necessity of inferring another answer from the figurative answer given by the trope, hence the crucial role of tropes in the history of rhetoric. They have an economic or time-saving function. Tropes are figurative answers aimed at sparing us from having to find *the* exact (literal) answer which renders its actual content. They are modes of suggesting an answer without literally expressing it. "Richard is a lion" is a way of saying that Richard is courageous, or that he behaves like the king of animals (the lion is the king of animals) or humans (Richard is the king of England) should behave.

[10] Aristotle, *Rhetoric*, III, 1405 b 13.

Similarly, saying "Washington has decided to raise its interest rates" is a manner of affirming that the United States have opted for such a raise. "Washington" stands for the place and people where the decisions take place in the U.S. and, as such, is a metonymy for American power and the locus where its major decisions are taken.

The fact that Kenneth Burke, following Vico, saw in metaphor, metonymy, synecdoche, and irony the four "master-tropes" is revealing.[11] These tropes embody the four basic operators of rhetoric: identity, similarity, difference (or addition with some distinct proposition, generalizing the position), and negation, which are the four modes of questioning a given answer, i.e. fixing in some way the adequacy of answers to questions. They are thus the four ways for a speaker to react to what is said concerning a given question, i.e. of actualizing a certain level of problematicity (high or low). One finds these four operators in all the classes of figures of speech, the other figures also being derived from these four basic operations, something that the barbaric names of the multitudinous versions and subdivisions of figures often obscure to the analyst. All tropes are enigmatic, but some are closer to an identity (metaphor) because of conventional signs, recognized symbols, or accepted opinions, while others are closer to opposition and negation. In between the two, there are various levels of differentiation of which metonymy and synecdoche are probably the best-known cursors. In rhetoric, the basic formula "to say A is to say B" raises the question of knowing whether there is a relationship of identity, inference, or opposition between A and B themselves, and not only between their utterances. To say A *is* to say B—as in "to say it's cold outside is to say one should put one's coat on"—raises the question of knowing whether A is or is not identical to B. An answer is all the more persuasive when "to say A implies to say B" is true *because* A is a *reason* for B. For example, to say that Socrates has a headache is another way of saying that he is ill, but his illness is also the cause of his headache, fever being the sign of

---

[11] Burke, *Grammar of Motives*, Appendix D.

his illness.[12] We thus have three possibilities when we say that "to say A is to say B": A and B are identical; A is a reason to say B; and B is the cause of A. This reminds us of Perelman's three classes of arguments: quasi-logical ones, such as identity; arguments based on the structure of the real; and finally, those establishing this structure.

Let us go back to the analysis of tropes. To say A is to say B, and in this way all tropes have this rhetorical structure by identifying what is in question with an answer that establishes some identity in spite of the literal differences in content which then fade off from this form of language. Consider the two examples of *metonymy* and *synecdoche*, since metaphor is already an identity and irony is a negated or denied identity in content in spite of the form ("That's really clever" refers to a stupid act or utterance, when said with a certain tone or within a given context, i.e. one in which it cannot be taken at face-value). A *metonymy* is a figure in which what is considered to be the major feature or property of *what* is in question is used to designate this "*what*." For example, if I say "My son, my happiness," this is a way of saying that my son counts more than anything else that would also be a source of joy. I identify my son through the property which I deem to be the most important to me, namely that he is the wellspring of my joy in life.[13] To take a classical example, I could speak of one hundred sails on the horizon to refer to the ships emerging out of the distance through what I first perceive of them, namely their sails, since the earth is round. "My heart will beat for you forever" is also a metonymy because the essential place where good feelings are supposed to originate in the body is the heart. The heart thereby becomes the symbol of what is essential in love. In all these cases, as in others, we have the following formula:

---

[12] We could also take the example of a *cause*: to say that Montgomery won the Battle of El Alamein is to say that he inflicted a defeat on Germany because this battle caused a defeat for the Germans.

[13] To take the cause for the consequence is a special type of metonymy called metalepsis.

A, which could be B, C, D, ... is essentially or above all B, therefore A can be replaced by B, and to say A is to say B, and, since it is a trope, A "is" B.

Let us note that metonymies, like all other tropes, provide answers to questions such as *where, when, what, how much*, etc., by conflating the chain of determinations embodied in attributes. We have "the heart, *which* is the symbol of feelings" → the heart = feelings. "Washington, *where* all political decisions are taken in the U.S." →Washington = the U.S., and so forth.

The same reasoning applies to *synecdoche*, but synecdoche is a trope which implies more distance:[14] "The one hundred heads of cattle" → heads = cattle," hence the sentence "I see one hundred heads in the field" → I see a huge number of cattle in the field, or "Age, *which* is the sign of people who are old," → Age brings wisdom. But the difference between metonymy and synecdoche remains. For the latter, the idea of a + is predominant, while for the former, the idea is that the attribute refers to the main qualification of the subject (±). In both cases, it gives rise to an identity, a trope which is its figurative rendering. The formula which sums up the structure of tropes is as follows: "q_1" = "q_2" → $q_1 = q_2$.

4) *The figures of thought.* Speakers resort to figures of thought when what is problematic is too strong to be "swallowed" by an affirmative discourse, as is the case for tropes, where the problematic is, so to speak, "openly there." Speakers explicitly refer to what the problem is even though they do so by offering an answer to it. Among these modes of expressing the figurative, we find concession, recantation, threat, doubt, euphemism or exaggeration, amplification or minimization, parallels and analogies, antithesis, inversion (*chiasmus*), etc. In these examples, as in all other cases of figures of thought, the four operators are again at work; =, ±, +, and −, with, respectively, repetition, similitude (analogy), amplification or minimization, and

---

[14] B. Dupriez, *Gradus: A Dictionary of Literary Devices*, tr. A. Halsall (Toronto: University of Toronto Press, 1991), p. 446.

finally, doubt or concession, as well as other forms of recanting. The latter figure of thought can highlight an opposition (through antithesis or irony, for instance), enable us to recognize a difficulty which should be minimized or amplified, make a concession in favor of some solution, make a retraction (or *epanorthosis*), or even come back on what has been affirmed (it can also be seen as ±), which suggests an identity (by allegory or exemplification, for instance). In all cases, the speaker explicitly mentions what he feels or thinks, but most of all what he *thinks of what his interlocutor thinks* about a given question, and how he reacts to it, even if this reaction is purely strategic. In figures of thought, the question dealt with through rhetoric is raised openly because it can no longer be treated through other rhetorical means, the question being too problematic and too pressing. As a result, the explicitness of this question in figures of thought allows them to be found similarly in argumentation, where the question is also explicitly raised at the outset. The question cannot be "swallowed" but needs to be discussed *pro et contra*. Confirmation and refutation are also seen as figures of thought. Another consequence of this explicit character of the problem is that the rhetorical operations =, ±, +, and − are embodied (generally in an explicit manner) in distinct expressions (figures). The use of Ducrot's connectives such as "but," "even," and so on, express figures of thought. To minimize the problematicity of the questions, speakers often resort to euphemization, litotes, or understatement (for instance, "I would not want to do this" to say "I might have to do this" or "Is he not dishonest?" to suggest "he is indeed dishonest"). Correlatively, the speaker can amplify his state of mind or position on a given problem. He can resort to hyperbole, exaggeration, or overstatement, and treat as present (or even personified as in poetry, i.e. *prosopopoeia*), a feeling or an answer. He can also hesitate to give a firm answer by using *praeteritio*, just as he can anticipate this answer by *prolepsis*, or express doubt by resort to a rhetorical question (a rhetorical question is one to which the speaker knows the answer, as in "Who would live in this area of town?" which has for an implicit answer a statement that everyone would sensibly infer: "Nobody, of course").

We can now understand the rational link tying together the three types of figures of language: *each reflects an increased problematicity of the questions dealt with by the speaker*, from the figures of sound to figures of thought. Figures of sound are, relatively speaking, less problematic than figures of construction and the latter are relatively less problematic than tropes, which nonetheless evacuate the problematic though expressing it in its very form, but the problematic is there in the impossibility of a literal reading. These figures are all economical since they spare the speaker from having to provide a literal answer. There are many tropes, just as there are many grammatical or phonetic figures, but they all reflect the general structure that we have identified here and give rise to an increased possibility of expressions from repetition to opposition. Tropes fall into one of the four classes: metaphor, metonymy, synecdoche, and irony, because they crystallize the four possible responses to what the speaker says: =, ±, +, and −.

We could reasonably invert + and ± in the scale of responses. This is the case if we see + as adding an answer which confirms the speaker's initial response, or if we see this new answer as an embryo of opposition, or renunciation of his initial position, which thereby brings the respondent closer to opposition (−). We can add a new answer to problematize that of the speaker, instead of literally (and maybe radically) contradicting it. In the case of ±, we can then have two interpretations: it can mean an orientation rather towards rejection (± → −) or a positive requalification of the initial sentence (± → =). This is why we can have two sequences of problematization:

=
± (± → +: leading to the confirmation of the initial answer)
+
−

We can then suggest the following order instead:

a) =
b) +
c) ± (± → −)
d) −

This second sequence merely indicates that between approval and disapproval, the audience can add an answer to go in the same direction (here the + of ± is stressed) and may even answer by modifying the initial one in order to generate wider approval, even if the difference with the first answer is greater. This new answer can also be uttered as a way of reinforcing the validity of the initial answer by adding another argument, or by drawing a new consequence worthy of consideration. But the added answer can also requalify the initial answer in order to stress its inadequacy and to emphasize the difference from the speaker's initial claim (here the − of ± is stressed). In this case, it is uttered to minimize the acceptance or validity of the speaker's claim, thereby coming close to its rejection (−). This is what makes the difference, especially in argumentation or in the figures of thought, between a "yes…, but…" − sentence (± → −) and a "yes…, then…" − sentence (± → +). This is why we can consider both orders (=, +, ±, − or =, ±, +, −) as equally valid arrangements of the operators as cursors of approval and disapproval (Figure 5).

In both cases, this structure gives rise to the four major tropes:

a) =: metaphor (identification: "Richard is a lion")
b) +: synecdoche (generalization, classification, taking a part for the whole: "*Society* is responsible for this crime")
c) ±: metonymy (a single property denotes the whole subject because it epitomizes its essential features: "*Washington* has sent its armed forces")
d) −: irony: (negation: "That's really *clever!*" meaning the opposite)

We can now complete the table of figures by including Burke's (or Vico's) famous master-tropes (Figure 6).

THE ELEMENTS OF RHETORIC *STRICTO SENSU* 155

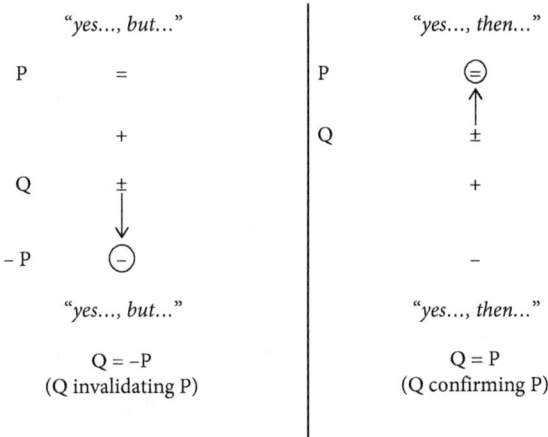

P = initial proposition

argumentative conclusion	operator or cursor on an argumentative scale of approval or disapproval	figures of thought
−	± → − (yes…, but: −)	restriction; minimization
=	± → − (yes…, then: +)	consequence; amplification

Figure 5 Opposed scales of approval (or agreement) and disapproval (or disagreement)

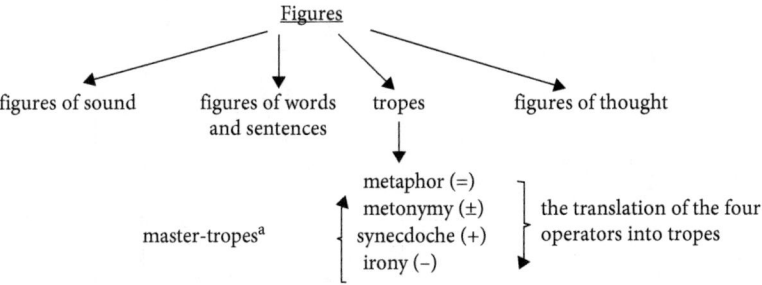

Figure 6 The catalog of figures and the inner working of the four operators on tropes as examples

[a] Following Kenneth Burke's terminology in his *Grammar of Motives*, Appendix D.

Table 4 Table of strategies and operators as a function of the level of problematicity

Increased level of distanciation expressed by answers →

	Rhetoric	*Logos*	*Argumentation*
	figures of language	figures of thought	arguments
increased level of problematicity of the question ↑ answers about the speaker's answers on the basis of the question dealt with	= identification, definition, reformulation + qualification with another answer ± amplification, minimization − contradiction [=, +, ±, −] *ad rem* / *ad hominem* pleasant or unpleasant influence / pleasant or unpleasant impact	= identity + addition (minimization or amplification) ± modification − opposition − contradiction [=, +, ±, −] *ad rem* / *ad hominem* agreement or disagreement effect / pleasant or unpleasant impact	= identity, analogy, definition (inference) + additional arguments ± qualifying arguments − contradiction [=, +, ±, −] *ad rem* / *ad hominem* agreement / pleasant or unpleasant impact

With this rational analysis of figures, we avoid becoming mired in further details concerning the multiplicity and arbitrariness of the figures of style and speech. We can now summarize the various rhetorical strategies as the interplay of the questions and answers with which rhetoric deals (Table 4).

7

The foundations of literary rhetoric

The basic, or most obvious, type of discourse in which the text itself must play the role that context itself cannot ensure, is literature. In literature, context is reduced to a minimum, and in poetry, it may even be close to zero. Literary rhetoric is characterized by the fact that context is replaced and produced by the *co-text*. The co-text is the discursive context in which questions handled implicitly in reality are integrated within the text, thereby allowing for questions to be recognized independently of what answers them. The aim of the text, as context, is to describe what we naturally perceive: men, women, places, smells, noises, the atmosphere in which people live, what we think they think, their physical description, and so on. Balzac, for instance, is well known for providing endless and overabundant descriptions, such as that of the Vauquier boarding house at the beginning of *Le Père Goriot*, which would be superfluous if we had lived there and met the people in real life.

The law of contextuality and the requirement of problematological differentiation

If language can express both questions and answers, one must always be able to recognize and demarcate the two. The most obvious embodiment of this requirement is *form*. Language employs syntax to differentiate interrogative and assertoric forms, the third syntactic form being the imperative, which can be interpreted as a stronger form of request than mere questions since it commands actions. The linguistic structure enables us to delimit what is and what is not in question as a means of differentiating the problematic and the non-problematic. As a result, interlocutors know their role: respondent or questioner, or indeed both successively. But as we all know from our own experience of language, we can assert, declare, uphold this or that, and still be posing a question, as in: "I wonder whether the current prime minister will win the next election." Even if this utterance is an answer, an assertion, or a proposition, it is mostly a way of expressing a problem. In a similar sense, we can use questions as a means of asserting something: "Is this man not courageous?" is not a real question, yet it amplifies or stresses the suspicion of cowardice we feel about him. How is this possible, if grammatical form bears all the weight of differentiating questions from answers? In spite of this inversion of forms, we still recognize in these two examples the question in the answer and the answer in the question. Would the task imparted to form be relinquished in some cases, and if so, how is this possible? The answer to this problem derives from what has been established so far: if the context is sufficiently clear and informative concerning what is in question and what is not, thereby generating more freedom in the use of form, affirmative statements can be used to express the problematic and questioning in general, just as problematological expressions can be employed to convey an affirmative or a negative answer. At the reflexive level, also called metalanguage, in which discourse bears on discourse itself (e.g. "I *said* you were not obliged to do so"), the problematological difference is upheld by distinguishing answers that express questions from answers that refer to other answers, respectively *problematological answers* and *apocritical answers*. This difference, inherent in any discourse, is thus preserved when we reflect upon it through meta-answers.

The more the context is informative about the question–answer complex, the less the form will be in charge of doing so. This *law of contextuality* is a basic law of language use which enables any language user to know from observing the context of a problem or a problematic (i.e. a cluster of related problems) the necessary information concerning what one can say (or answer) about the problem. This is why we do not have to describe what we see through words, as some novelists do. We see people, objects, situations; we perceive their colors, their forms, how objects and persons are related, how they behave, where they live, and so forth. In many novels, long descriptions fulfill this role of "letting us know" because the context can only be in the text, constituting its "co-text" as linguists characterize the linguistic environment of discourse which gives it its consistence, if not its relative autonomy.[1] Both context and co-text complete each other to enable the speaker and the audience to recognize the problematological difference, given the information that either provides.

To maintain that everyday language is contextual means that most of our information stems from what we perceive, hear, and observe. Situations into which we are plunged inform us about the particular problems we face. To be rational, let alone reasonable, is a question of adequacy: it is the way we respond adequately to these problems that makes the procedure rational, and the individuals, by complying, reasonable. Answers we give to others and hear from them emphasize our respective standpoints; they complete, qualify, countenance, or counterpoise these standpoints. But this knowledge of the questions which form the core of our exchanges (or merely of our observations) is very often left implicit; the questions thus belong to the "landscape," so to speak, or the background of the situations we face. We do not have to render explicit what we see; we simply know it from seeing it. This is sufficient to establish and know the distinction between what is problematic and what is not in a given context. The more context is informative about the questions raised and what is answered about them, the more the forms of language we may subsequently use are free from the necessity of rendering explicit the problematological difference. Conversely, the less the context is informative, the more the form has to fulfill the function of

---

[1] The term "co-text" was coined by the linguist M. Halliday. See G. Brown and G. Yule, *Discourse Analysis* (Cambridge: Cambridge University Press, 1983), p. 46.

characterizing the difference between what is in question and what is not. Rationality, as said before, lies in this capacity of differentiation (if not, adaptation) between problem and solution. It is an expertise or know-how, a technique, what the Greeks called a *teknè*, which is nothing but the capacity to adapt to the situation in which a particular problem has to be solved. As a consequence, the *Teknè rhetorikè*, to use Aristotle's term, is the art of giving an adequate answer to someone in a given situation. A rational person knows how to adapt the answers he or she gives to the questions raised in the situations in which he or she happens to be. There is a burden of form, as I have called it, when the context is more indeterminate concerning what may be problematic in the situation and what counts as apocritical. This burden compels locutors to auto-contextualize the process of problematological differentiation, since to speak or write is to have a question in mind, one which must be dealt with by a discursive response. Texts which do not rely on the external context to express the problematological difference are addressed to no audience in particular and therefore bear the whole weight of translating on formally suggesting it. This is a particular case of textuality as it is found in literature.

Texts or discourse express what is in question by raising these questions through the text. Advertising has this capability too, even suggesting that *you* have a problem that is now answered by the product advertised, a problem which you might not even have perceived up to that point as a necessity or as a potential pleasure. The basic difference between literature and advertising is that in literature it is someone who does not exist (the narrator) who establishes the problems. The problem of the literary character is usually less trivial and less common than that of the "hero" of commercials. The literary co-text is a discourse which situates the problematic of the characters and gives a frame to the narrator through the text. Literature is not a report on actual problems faced by real people, but invents problems that do not pre-exist their co-text, since it invents it, even though these may remind the reader of real problems. This is why Roman rhetoricians concerned with literature, whether poetic, dramatic, or more narrative-focused (e.g. novels in later periods) spoke of *inventio* as the first rhetorical step in literary construction, as a preliminary step to verisimilitude in any discourse. Literary rhetoric is characterized by the textual embodiment (co-text) of the questions dealt with in the text and of the answers deriving from those questions. This varies from the unfolding of the text as resolution to the solution which consists in expressing these questions as the text being itself.

In conclusion, the context is in the text, hence the numerous descriptions of places and characters we find in realistic novels, for instance, whereas in everyday life such descriptions are useless, since we immediately perceive them. *Literature is the auto-contextualization of the problematological difference, hence the possibility of increasing figurativity in order to express the problematic, when the latter is not explicitly staged in the text itself.*

From everyday life to literature: inverse problematicity as the basic principle of auto-contextualization

The context enables the speaker to recognize and differentiate what is problematic from what is not. As a consequence, the forms of language are intended as answers, even when answers reflect and express the problems faced by the speaker in the form of speech acts such as: "I want this," "I promise this," "Do this!" (i.e. I want you to act this way), and so on.

We can now imagine a world in which the context is largely nonexistent or scarcely informative. Would it still be a context? Logically, the consequences would, in any case, be the following: what the context does not tell the audience or the locutor about the question–answer difference must be legible in the text or from it, and the forms of language which are used must be subordinated to the necessity of instantiating the difference of the problematic and the non-problematic. This is how the audience can demarcate the two and identify the responses to the problems raised in the text. In general, this is implemented thanks to the use of form, which can be used more loosely when the context has already informed the reader or the viewer of what is in question (as prescribed by the law of contextuality analyzed in the previous section of this chapter). If not, the text bears the entire burden of informing the audience and it does this by raising questions in the very answers it proposes.

As we saw earlier, we can imagine a world in which the context is reduced to the text, which should then be called a co-text, rendered explicit by giving all the necessary meaningful information that we usually find in the context as an outside world. A world without context is not usual in everyday life because it is the *world of fiction*.

The problematological difference (and the dynamics leading to its establishment, called the resolution) falls within the text. The author has to imagine and put into words what people usually know with their own senses in everyday life. He has to select the relevant information he wants to convey; and sometimes, as in the case of thriller stories, the author will squeeze in some irrelevant details in order to lead the reader astray, thereby rendering the resolution of the suspense more unexpected.

Can we derive a law proper to fiction from this requirement of auto-contextualization of the problematological differentiation, one which would cover the way all of fiction operates, from poetry to narratives and theater? It would be indeed a significant advancement in our understanding of literature if we could establish the unity of literary rhetoric by discovering a single law or principle that would account for the variety of literary forms and for the corresponding major schools of literary interpretation. Such a law could only be based on questioning, and more specifically, on the way literature evinces the problematological difference. Given that questioning has forever been repressed as the unity and foundational component of thought and language use, it is no surprise that this fundamental law of fiction has escaped notice, even if theoreticians like Bakhtin, Lukács, Gadamer, and Hans-Robert Jauss have already sensed the critical role played by questioning and dialogue (or dialectic, as the interpersonal play of questions and answers) in the discovery of meaning in literature, in novels, theater, or poetry.

As we have already seen, the more a problem is expressed literally in a text, in a narrative, or in a spoken address, the less the form counts in demarcating the problematological difference since the problem is already specified and recognized at the outset, and clear all along. The less literally the problem at stake is expressed in a text, a narrative, or any other type of discourse, and without any outside context which would enable the reader, the hearer, or the viewer to identify it univocally, the more the forms must take over the charge of differentiating problems and solutions. Style or, in spoken discourse, eloquence, are the means of achieving this. How does the author or speaker proceed to convey the problematic character of discourse if not precisely by *de-literalizing* the latter, by using figurative language to embody the enigmatic in discourse for the reader (viewer or hearer) and to solicit a response from him, let alone to decide what is ultimately in question in the text? Literature embodies questions and answers, and if necessary, questions *as* answers. This feature is even the specificity of literature, its *sui generis* form of textuality.

We can now formulate with precision the basic law of literature and literary historicity. Since in real life it is the context which fulfils that role and enables each of us to identify what is and is not problematic, the question here is how the problematicity of the question is taken into account as literature, as fiction. In fiction, the problematological difference is integrated within the text (i.e. autocontextualized) in the following possible ways:

The more literally the problem is expressed, the more literal its resolution will be. The language of realist literature is more referential and similar to everyday discourse. Realist discourse is literal and the questions are clearly specified as the motive underpinning the story, giving the key to its plot. The distance between the narrator and his audience here is small and is negotiated within the text thanks to a spoken style that is shared by many in the society of the time. The whole difficulty of such a style is of capturing and captivating the reader with the resolution of a particular plot. The text itself unfolds as a solution, and examples of such narratives are thrillers or love stories. In such narratives, the problem is clear at the outset and the stories usually end by offering the solution. If the style of the text is not sufficiently captivating, the reader will feel that the fictional aspect of the story is rather fictitious and construed. She will probably close the book before the end and relinquish her "willing suspension of disbelief."

Conversely, the less literal a problem is, the more problematic and figurative the text will be (style is here the instrument of problematological differentiation) and the more active the reader must be in order to discover, if not provide, its meaning. Distance increases through recourse to a more enigmatic form and a more unusual style than the one used in everyday life. The consequence is a greater distance between the figurative and the literal, the latter being less and less in the text and more and more outside of it, as the meaning sought. The greater the distance between the figurative and the literal, the less literality can provide a **re-presentation** *of what is figuratively expressed in everyday language, and the more the reader faces an implication, an inference, a suggestion to be made. Finding the meaning then falls more and more on the shoulders of the reader, who must actively search for it or, as in recent modes of fiction, admit that there is nothing which can be discovered with certainty concerning the meaning of this text and in the end, that meaning itself has become the problem, to specify as such.*

Is meaning deconstructed or is it only as an answer that meaning has become increasingly difficult to identify univocally? Unless, of course, one accepts the fact that there are answers capable of describing the problematic, i.e. problematological answers, we here face the crux of a debate between deconstruction and problematology, the latter abandoning the propositionalist point of view, the former continuing to see the lack of propositional meaning as a void, a *nihil*, a deconstruction or an "other" of Reason, Reason being seen only as a propositionalist construct. Nonetheless, the world has meaning, even though it is made of problematical statements, of open questions posed to the reader stemming from the fragmentation of his or her previous certainties. We find such an increased problematicity in modernist literature in Joyce, Calvino, Borgès, or Kafka for example, but also in modern poetry from Yeats to Pound, from Montale to Vincente Aleixandre, from Mallarmé to Paul Celan. The object of such literature is to open literature to questioning itself, reality having become a problem per se. Literature has become figurativity without an available external literality, one "lying" there to serve as a rock of established meanings for everything. Literary meaning is the discovery that meaning cannot be put forth any longer as an answer typical of other discourses, but that is itself in question each time. And this is the only answer left at our disposal when we usher in contemporary literature and the avant-garde.

We can see how this *law of inverse problematicity* ("the less..., the more...") also covers the development of literary forms. This law expresses the various historical responses to increased problematicity under the forms not only of interpretation but also art itself, from the simple representation of an action (what Aristotle calls *mimesis* in his *Poetics*, to characterize the fact that literature offers representations of acts and facts in narrative succession, reproducing through fiction the usual order of succession in life) to total enigmaticity, reflecting a contemporary world of broken identities and turmoil in which everything, from family to politics, has become problematic. We live in a world of uncertainty and questioning, a fact that contemporary art expresses in multifarious forms, from abstract painting to dissonant music, from non-representative sculpture to urban architecture. This does not mean that the old forms of art and literature have disappeared, but rather that they coexist alongside the new ones. We still take pleasure in reading a love story or a thriller, as much as we still appreciate sculptures which represent the people we like or belong to our family, as the Romans liked to have in their houses or in the Forum.

At first glance, the basic law of literature is formal because it seems to be merely compliant with the requirement of problematological differentiation. In fact, there is more to it than that. If the basic requirement of such a law is a certain respect for the problematological difference, the variations in the possible expressions of the latter not only give rise to various literary genres, such as the novel or poetry, but also respond to historical change. Increased problematicity in history spurs an increased problematicity in fiction, even in the traditional modes of fiction. Meaning is less a given within the text, than it is the text itself which becomes more problematic. The only response left to the problem of meaning will be that meaning lies nowhere else but in the acquiescence and recognition of the problematic aspect of meaning, that meaning is always a question, and all the more so if our world has become more and more absurd and seemingly more meaningless than ever. It is a world in which meaning is no longer simply given (by whom?) or easily found (*where* would it be?).

The distance we refer to in rhetoric is embodied in the relationship between *ethos* and *pathos* that can be found in the text. It is evident in drama and in most dialogues found in novels, where discussion or confrontation is the key to the unfolding story. Realistic narratives often use *logos* literally, in the same way that poetry resorts to a specific form of style or *versification*, though most contemporary poetry has ceased to make use of the latter. *Pathos* is the emotional response contained in the work of art and created by it or in it through the interaction of characters. The audience will more or less reproduce such *pathos* (i.e. *mimesis*, according to Aristotle's view of re-presentation). The intensity of emotions and of passions in general is typical of a greatly reduced distance, in which individuals are more "touched." Proximity is here a byword for affect, or at the very least, its metonymy.

The four stages of literary evolution and the corresponding theories of literary criticism

We now have two subsequent questions: what are the main stages in the evolution of literary analysis? And how do they correspond to a continuous increase in textual problematicity?

1) The first stage of literature and its theorization is given by the Aristotelian word *mimesis*, or the representation of action. For Aristotle, the main advocate of art as *mimesis*, art imitates nature and the natural course of action: it thus has a beginning and an

end, and in between the two, a resolution. This is the non-problematological version of a double operation: the setting up of the problem and the resolution or conclusion of this problem. A primary aim is to captivate the reader, from the introduction of the problem to its eventual resolution. *Mimesis* plays a key role in this because the reader is asked to follow the resolution to its concluding term as it unfolds in the story or in the play, thereby reproducing the course of action of the internal problem-solver (a narrator) in order to arrive at a conclusion. This re-presentation—which follows the initial narrator as closely as possible, reproducing what he or she accomplishes—is, of course, mimetic as a piece of literature, as it is for the audience, which is called to represent for itself these same actions. Figurativity is therefore residual because what is essential is the literal resolution brought out by the text. Figurativity nonetheless plays a role, if one looks for a meaning underlying the text as a whole. As for the reader, she must abandon her "will to disbelief" and let herself be taken in by the action: this is what is meant by the expression, "a captivated reader."

However, there are two versions of this mimetic movement of interpretation which Collingwood called the "re-enactment of events."[2] The first version of the reader's interpretative movement is propositionalist; the second is problematological. A propositionalist view of meaning, at this representational and referential stage of mimesis, is based on the search for identical representations: A for B, where A means B, since it repeats the original message in terms that preserve its meaning, albeit in different ways. For example, what is the meaning of the expression "human being"? A human being is a rational animal. The second expression here preserves the identity of what is said in the first and preserves the truth-values of propositions constructed using these terms. An expression meaning this or that has to refer to the same reality, in the same way, for example, that the

---

[2] R. G. Collingwood, *The Idea of History* (Oxford: Oxford University Press, 1996), p. 282.

meaning of "The author of the 18 Brumaire coup d'etat" is identical to "Josephine's husband," and maintains the truth-value of all the phrases in which they are used, for both expressions refer to the same person. A means B because A stands for B. It is important to point out that in this propositionalist version of meaning, essentially based on isolated statements and not on texts taken as a whole, no reference is made to the underlying questions which might explain the particular use of two substitutable expressions. It is true, however, that when someone asks me the meaning of what I have just said, I usually repeat it with different words, words which are supposed to be equivalent. Let us note in passing that if two expressions mean the same thing because they refer to the same thing, this is due to the fact that *what* they are is identical. Interrogatives like *what, which, where, when,* etc. have a referential function. This function is a consequence of the denoting role of interrogatives, which pinpoint in a unique way what we talk about. But can we reason in the same way when we deal with whole texts, such as novels, plays, or poems? An ironic answer can be found in the work of a master of storytelling, Jorge Luis Borgès, in his short story "Pierre Ménard, author of the *Quixote.*" Borgès introduces us to a character who devotes himself to rewriting Cervantes' book in one substitutional, epitomizing version, one which is quite literally a *tautology*, since it is an exact reproduction of the original text. The interpreter merely reproduces the original *Don Quixote* in another text which is identical, in order to avoid any interpretative move that would alter the words of the novel, therefore literally rewriting it term by term. The only possible substitution must then be identical with the original text. Hence, in order to grasp the intrinsic message of the *Quixote*, Ménard sees no other course than to rewrite it entirely as it was in the first place, thus committing himself in the most absurd manner to the substitution view of meaning, extended this time to texts. This extension is clearly the logical consequence of the semantics of the propositional theory of language. But what can be more quixotic than literally reproducing the *Quixote* word by word? Pierre Ménard appears here rather as *Don Xerox*. His project is, of course, absurd, yet Ménard pursues it to its logical conclusion with the consistency of a stalwart follower of the propositional theory. Once we—the readers—accept his methods, Ménard appears just as reasonable as many a logician or philosopher of language. Is not the perfect substitutionalist version of a text, the text itself? "Cervantes' text and Ménard's are verbally identical, but the second is almost infinitely richer," Borgès concludes with irony, both as a literary project[3] and as a literary achievement.[4]

Aristotle's views on literature and more generally on art were also influenced by Greek theater and epic. Nowadays, the same narrative structures can be found in stories which increase the suspense by manipulating the chronology, hence the amplified problematicity of the plot. The readers (or the viewer) and the narrator remain in close proximity by means of common natural and referential language, the same language that is used by most people and which renders superfluous any questions on the acceptations of terms for this very reason. The reader has then a more passive role when following the resolution of the intrigue represented in the text.

Mimetic or representational art has remained very popular throughout Western history, but is no longer understood by means of some substitutional theory (which, as we have seen, proves absurd when generalized beyond the analysis of terms). In fact, textual understanding relies on the inference of answers from the work of art, considered as figurative to a minimum degree. However close they may be, some minimal distance always remains. The bridge between text and meaning is one of implication, of causality, as can be found even in love stories ("These roses he gave me must mean he loves me," the heroine might say). The *implication* from something enigmatic to its resolution can even pertain to the very text itself. The enigmatic can be weakly problematic and very conventional ("to give

---

[3] "To compose the Quixote at the beginning of the XVIIth century is a reasonable undertaking, and perhaps even unavoidable; at the beginning of the XXth, it is almost impossible." J. L. Borgès, *Labyrinths* (Harmondsworth: Penguin Books, 1970), p. 68.

[4] "The contradiction in style is also vivid. The archaic style of Ménard—quite foreign after all—suffers from a certain affectation. Not so that of his forerunner, who handles with ease the current Spanish of his time" (Borgès, *Labyrinths*, p. 69).

roses means affection"), and gives rise to a passage from a question to its answer, carried out here by the main character of the story himself or herself as much as it is by its readers. *Mimesis*, as a mode of reading and interpretation, even when it is not merely substitutional, is a *re-presentation* of the initial text. The operation of interpretation at work is nonetheless similar to a form of identity, even if it is a loose identity: =.

2) The second stage of literary evolution is the search for meaning and the reign of *hermeneutics*. For hermeneutics, words have a hidden sense which bestows consistency and meaningfulness to texts which might otherwise appear inconsistent and unrealistic, such as certain passages of the Bible. Protestantism introduced hermeneutics as a method of resolving contradictory passages in the Bible. Methuselah's canonical age (969 years old) or the walls of Jericho which collapsed at the sounds of trumpets, and many other similar assertions, could not be taken literally, hence the need for interpretation. With hermeneutics, the distance and the complexity of inference is all the more taken into account if the pace of history has increased and, as a consequence, has rendered previous identities more figurative.

Mimetic art and the mimetic representation of art have endured for centuries and are still among the most popular forms of art, especially in literature. *Mimesis* continues to be linked to representation and more generally to realism in art. As for mimetic literature, textual resolution, being the matter of its works, is the key to their understanding. The unfolding of the story is itself an answer to some initial question. With the acceleration of history, identities change and are more and more permeated by difference. Identities can only survive by ceasing to be taken literally. They then become metaphorical (a metaphor is a difference expressed as an identity), translating differences into figurative identities. What is, however, in other words, the real, turns out to be different from what it was. However, minimal differences plunge identities into the realm of *fictional* identities. A metaphorical identity such as "Richard is a lion" is a figurative identity covering two distinct and even opposed terms: Richard is human, *x*, and not human, *not-x*. This formula involves a conundrum, since we have *x* and *not-x* presented as though they were not contradictory. But the formula covers a literal contradiction because Richard is not literally a lion—he *is* so only figuratively. Through fiction, difference can maintain the feature of identity. But it is a shortcut for an answer that is absent, even if it is one in a sense. Figurative identities such as metaphors remain enigmas for us when we need to formulate what they literally mean. Richard is both a man and an animal, but this is a fiction. Figurativity and realism are the two complementary modes of fiction and art in general. They are, of course, often mingled in various proportions. History is a difference and rather "metaphorizes" discourse in response to those generalized differences.[5] Literature is very often a mixture of both, even if some genres, like the novel, can be more realistic, while others, such as poetry, tend to be more figurative, as if modes of fiction had to be complementary in order to fill the voids of fiction created by the destructive differentiation imposed by historical changes.

In the arts, the demarcation lines are clearer: sculpture is often more representational, or at least has been, while music is more figurative. The acceleration of history increases the difference between what is and what came before and hence generates more figurativity which needs a realistic counterpart in the guise of new answers. As a result, history spawns more enigmaticity in art as in literature. Hence the increasing active role played by the viewer or the reader when making sense of cultural objects. Characters, stories, plots, and intrigues multiply and intertwine, so that the meaning of the narrative becomes more and more enigmatic for the reader. Hence the reader's questioning focuses on what the question of the narrative *is*. The increasing complexification of the story renders it less readable with "black and white" categories of reading which are less and less easily distinguishable. Once again, the questions raised are multiplied. The mimetic reading, which follows the narrator in his

---

[5] See White, *Metahistory*.

progressive discovery of a much sought-after response, is no longer available because there is no univocal and unique text which provides answers for such a query. The questions, the queries, the problems, their consequences, and their failures or successes, all collide with one another and intermingle, giving rise to complex stories in which there seems to be no single solution that can emerge univocally, i.e. as providing the meaning of the text. The reader is therefore all the more solicited and questioned in multifarious ways. In sum, the text is just like real life, in which we fail to overcome difficulties by finding one meaning which would unveil once and for all the secrets underlying the events that happen to us. These events are sometimes so unrealistic and staggering that no one would dare put them in a novel, not even of science fiction.

The task of *hermeneutics* is to seek and discover what is in question in the answers given in the text, or inferred from the text as answer. The reader's questions express the problem encountered by the characters themselves, embroiled as they are in the multifarious experiences of their own lives, whose meaning is problematic for them: "A person who wants to understand must question what lies behind what is said. He must understand it as an answer to a question. As these considerations show, the logic of the human sciences is a logic of the question. We can understand a text only when we have understood the question to which it is an answer."[6] Such a question is itself an answer to the questioning process of the reader, who must reconstruct those questions from the text itself. Moreover, "this is not to open the door to arbitrariness" since the question emerges from the traditional *horizon* in which texts take place.[7] The questions we can raise about a text are, in a way, embedded in the text itself (though they are not *given* by it). Does this mean that the understanding of all the possible questions about a text unfolds like the successive stages of history as in Hegel's logic, or as T. S. Eliot could have said, points to an end which would already be in the beginning? On this view, the

---

[6] Gadamer, *Truth and Method*, pp. 363–4.
[7] Gadamer, *Truth and Method*, p. 367.

reader would be nothing more than an instrument in the unconcealing and unfolding process that clarifies the questions raised by a text. According to this view of meaning, the history of all interpretations would be a self-contained block, historically folded with the text itself, only historically bound by virtue of accessory readers, succeeded by each other in time (and space). Hermeneutics is, on this view, a form of Hegelianism in which there is a plan right from the outset for any understanding that happens thereafter. The reader is the passive instrument of this process. She operates as someone who requalifies and reformulates what is said in acceptable and comprehensive terms as if she were restoring the underlying identity of some opaque or implausible speech: her operation is similar to rendering ± the original intention of the text. An alternative solution is offered by Reception Theory.

3) *The progressive disintegration of meaning: the compensatory role of the reader.* The real question here is to know which general view could really be tenable, if hermeneutics is not. We can reasonably doubt that all questions that can be raised *by* or *within* a text are already "there," present right from the beginning, as though all possible readings were predetermined by the text itself regardless of what might occur thereafter, which is after all largely unforeseeable. Societies evolve and may even disappear. The interests of readers change with the social and political framework. A reader of Plato in the Middle Ages was probably more interested in the question of God than a reader in the twentieth century, who has experienced Fascism or Communism and is more focused on the problem of totalitarianism, a subject to which Plato also alludes.[8] *Reception Theory* is the counterpoise of hermeneutics' immanentism. In it, it is the reader who matters and makes all the (problematological) difference. The questions asked are not "in" the text as such but depend on the choices of the reader who formulates them at each moment (+).

---

[8] Karl Popper, *The Open Society and its Enemies*, vol. 1 (London: Routledge, 1962).

Reception Theory is the basic tenet of a view which opposes hermeneutics, initiated by Hans-Robert Jauss and Wolfgang Iser in a famous debate with Gadamer.[9] The reader or the viewer makes a difference by the questions she poses to the work of art. Audiences are always historically variable: "The work of art, as a *work*, has an effect, a questioning effect, taken up by the audience which questions it in turn."[10] The questions asked are conditioned by what does and does not count as problematic at a given time, even if what is contained in the work of art limits, to a certain degree, the variability and the arbitrariness of interpretation (or its subjectivity, as we would say today). A work of art, whether a text or not, provides answers to what, within it, is posed as a question: "The reconstruction of the horizon of expectations, in the face of which a work was created and received in the past, enables one, on the other hand, to pose questions that the text gave an answer to."[11] Literary genres constitute the framework for such questions; they enable us to categorize, recognize, and formulate the questions which are adequate and relevant at a given time. Nevertheless, if questions are historically conditioned, does this mean that texts have to embody the totality of answers embedded in the text to which the text is itself an answer?

The interesting claim of hermeneutics as well as reception theory is that the distance created in and by the work endures, whereas it would be abolished if we held to the mimetic theory of interpretation. According to the theory of *mimesis*, we are fully absorbed in the story, while in hermeneutics and reception theory we must *seek* the meaning of the work precisely because the text or the work of art is problematic, thus creating a wider distance (or relying on one created by history which requires us, the readers or viewers, to search for an answer that is not given *by* the text itself). This means that the

---

[9] In English, in S. Suleiman and J. Crossman, eds., *The Reader in the Text: Essays on Audience and Interpretation* (Princeton: Princeton University Press, 1980).

[10] H. R. Jauss, "Literary History as Challenge," in *Toward an Aesthetic of Reception* (Minneapolis: University of Minnesota Press, 1982), p. 15.

[11] Gadamer, *Truth and Method*, p. 28.

historical distance from the past (the "horizon of expectations") has increased and must be actively explored by the reader, since it is no longer given. In short, we are distant readers by virtue of history. We cannot look at a Roman painting with the same common grid as the contemporary Roman viewer:[12] we need more information to formulate and direct today's questioning.[13] Theater has always been a privileged mode of art (spectacle) for expressing distance in society. We can laugh at husbands who have been cheated on (a fact which would not induce a smile on our part were we in their situation), at mythological creatures, or at improbable characters such as Oedipus because theater renders them observable in spite of the distance generated with respect to the spectators by fiction. We shall return later to the theory of genres as a means of expressing distance in literature and in art in general. Genres, like categories, are ways of recognizing what precisely is in question each time when we are compelled to search out the meaning of a work. They represent the frames of literary interpretation, i.e. the categorization of questioning in literature.

4) The fourth moment of literary analysis is called *Deconstruction* and is probably the final moment in the breakup of meaning which occurred in the twentieth century.[14] For deconstruction, works of art are so rich in form and content that they entertain a plurality of meanings and thereby deconstruct the possibility of having just one meaning which would be the right one—and this is not just the case for avant-garde art. Deconstruction went even further and claimed that the only answer to the question of meaning was that there was no answer. Hence, what is left is *nothing*, a void, since without an answer

---

[12] J. Elsner, *Art and the Roman Viewer* (New York: Cambridge University Press, 1995).

[13] See M. Meyer, "Preface," and M. Meyer, "The Rhetoric of Roman Painting within the History of Culture: A Global Interpretation," in J. Elsner and M. Meyer, eds., *Art and Rhetoric in Roman Culture* (New York: Cambridge University Press, 2014).

[14] See J. Derrida, *Of Grammatology*, tr. G. Spivak; J. Derrida, *Writing and Difference*, tr. A. Bass (Chicago: University of Chicago Press, 1978); J. Derrida, *Margins of Philosophy*, tr. A. Bass (Chicago: University of Chicago Press, 1982); and concerning literature more specifically, P. de Man, *Allegories of Reading* (New Haven, CT: Yale University Press, 1979).

there is nothing that can be said in a propositionalist order of thought as the one which has so far prevailed. The propositionalist model reduces to nothingness (operator: –) what it cannot conceptualize, namely the problematic as such. This nihilistic view seems to be confirmed by the figurativity of contemporary texts which very often have no literal translation. In poetry (Mallarmé, Yeats, Eliot, Pound, Mondale, or Aleixandre), or in the novel (Calvino, Borgès, Kafka, Joyce), texts embody the enigmas of a world that has been broken in the wake of the First World War. More and more, the audience (and hence *pathos*) plays a determining role: interpretation is subjectivity, and as such is multifarious, equivocal, and never beyond dispute or questioning. What exactly is hiding behind this figurativity of trivial objects, as in conceptual art (like Duchamp's urinal) or in the most literary texts? Perhaps nothing, but to say so is, paradoxically, also to affirm something. As such, this very statement is self-defeating and deconstructible. Kafka's short story, *die Prüfung* (*The Test*), offers a good example of such a deconstructivist reading, one which can also be read as a coherent whole if the problematological perspective is adopted. Kafka recounts the story of a servant who wants to be hired but never quite succeeds. One day, he goes to the tavern where he meets the person in charge of hiring people at the local castle. This person asks a great many questions, which the servant is unable to answer. Feeling he has once again failed, the servant gets up to leave. His interlocutor then replies: "Stay, that was only a test. He who does not answer the questions has passed the test."[15] This, of course, is quite absurd: how can we solve problems if we do not even understand the questions which express them? But this is not Kafka's conclusion: the conclusion, rather, is that we should accept questions as irreducibly open, and that in itself is the answer. This acceptance of the problematic as irreducible is, metaphorically speaking, the price one must pay in order to gain access to the high figurativity of contemporary literature, a literary novelty of

---

[15] F. Kafka, "The Test," in *Parables and Paradoxes* [1935] (New York: Schocken Books, 1975), pp. 180-3.

which Kafka's text (and test) is but an allegory. This acceptance of questioning, of figurativity without a literality which could "translate" what is meant or simply convey it, is the key to contemporary literature. As in modern theater, figurative literature operates through the impact its texts exert on their audiences. Literature and art in general have become openly rhetorical due to the increasing role of the very notion of impact.

The problematological consciousness of the historical process

The problematological approach to literary rhetoric is a kind of *fifth* stage. It embraces all preceding stages by giving them a theoretical place and a rationale. Mimesis represents a form of a re-presentation which can be symbolized by the operator =. Hermeneutics is a way of requalifying or defining in other terms what is said in the text as being its figurative meaning: it is ± the same thing. Reception theory adds to the meaning of the text what it means for the reader: +. Finally, deconstruction is the literary version of an operation which can be expressed with the symbol −, since it denies the text any literal meaning. Interpretation serves to deconstruct what is said into what is not literally translatable as a unique answer. The problematological stage is then the recognition that questioning in itself is an answer and that there is a new way of understanding figurativity and the figures of interpretation as the expression of the problematic. After all, Kafka's text *could* also mean the following: the fact that we have to accept questions without looking for an answer is in itself already an answer, indeed a new one which reflects our fragmented and often meaningless (or absurd) world. "Meaningless" should be understood in the traditional, i.e. propositionalist way of understanding meaning: the lack of propositional truth is the sign (if not the proof) that there can be no propositionalist "answer," no meaning. In other words, the lack of meaning leads to a void since in such a model there is nothing outside of propositions which can be thought or expressed. This lack, this void—in Latin, *nihil*—is the key to nihilism.

It would be more appropriate to say that we can no longer reduce thought to propositional thinking. Questioning and answering are the new forms of thinking. There is no void in this, only another way of envisaging reason and thought, one which leads to an alternative way of thinking about thought itself: as a way of answering questions, or expressing them. This solution is certainly more adequate for developing not only philosophy, but more particularly, rhetoric.

8

The rhetoric of the arts

The structural complementarities of art and literature

Rhetoric is the negotiation (answers) of the distance between individuals (*ethos* and *pathos*, speaker and audience) on a given question (*logos*). The speaker can proceed in two ways:[1] 1) by submitting, raising, or handling a question that is already "on the table," before proposing an answer to be agreed upon or accepted (this is consent), generally after some debate; 2) the speaker can also produce a discourse which is intended to provide the answer (convincing or pleasant) to an underlying question. He invents, recounts, and draws a conclusion. The speaker *expresses* his point of view (*ethos*) on a question, then lays out the cluster of answers (*logos*) which lead to the solution he advocates, before finally concluding his speech in expounding the reasons why the audience (*pathos*) should agree and accept his conclusion (or draw the same conclusion).

In literature, narratives and novels in general seem to have taken the upper hand. *Ethos* and *pathos* are differentiated by *logos* which represents them. Even their distance is modulated by fiction itself. Fiction creates individuals who express themselves, confronting one another in dialogue or debate. It can take the form of a novel or even a play. *Catharsis* is the rhetorical impact of fiction upon the characters themselves, but also on the reader who, by her external situation, is more at a distance and can be less affected by the emotions than the

---

[1] To put it in succinct terms, we can speak of a Greek way (Aristotle) or a Roman way (Cicero, Quintilian).

What is Rhetoric? First edition. Michel Meyer
© Michel Meyer 2017. First published 2017 by Oxford University Press

characters at work in the fiction. Distance, here, is what makes a work of art *aesthetic*:² it represents the responses of the audience to the work, ranging from contemplation to approval (or rejection). Aesthetic involvement should be differentiated from ethical involvement. Aesthetics creates distance. I may feel shocked by a violent murder in a movie, but this experience will be less emotional than if I had lived through a real one.

In including *ethos, pathos,* and *logos,* fiction can also make one of these elements prevail over the other two. When fiction focuses on *ethos*, the speaker is an "I," an ego who expresses his feelings. *Ethos* is usually associated with the specific literary genre of poetry or lyric. Alternatively, when *pathos* is at the center of a fiction, it is the relationship with others which takes precedence: since Aristotle, *pathos* has been associated with drama.³ For him, the dramatic and the lyric genres are complemented by a third genre; that of the epic, which draws on *logos* as the intellectual mirror of reality and of the main social values put forth by the reigning political order, as an act of legitimacy (e.g. *The Niebelungen,* for Germany; *Beowulf* for the English; *la Chanson de Roland* for the French; the *Odyssey* for the Greeks; and the *Aeneid* for the Romans). Poetics, by making use of *ethos, pathos,* and *logos,* is closely associated with rhetoric. The difference between them, however, lies in the fact that poetics, and literature more generally, does not deal with real interpersonal relationships, i.e. relationships between existing interlocutors, but only those which fall within the *logos* of fiction *as the components of a represented or enacted distance.* It could be a social distance or a hierophantic one, which separates the sacred from the profane. When used independently, *logos* is seen as the discourse reflecting the world order, for example as created by God in John's Gospel. It could also be any story invented by some author. If focused on the

---

² "From this we may conclude that the literary work has two poles, the *artistic* and the *aesthetic*: the artistic pole is the author's text and the aesthetic is the realization accomplished by the reader." Iser, *The Act of Reading,* p. 21.
³ This is the basis of the G. Genette's analysis of Aristotle's *Poetics* in *The Architext* (Berkeley: University of California Press, 1992).

Ego or the on Other(s), the expressive language of the I who speaks is used to declare his feelings or, when others are present in the literary work, Ego and the Other are usually the characters of some play. Logos could also represent their interaction within novels, although the Greeks did not know the novel form until the fourth century AD.

Genette summarizes these three Aristotelian genres in the following way:

Ethos	Logos	Pathos
lyric genre	epic genre	dramaturgic genre
("I")	("It")	("Thou")

He quotes Austin Warren: "The three major kinds are already, by Plato and Aristotle, distinguished according to the matter of imitation (or representation): lyric poetry is the poet's own *persona*; in epic poetry (or the novel) the poet partly speaks in his own person, as narrator, and partly makes his characters speak in direct discourse (mixed narrative); in drama, the poet disappears behind his cast of characters. Aristotle's *Poetics* roughly nominates epic, drama and lyric poetry as the basic kinds of poetry."[4] Indeed, Aristotle's distinction between *ethos, pathos,* and *logos* has greatly enhanced our understanding of literature and, in many ways, it still underlies the basic views concerning the various conceptions of literary work developed so far, if not art in general, from sculpture (*ethos*) to architecture (*logos*) to painting (*pathos*). What, then, is the rhetoric of art developed along the lines of this famous triptych? First of all, we should recall a distinction made by Aristotle himself, when he deals with the modalities of theater which need to be divided into comedy and tragedy, even if he speaks very little of the former, as readers of Umberto Eco's *The Name of the Rose* will no doubt remember. Rhetoric is nonetheless present in all forms of drama. Drama stages conflictual encounters between an Ego and an Alter Ego concerning a divisive issue. According to Aristotle, there are three differences

---

[4] A. Warren, "Literary genres," in R. Wellek and A. Warren, *Theory of Literature* (New York: Harcourt, Brace, 1956), pp. 217–23.

between a comedy and a tragedy: 1) a difference in object—common people or inferior individuals in comedy, high deeds or noble characters such as princes and kings in tragedy; 2) a difference in form—prose in comedy, verse in tragedy; and 3) a difference in effect—laughter in the case of comedy, fear and pity for the hero, in the case of tragedy. But why is this the case? If we return to what has been said about rhetoric so far, i.e. that it is founded on an *ethos–logos–pathos* relationship, the nature of these differences become quite clear: the nature of the characters in the play (high or low) is a feature of *ethos*, the type of discourse characterizes *logos*, and the impact on the audience relates to *pathos* (the word *pathos* is here metonymical in appealing to the essential feature of the effect undergone by the audience, since *pathos* also refers to the audience itself as much as to its feelings).

It is essential to the comprehension of art to differentiate its *realistic* from its *figurative* components, which is the aesthetic embodiment of the problematological difference, namely apocritical vs problematological answers. Normally, this differentiation emerges as a historical process. The acceleration of history brings with it new identities, breaking up older ones which become less and less valid or relevant except as figurative ones, conceived of as fictional manners of speaking. Literature aims at mixing the old and new, at synthesizing them, and thus gives rise to a confrontation in drama, in the form of an opposition between answers which represent the old identities that have broken up with the emergence of new ones. But this is a fiction and can even be said to be the object of fiction, in which old answers may appear, rightly or wrongly, problematic to various people, hence the confrontation. The effect of art is to question us about the world, as it was and as it has become, by mingling what is problematic and what is not. What *was* has become something other and *is* only metaphorically what it used to be. A metaphor is a figure of style in which what is different is treated as identical ("Richard *is* a lion" refers to a literal difference, but is also an identity as a figure of speech). The identity being fictional, metaphor always raises a question, according to Aristotle, namely; "what *is* Richard actually?", the answer being given by a *topos* associated with lions, courage.

The essential movement of aesthetic change is thus dual. On the one hand, the acceleration of history creates differences where there was once identity. In order to preserve their identity as answers, there is no way other than to transform that literal identity into a figurative one. As a consequence, however, this increased figurativity is bound to stress more and more the problematic aspect of the answers retained. On the other hand, the relationship to the world as it has changed requires new answers, which are meant to be realistic in a counterpoint to this increased figurativity. Figurativity and realism form the basic couple of artistic creation. The metaphorical aspect of answers increases at the same time as new forms of realistic art are created to counterbalance the former, just as a question needs an answer. In the time of the Renaissance, for example, Flemish painting embodied the realistic expression of the world that had changed, rendering Flemish sculpture redundant as a realistic invention and almost non-existent, or at least unoriginal insofar as it too could resort only to realistic forms. In Italy, figurative painting became the order of the day; to create an original Italian sculpture was, by contrast, the essential complementary response to this figurative movement. The same occurred in music when Italian painting later became far too figurative; the paintings were crowded with angels and a multitude of characters from top to bottom, creating a setting that was enigmatic for the viewer. Since nothing more could be added, a new form of art was necessary to render and capture formally the increased pace of history as well as to materialize the realistic counterpoint of such a formal way of painting (mannerism). Italian music served that purpose. It developed the realistic counterpart in form by substituting opera for chamber music and thus assuming the position of the new leading form of Italian art. Today's art is mostly figurative, abstract, symbolic, in sculpture as well as in painting, and cinema has replaced the opera as a means of offering a realistic vision of the world. History has effectively experienced an incredible acceleration in pace. Many other examples could be added here which would verify this dual movement (figurativism vs realism) in all forms of art, but let us first focus on literature (Table 5).

THE RHETORIC OF THE ARTS 185

Table 5 Literature in Aristotle's time

	Ethos	Logos	Pathos
Figurativism	Lyric (Homer)	Epic (Homer)	Tragedy (Aeschylus, Sophocles, Euripides)
Realism	Eloquence Philosophical Dialogues (Plato) Novels, after the 2nd century CE	History (Herodotus, Thucydides) Philosophical Treatise (Aristotle)	Comedy (Aristophanes)

The same schema can be used to organize the fine arts, as in Table 6.

Table 6 Greek fine arts

	Ethos	Logos	Pathos
Figurative		architecture	geometric painting
Realistic	sculpture		vase painting

The two tables can then be combined, as in Table 7.

Table 7 Greek fine arts and literature

	Ethos	Logos	Pathos
Figurative	lyric	architecture epic	tragedy symbolic painting (geometrical style in Greece; First Style or brick painting in Rome)
Realistic	eloquence sculpture (representing the Gods, and later in the Roman Era, ancestors)	history philosophical treatises	comedy representational painting (landscapes, cities, gardens)

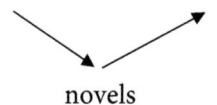

novels

Table 7 can help to clarify the evolution of forms, when *ethos, logos*, or *pathos* must be expressed, but also when a certain type of art eventually imposes itself as dominant at a given time, sometimes in conjunction with another art form, often in another country. It is well known, for instance, that Romanticism culminated in poetry in England, in theater in France (e.g. Victor Hugo, Alfred de Musset) and in opera in Italy. But Table 7 can also account for the succession of various dominant forms of art in the same civilization. For example, when Roman theater ceased to be inventive after the death of Terence (155 BCE), painting replaced it symbolically by becoming highly theatrical, e.g. by introducing depictions of theatrical masks, before Augustus decided to rebuild Rome and other cities as theaters, with columns and busts offering a new spectacle of harmony to the inhabitants of these cities. Music is absent from the tables shown here, but as mentioned before, it became a dominant form of art in the Baroque era as a figurative counterpoint to painting. We can even say that different nations favored different forms of art, often for political and sociological reasons. France, with its strong centralized state and powerful aristocracy, preferred theater to opera because theater stages hierarchies better, with kings and noble deeds, while Italy created a more "bourgeois" style of realistic art, namely the opera, which better mirrors a society in which the state is weaker and several classes share power. One could multiply such examples, but they would all still embody the Aristotelian tripartite view of literature, which we have completed by adding the dual orientation of realism and figurativism, thereby extending Aristotle's model to art in general. This has enabled us to single out the rhetorical structure of art, since it relies on *ethos, pathos*, and *logos* as sources and resources for its *inventio*.[5]

---

[5] For a more detailed analysis, see Meyer, *Of Problematology*.

Literary and non-literary rhetoric: the role of auto-contextualization and the externality of questions

The *law of inverse problematicity* explained in Chapter 7 stipulates that, when the questions dealt with are not literally mentioned, they are expressed with increased figurativity, which makes them look resolved, even though figurativity is meant to express problematicity. This process, characteristic of literature, is also present in everyday life, where the problematic need not be mentioned in order to be known by the addressee. In literature, this process has been called auto-contextualization because what counts as the context of speech in everyday life becomes in literature a co-text. In theoretical terms, this process means that the problematological difference, i.e. the difference between questions and answers, falls within the text or is indicated within it. But is this a process specific to literature, or can it also be found in law, in political discourse, and even in advertising?

The distinction between literature and these other forms of discourse may, of course, seem tenuous. Let us consider the different types of rhetorical "genres" in order to see what makes them different from literature. The obvious answer is that all these types of speech or texts deal with *external* questions, clearly identified in the context of real life from which they emerge and giving rise to the responses we have just characterized as specific modes of discourse: political, legal, advertising, and so forth. This also leads the speaker or writer to first specify the questions dealt with, in order to justify or convey the type of answers that will be privileged by determining the *exordium* or prologue that will demonstrate the interest or relevance of the questions raised. Such questions can also be dealt with implicitly, leading to a greater figurativity of language, as is the case in literary writing. But the argumentative procedure is also quite usual in cases of advertising. When a product, A, is claimed to be "better" than a rival one, B, then the question of the efficiency of the product is clearly raised, and a demonstration of the better qualities of A has to be made by the advertisement, generally through a comparative test. A washing powder, A, is said to be better than another, B usually, by showing that the same T-shirt is whiter after using A than after using B.

The same type of advertisements can be observed with cars. A brand, A, is more economical than models of another brand because it consumes less fuel, for instance. But the advertisement can be more subtle, more "figurative" than this, more "rhetorical" and indirect when dealing with the reasons why a given brand should be preferred. The driver of A, for example, is shown to take enormous pleasure in taking side roads to reach his destination because to drive with such a car, A, is quite pleasant due to the silence of the motor and the comfort of the seats. The beauty of the landscape can thereby be more fully appreciated, allowing the driver to take his time and enjoy the journey. In fact, the reasons for buying A are merely suggested in the advertisement without being fully and literally expressed. It is up to the viewer to figure this out and to conclude that brand A offers not only utility but also pleasure. In sum, an advertising campaign will be all the more argumentative if the question is explicitly posed from the outset; and it will be all the more rhetorical if the same question is indirectly treated and need not be specified as having to be resolved. The underlying problem dealt with in the ad is presented as already resolved, thanks to the advertisement which presents itself pointing toward the best solution. The former is more direct and generally addresses products based on self-evident utility at a relatively (or comparatively) low cost. An advertisement, then, can be more argumentative than rhetorical, and vice versa, according to the type of problems encountered in real life by the target buyer.

Even if there is a short narrative recounted in the ad, we should keep in mind the specificity of literature. There is no auto-contextualization of the problematic in advertising because ads refer to an external problem, linked to selling a product that must be rendered more attractive to that effect. Legal pleas too can be full of eloquence, just like advertisements or powerful political speeches, such as those of Winston Churchill or Martin Luther King. But in all these cases, what is recounted must not be confused with literary rhetoric, for a basic reason: the question is either known beforehand by the audience (which has such a problem) or is evoked as being a problem in real life. This question is based on the audience's wishes, namely to buy a car, a fragrance, or an efficient brand of washing powder. The story contained in the advertisement may pose such a question by evoking it or by explicitly mentioning it. Nevertheless, we cannot speak here of an *auto-contextualized presentation* of a question, as we can in literary texts where such a question is invented. The distance from the audience and its real problems is maintained in literary fiction, but it is irrelevant when someone has to sell a particular product, defend a political program, or plead for a defendant in court. Literature creates its own distance through form (*logos*), through an implied reader (*pathos*), or through the narrative voice (*ethos*). It can even combine the three.

Rhetoric in everyday life is often based on the discussion of questions which are implicit, i.e. which are more or less presented as resolved (the speaker expresses his "point of view" or "gives his opinion," as we usually say under such circumstances). The speaker does not have to vindicate any point of view in order merely to express it. He can be more figurative, or more literal if the question is "there" beforehand, either raised by the audience or suggested to it by his discourse. Nietzsche maintained that even the most literal discourse one can create is composed of old metaphors which have, at a given moment, crystallized into a single meaning which we term the "literal" meaning ("the face value" of something, for example, has no face). In any case, rhetoric is the mode of speech of everyday life since interlocutors share questions they want to speak of and also to debate, because they discover from their linguistic exchange how much these questions are relevant to their interests or to the problems they encounter in their lives at a given time.

9

The role of *ethos*: the voice of values

Logos: what else?

Asking "what else?" is, of course, a rhetorical challenge, since we already know that rhetoric is equally based on *ethos* and *pathos*, and not on *logos* alone. My definition of rhetoric, as the negotiation of the distance between individuals on a given question, has led us to examine the role of *logos*. It is now time to investigate the contribution of *ethos* and *pathos*. As we have seen, *logos* is the place of exchange in which questions and answers are literally or figuratively expressed, where questions are posed as well as answered. In this respect, *logos* may be a visual discourse, a spoken or written one, a gesture, a posture, a painting, or any work of art or literature. This is because *logos*, in each case, allows the speaker to offer an answer to a given question, as well as to express its corresponding question or merely suppose it by interesting the audience. He will resort to argumentation if the question is highly problematic and therefore more divisive, which will lead to a debate with conflictual arguments. But he may also simply suggest an answer, implying that the underlying question has to be taken up by his audience, if it is not shared with it beforehand. Rhetoric begins when some question receives an answer in order to evoke another answer. The former answer is all the more "rhetorical" insofar as it makes the latter the underlying question which is thereby solved. Rhetoric is also a social tool, since it enables individuals to work on the distance between them, to diminish, increase, or reaffirm it. Rhetoric is often used to evince or recall the distance that exists between people in everyday life, just as a uniform displays the distance within the army by displaying rank; or a physician's stethoscope, when wrapped around the neck or stuffed in a pocket in a desultory fashion, refers to the place he or she occupies in the hospital's hierarchy, in spite of—or rather, because of—the uniformity of color in the dress of hospital staff. Rhetoric can operate either on distance itself or on the question translating this distance: this is the basis of the distinction between an *ad hominem* strategy and an *ad rem* one, as defined by Cicero and the other classical Roman authors on rhetoric.

Another specificity of rhetoric is that it addresses questions indirectly, hence the necessity of giving reasons when there is a debate or an equivalent affirmation when the question *is* the expression of another question, implying a figurative answer. We have encapsulated this phenomenon with a formula: $a_1 \rightarrow q_1 \bullet q_2$, which can be read either argumentatively, a_1 therefore a_2, or rhetorically *stricto sensu*, $a_1 = a_2$ (i.e. to say a_1 is to say a_2), which is another way of saying what the speaker thinks without affirming it literally. A_1 can be an argument for a_2, but it can also be another way of figuratively translating (or hiding) it. In the argumentative reading, we are confronted with an inference to be drawn: "it's cold outside" is an *argument* to put one's coat on (and this action reflects the "real" question at stake) or is another way of expressing that solution, which is to put on one's coat, albeit the fact that it is not literally expressed as such. The audience then raises the question of what the speaker's beliefs are and this is the source of the interpretative process in general, and of any dialogue. No immediate literal answer is rhetorical unless it becomes the sign or the source of a different one, which may also emerge by virtue of some emotional impact and not merely as the final result of some reasoning. This response may be negative and give rise to rejection, or it may be positive and lead to an agreement or a feeling of pleasure. There is here no value judgment attached to the concept of "positive" or "negative" because what is at stake is merely the marking of a possible opposition or acceptance in the response of the audience.

This does not mean that there is no value implied in the speaker's strategy. Indeed, just the contrary is true, since we cannot argue, debate, or more generally convey answers to someone without implying values, which themselves may confirm eventually (or oppose) those held by the audience. Perelman would speak here of association or dissociation.[1] By way of metonymy, *ethos* refers to all the possible values on which the speaker draws when he entertains a rhetorical relationship with an audience. The question is one of knowing whether we can establish a basic and finite list ordering those values. Without criteria for such an order, this could be an endless task, as superfluous as establishing a catalog of figures of speech or of arguments, when we had to propose a similar classification. But there is a way out of what would otherwise seem a Sisyphean task.

No *ethos* without values

There is no action or *ethos* in general which does not implicitly rely or extoll some value or values. What exactly do we understand by "values"? Values refer to the components of social action and judgment which orient them in a precise direction (or sense) and, as such, they constitute the premises of our behavior as it is oriented toward others, whatever the goal pursued, from opposition to cooperation. From an argumentative point of view, values are not just the guidelines of our conclusions on social and personal issues; they are also the means of arriving at such conclusions. In rhetorical terms, values are the "answers" we usually consider to be out of the question in everyday issues encountered in society. They ought to be viewed as the interpersonal premises of any argumentation.

Values thus seem to correspond to what Aristotle, and since Aristotle argumentation theory, has called *topoi*, i.e. shared statements enabling an audience to infer something unproblematic when confronted with something problematic. This also includes, at least for Aristotle, the formal rules of inference. The difference

---

[1] Perelman, *Realm of Rhetoric*, p. 49.

between values as we envisage them and *topoi* as they were analyzed in ancient rhetoric is the relationship the former entertains with *ethos*. *Topoi* transform *ethos* into *logos* by expressing the orientation that the speaker wants to give to his values by relying on what can be shared in them by *ethos* and *pathos*.

Ethos is not only the speaker, but also, by extension of meaning or usage, the properties of the speaker required to gain credibility and to show authority on the questions addressed. In this respect, *ethos* is a metonymy, and a very useful one in the study of rhetoric. Values are the instruments linked to *ethos* for convincing (argumentation) or for influencing and pleasing an audience (rhetoric). They are answers or tools for arriving at answers that are acceptable to both speaker and audience. In fact, values are the premises of answers or the embodiments of answers. The difficult question is to determine what these answers are and in what order they should be arranged, since everybody upholds different ideas concerning what is good or bad, what is useful or not, what is preferable or negligible, according to the circumstances. We need a criterion of order and a criterion of content. The problem we face in defining both is that they might appear highly debatable. We can overcome this hurdle if we agree to proceed as most people actually do, and put at the top the most general and universal values, alongside those which are the most necessary to the survival of the group and to the individuals belonging to the group. In every society, the most important are those values that enable the group to express itself as such and to survive: religion, respect for life and rejection of death, family values, and all the values which provide a sense of group coherence. After that comes whatever enables the group to pursue political life (organization and norms) and economic existence (the appropriation and distribution of goods). At the bottom of the list we find the most individual values, such as opinions and personal desires, which are even more variable and debatable. *De gustibus non disputandum*,[2] affirms a famous Latin saying, but tastes and personal opinions do give rise to many a quarrel. We may thus

---

[2] "In questions of taste, there should not be any dispute."

Table 8 Table of collective values

Ethos (the "I" or the speaker)	*Logos* (the "It")	*Pathos* (the "Thou" or the addressee)
Respect for life and avoidance of death	Respect for nature as a common world gives a primacy to religion, which explains it and ascribes our place within it. By extension, the most important value here is the definition of the relationship between men and women, since their union is the condition of that common world and of mankind in general	The cult of family, and by extension, respect for one's parents, extending to ancestors

have found a rule of thumb for specifying and ordering the values used in rhetorical interaction as expressing the plurality of the voices of *ethos* when dealing with questions and answering them.

Let us then begin with collective values (Table 8), those that are supposed to warrant the very existence of the group, in all the senses of the word "existence."

This view is a classical one: "Perhaps the simplest way of putting the state of the case is this. Every human being, without choice on his part, but simply in virtue of his birth and upbringing, becomes a member of what we call a *natural* society. He belongs, that is, to a certain family and a certain nation, and this membership lays upon him definite obligations and duties which he is called upon to fulfil as a matter of course, and on pain of social penalties and disabilities, while at the same time it confers upon him certain social rights and advantages. In this respect the ancient and modern worlds are alike."[3]

---

[3] W. Robertson Smith, *The Religion of the Semites* [1889] (New York: Meridian Books, 1956).

From a rhetorical point of view, the most compelling and universal arguments are those which appeal to family or tribe membership and which provide accepted (or socially constrained) judgments. This is why religion, family, or integrity of life are always touchy subjects in everyday conversation: they belong to our most fundamental commitments and to what also determines our deepest emotional being. They speak to most people in society, whatever the society. To appeal to the respect for or sacred aspects of life, of religion, and family gives rise sometimes to strong, forceful, and convincing or convinced points of view. They represent what we could call "natural" commitments for everyone. To call these premises into question is also quite difficult to achieve, since there are no higher values to invoke for the group. As a result, most people will likely refuse to hear anything that goes against what constitutes their beliefs concerning these values, because the latter define their belonging and self-definition (i.e. their identity in a largest sense of the word). More problematic because less universal are the arguments derived from the ones mentioned and which express goods related to the *body* (hence the ongoing nature of debates on euthanasia or abortion, still raging today in some countries); arguments vindicating *economic goods* drawn from commerce with the world (and with nature); and arguments extolling what are considered to be founding political goods (or even privileges) pursued by others, even if they are said to be dedicated to the common good. Hence, the second line of our table of values (Table 9).

In any society, indeed in every society, these goods are the objects of the most fundamental debates but, most of all, they are pursued by

Table 9 The first two lines of the table of values as an instantiation of its logic

Ethos (the self)	*Logos* (the world)	*Pathos* (the other)
life	nature	family ties
physical goods	economic goods	political goods such as rules, norms, and laws

the members of any society as though obvious to everyone and as mostly out of the question. The debates bearing on "life" or on the "good," when defined politically and economically, usually make the different points of view on such topics a source of highly adversarial debate. For example, capitalism and communism are well known for being opposed with respect to what constitutes the best way of life, economically as well as politically, just as those in favor of or against euthanasia have defended a certain view of life, feeling that it is more "just" than the contrary viewpoint. These debates are all the more fierce or radical in that they cannot rely on more general premises than those already present in the first line of our table of values. Debates arise, then, from different interpretations of what, on the same line, *ethos* owes to *pathos*, and reciprocally. Which is "better"; values of life or family values?

How do we formulate arguments based on values or using values? In order to answer this double query, we must draw two major conclusions from the table of values which will also highlight its functioning: 1) an argument opposing two individuals is a different reading within a single line as to what *ethos* expects from *pathos*, and conversely. It then gives rise to personal disagreement. For example, the way I understand pleasure, the right food to eat or not to eat, or sexuality, are related to a certain conception of the body which may be at odds with what others understand by these terms, such as our parents for instance. If the reciprocal view of *ethos* on *pathos* and of *pathos* on *ethos* is in contradiction, debate is unavoidable. 2) Each line is the locus of possible premises for a debate, corresponding to a line below, taking place between *ethos* and *pathos*. That is why, when we discuss particular issues, we always invoke more general, universal, and (often) indeterminate (fluid or fuzzy) concepts or principles, such as "democracy," "justice," "freedom," and so forth, about which agreement with each other is proportionate to the relative imprecision of these concepts. As a consequence, the more a debate bears upon collective issues, the more its arguments must be concrete, and conversely the more a debate deals with practical and individual issues, the more it appeals to general premises.

Ethos as the source of values and their hierarchy

With the same principle of increased subjectivity and particularization, we can now establish the whole table of values (Table 10).

Let us now look more closely at the remaining lines of the table of values. The *third line* deals with the various ends people normally pursue in life: i.e. ends that are socially, economically, and politically defined. In this sense, they are "collective," but we all know that they

Table 10 The general table of values
Collective (resort to these collective values relie on concrete cases)

Ethos (the speaker)	*Logos* (medium of exchange and communality)	*Pathos* (the other)
life and death	the nature of the world and the world of nature (religion)	family ties
the body: physical and intellectual goods (age, health)	economic goods	political goods (norms)
the mind or spirit: personal ends (salvation, intellectual, ethical, aesthetical, satisfaction)	external ends (economic interests: profits, capitalization, etc.)	social ends (general and personal interests)
identity	negotiation	difference
status rights	income capabilities (competences, expertise)	power duties
virtues	efficacy	demands (for personal satisfaction)
desires opinions	needs facts (signs and causes)	emotions questions

Individual (resort to individual values requires resort to abstract premises)[4]

---

[4] One's arguments must be all the more predicated on abstract and general concepts (democracy, freedom, etc.) if the discussion takes place at the level of opposable opinions and individualistic points of view.

are differentiated according to social groups, as the usual statistics on societal issues demonstrate. Even individualized ends are socially "marked," as we know from Bourdieu. The attributes on the third line are nonetheless more personal than the ones above, without being susceptible to being called thoroughly individualistic on account of their being more personal. In fact, they are mostly defined by group-belonging.

The turning point between collective and individual values undoubtedly lies in the *fourth line*, identity–negotiation–difference. This is the line of conflation of social with individual premises. The embodied triptych *ethos–logos–pathos* here represents the rhetorical relationship in its very structure and components. At this stage, being able to entertain rhetoric as a relationship becomes a value in itself. It embodies the need if not the necessity of negotiating with others, however different they are, in order to pursue collectively our respective goals in a peaceful manner. We try to impress and to express; we demand assent or consent; we want to share our intentions, our arguments, and to render them agreeable or convincing (or both).

The lines below the fourth line are more representative of values bound to individual preferences and qualities. They are used to defend or propound arguments based on personal choices and values we may share through empathy, sympathy, or reciprocity. They may also oppose individuals and separate them from each other because of divergent interests, opinions, desires, and passions.

The *fifth line* explicitly embodies the social parameters determining individual life and guides the premises and arguments of our social insertion and our social roles. Status is the image of ourselves in social life. It is mostly linked to our professional position. It gives others the image of what we are through what we do: a doctor, a lawyer, a farmer, an employee, and so forth. Here *ethos* is what we represent for others, just as *pathos* is the other for us, i.e. a question for us just as we are for others. "Power" is the concept that epitomizes influence, i.e. the effect we have on others as well as the impact they have on us. The link between the other and our image of ourselves in a professionalized society is measured by our income, our "value"—in the two senses of the word—in society as assessed by the usual means of exchange, giving a value by doing it. Money is in many ways the embodiment for others of our social value. In everyday life, money is an issue often talked about, but behind this, the real issue seems to be the money that we earn because it enables us to get what we want. When there is a debate about status, income, and power it may take many forms, but it always presupposes these three parameters. Our social relationships thus represent important values which matter for everyone in society. This is why we are shocked when we read about a CEO who receives too much money when leaving his job, or about a politician who has misused his power by granting undue favors and positions, and this is also the reason why image, the status of people, is so important to them, if not to us, who also have one.

The triptych of status, income, and power is one of the most commonly used in the social sciences. Marx used the concept of social class to characterize these three elements: a class for him is at the same time the consciousness of our social position (status), our role and dependence in the production of goods and services (income), and what opposes us to others in the political struggle for power. It was Max Weber who first realized that these three components of social class did not necessarily overlap and could vary in different directions and at different paces.[5] They must be differentiated if they are to become really explanatory in the analysis of social behavior. Before Weber, these three parameters of social life had been subject to a more theological reading, even if the consequences of such a reading were also social. They were linked to *passions*: status, income, and power were the laicized words for vanity, cupidity, and desire, the most powerful of these desires being lust. With these three elements, we have what Augustine called the components of "original sin."[6] More than simple passions, they were vices to be overcome, if possible by

---

[5] Max Weber, *Economy and Society*, ed. G. Roth and C. Wittich (Berkeley: University of California Press, 1978), pp. 302–11.

[6] Augustine, *The City of God*, bk. 14.

ourselves and if not, with the help of the Church. Someone who enters the Christian Church to be ordained to the priesthood must even renounce them by pledging vows of humility, poverty, and abstinence. The minimum that common people ought to accomplish, then, is to confess their sins to a priest in order to obtain some forgiveness and absolution. In the eighteenth century, these three cardinal passions ceased to be viewed as sinful but progressively became interests that could legitimately be pursued; if contained they could even become respectable life goals. In other words, they became, as Hirschman underlines, *rational*.[7] In the sixteenth century, Machiavelli had already transformed the thirst for power into a rational motive to play a political role in the City, and Adam Smith did the same by rationalizing the accumulation of wealth as a source of common good and not merely as a legitimate personal goal. The pursuit of wealth ceased to be a vile passion and became a rational interest. Finally, Freud, in his turn, did the same for sexual desire and its derived forms by rehabilitating the libido. For each of these thinkers, the aim was not to extoll these motives but simply to show that they were shared de facto by all human beings and that explanation was better than condemnation.

These three kinds of motives have a rationality of their own and must be taken into account if we want to understand and explain human behavior in the larger sense. Political ambitions, economic interests, and the quest for social status have positive effects on the whole of society and they are, at any rate, the *real* motives of our actions. They represent the value of "values" in our lives: pleasure, desire, and image are thus good arguments for motivating and influencing our fellow human beings, as they are also the underlying (and often veiled) conclusions of arguments which seem, at first, to have nothing to do with them. It is thus seen as legitimate to pursue these various goals, or at least to take them into account even if they turn out to be in conflict with others who have the same goals. This overall rehabilitation of our basic passions did not mean that everyone, except

---

[7] A. Hirschmann, *The Passions and the Interests*, Part One [1997] (Princeton, NJ: Princeton University Press, 2013), pp. 7–67.

theologians or moralists, was ignorant of the evils to which excesses did lead. Marx against Smith, Montesquieu and Rousseau against Machiavelli or Hobbes, and Freud against himself, bear witness to the fact that unrestrained passions can induce poverty, corrupt power, or bring social contempt and violence towards the weaker members of our society. But at least the real motives of human behavior, once unveiled, could become studied in all their aspects, negative and positive, as *values*.

On *line six*, values are even more individualistic: the rights (*ethos*) of the person must correspond to the duties (*pathos*) that others have toward us, and if they do not match, conflict is bound to arise. Argumentation and debates in general stem from the contradiction between *ethos* and *pathos* situated on an identical line (if they are not on the same line, the debate becomes an unsolvable conflict that argumentation cannot settle). In fact, different readings of what *ethos* is to *pathos* and *pathos* to *ethos* are the sources of such debates. If I understand my rights toward my interlocutor as different from her duties toward me, the two readings will necessarily come into conflict and begin being expressed through disagreement between the two individuals.

The last three lines are even more individual-oriented: virtues are personal, but certainly less so than one's desires and opinions. They have to satisfy the other's emotions, needs, and questions in order to avoid disagreements. The link between the values of *ethos* and *pathos* is given in the *logos* column. Desires meet the others' demands on the basis of the utility of these needs being satisfied, just as virtues are convincing by their efficacy in bringing about positive emotions in all. My opinions do not necessarily respond to the questions of the audience with which I am speaking, unless I can rely on facts admitted by both sides to bolster my answers. Otherwise, the alternative (question) is bound to remain a subject of debate.

Values in rhetoric *stricto sensu*

The table of values does not only highlight how the speaker proceeds when he is arguing, but also how values are "figured out" in rhetoric *stricto sensu*. No question is really just put forward at the outset, but only the eloquent speech is offered directly as an answer, i.e. as a sign, as a "proof," as a demonstration. A painting, for example, or a piece of architecture are often meant to illustrate some virtue, i.e. some value shared by the community which the speaker wants to remind his audience that he is his voice, often under the order of some sponsor, private or public. Values, then, are presented as unproblematic to the eyes of the audience, being obvious for ethical, religious, or socioeconomic reasons. Debates about them when they arise usually come in the second instance, like any other criticism. Collective values need more reinforcement for individuals but are also more self-evident and more current. The struggle between them is present in our contemporary democratic societies for that very reason.

10

The role of *pathos*: from argumentative responses to feeling and emotions

The nature of *pathos*: the response of the audience

The *persuasive force* of an argument lies in its appeal to a line of values which match *ethos* to *pathos* on the same line in our table of values in Chapter 9, because "they are aligned." *Persuasive force* is to argumentation what *rhetorical impact* is to rhetoric *stricto sensu*.

An audience is impressed, convinced, persuaded, moved, determined to act, astonished, or pleased. The same gamut of qualifiers can, of course, be found in the opposite direction: repelled, disgusted, shocked, displeased, unconvinced, indignant, and so forth. The major works of art in the past, from the Roman Triumphal Arches to the Italian paintings of the Renaissance located in churches have a rhetorical impact: they convey a message. In the former case a message of power and grandeur, in the latter a message of humanity, of shared human suffering, even though it is also a sign of the power of the Church.

All this shows that *pathos* can mean several things in rhetoric: the most immediate of which is the *audience* itself, but by extension (or metonymy) *pathos* can also signify the responses of the audience and thus refer in the end to the problems the speaker wants to address by using rhetoric in the wider sense of the term (which includes argumentation and any other form of discourse, such as images). Influence, impression, agreement, uneasiness, and pleasantness are just some of the feelings and impressions that discourse can spur in *pathos*, and make *pathos* what it is in particular. The impact of the speaker upon his audience is variable and distance should be considered here as an essential parameter. Rhetoric as negotiation is used to modify that distance, thereby abolishing the problems which have initially arisen, or dealing with new ones linked to this modified distance. As a result, rhetoric alters distance as much as it commands it. It commands the use and force of affect over or in arguments when the distance is short, and an optimal rhetorical strategy will stress emotions rather than values, with the reverse when the distance is wider.

Just as *ethos* means expertise or virtue and requires art (*teknè*) when the speaker invokes them, and is rooted in authority and credibility, *pathos* can range from rational response to the expression of feeling according to the distance between individuals and the type of problematicity that divides them or unites them.

The transformation of values into passions: the emotional impact of rhetorical discourse

As we have seen, *pathos* is what characterizes the audience and, by extension, its reactions and its movements, either of aversion or approval. *Pathos* refers not only to the audience but also indicates the state of mind of those who react to the speaker. This is why *pathos* has been associated with passions, emotions, or simply with judgments of approval or rejection, of agreement or distanciation. An emotion is a weak form of passion. Distance gives tonality to the passions. The closer the audience and the speaker, the more their reactions to one another are personal and strong—today we would label them "emotional"—and the more that distance is great, the less passionate and emotional is the interpersonal relationship. On the other hand, the shorter the distance, the closer the protagonists are in their views and in their emotions. Sometimes we have different words

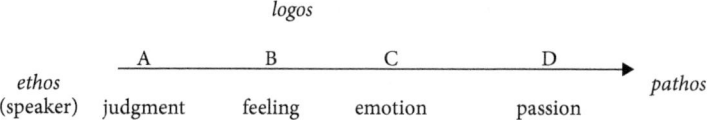

Figure 7 The transformation of emotional distance

for the same type of emotion or passion according to the distance in question: we *love* our friends and our relatives, but we *like* the Prime Minister, the President or the Queen. To speak of "hating" or of "loving" the President of the United States as if he were as close to us as a friend or parent would be an abuse of language, since we do not know him personally. There is an undeniable truth in the famous saying "out of sight, out of mind," which underlines that the strength or vividness of an emotion hinges on the proximity of its object. A passion fades off into an emotion, and then into some feeling or value judgment after a certain lapse of time or simply a physical distance (Figure 7).

When *ethos* is very close to *pathos*, say D, then the response is nearly physical, to say nothing of the role of sight and of the body in the reciprocal relationship between people. The result may go in either direction, but violence is not excluded as a means of responding to that distance, especially if it is deemed insufficient (Hobbes).

Passion—called emotions or feelings by the various authors who have dealt with the problem of passions, though without relating them to the variation of distance in human relationships—is indeed a very old topic in the history of philosophy, psychology, theology, and science (at least since Darwin).[1] Aristotle devoted the second book of his *Rhetoric* to the *pathè*, the passions. For Aristotle, passions are the mirrors of our individual differences in a world in which to speak of individuals or individualism would have been anachronistic. Passions are rhetorical in the sense that they reveal to others what brings us closer to them or, on the contrary, what distances us from

---

[1] C. Darwin, *The Expression of Emotions in Man and Animals* [1872] (London: Penguin Classics, 2009). For a more contemporary account of bodily emotions, see Paul Ekman, *Emotions Revealed* (London: Weidenfeld and Nicolson, 2009).

one another. They also highlight our wishes or desires, as well as the contrary movement of aversion and fear. Passions are then just as spontaneous as they can be reflective, in all the senses of this word. They inform our interlocutors of what we think about them, but also of what we think about what they think about us, revealing discrepancies of judgments or even disagreements (anger or sadness can ensue from such a reflective judgment) or indeed just the simple pleasure we take in the relationships we have with them.

They also allow us to hide ourselves behind facial or bodily expressions, to dissimulate, with more or less success, what we really think or feel. In Greek, the *"hypocrite"* is the actor who wears a mask when he is on stage. As an actor rather than a real person, he is the "respondent." Passions are expressions which enable the speaker—and the audience—to mark distance and express where he stands with respect to his audience (and vice versa), and to hide himself thanks to that distance, let alone to manipulate the other's mind. At a short distance, my body, and not only my face, will nevertheless denote what I feel, what I want, and what I do not want or what I fear. That is why passions also reflect distance in their social features: what is socially appropriate and what is not appropriate to a certain distance will give rise to emotional responses of anger or calm, contempt or pity, and so on. Passion is not simply the response to what the other thinks of me; it is also a response to what I think she thinks of me, *insofar as I accept it or not*. Passion is therefore a rhetorical response, an answer (i.e. it has an impact and conveys an opinion), to a social attitude whose effects are also psychological. The purpose of the passions, according to Aristotle, is to make known an evaluation of the "interpersonal" aspects of civic life.

Passions express an opinion on social distance. As such, we have seen that for Aristotle they relate to the positions of inferiority, equality, or superiority. More generally, they indicate to the various protagonists where each stands with respect to the others and how they themselves mark their positions (i.e. view themselves) and adopt a certain distance, just like us (hence a possible disagreement or misunderstanding in the messages conveyed). For Aristotle, some passions reflect equality (as in love or hate, which suppose a relation of equality and reciprocity, since we seldom hate people who do not hate us in return), superiority (as in contempt or benevolence), or inferiority (as in shame). The matrix of all passions in Antiquity up to the Romans, however, was anger and calm—Seneca even wrote a famous treatise on anger, *De Ira*—two distinct ways of establishing distance when one feels threatened. With the subjective approach originating in Descartes, passions became less social and more individualistic, although they were still viewed as altering judgment, in contrast to Reason.[2] After Aristotle, passions ceased to belong to the field of rhetoric even if they have once again become of interest to philosophers.[3]

Everyone seems to agree on three basic features of emotions or passions:

1) A passion contains—if only in an embryonic way—a judgment, and is at the very least the modification of a judgment (for Aristotle, *pathos* is that which affects men's judgments).[4]
2) A passion gives pain or pleasure.[5]
3) A passion is the evaluation of a solution to a problem in respect of the distance between individuals (fear is about an impending negative event or answer, hope is the response appropriate to an impending positive answer, while despair is the response adopted to a solution which fades away in the distance, and so forth).

The issue of precisely how many passions exist is as scholastic and debatable a question as that of the number and types of arguments or figures of speech. The catalogs propounded by Hume, Descartes, Spinoza, or Aristotle all differ from one another, with rationality proper to each according to their particular philosophical outlook.

---

[2] For a historical analysis of passions from the Greeks onwards, see M. Meyer, *Philosophy and the Passions*, tr. R. F. Barsky (University Park: Pennsylvania State University Press, 2000).

[3] M. Nussbaum, *Upheavals of Thought* (New York: Cambridge University Press, 2001); Robert Solomon, *The Passions* (New York: Doubleday Anchor Book, 1977).

[4] Aristotle, *Rhetoric*, 1377 b20.   [5] Aristotle, *Rhetoric*, 1377 b21.

In Descartes, for instance, the matrix from which all passions are derived is composed of six primary passions, while in Spinoza this matrix comprises three passions, and it was fourteen in Aristotle's *Rhetoric* and eleven in his *Ethics* (1105 b21).

As for the third component mentioned above, some additional comment should be provided because its justification is less obvious. Let us consider several passions, such as fear, anger, or hope. They all bear on a single alternative: each is measured according to a problem with which, sooner or later, here rather than there, I shall be closely confronted. Fear, joy, hope, and so forth, bear on an answer to a given problem in relationship to its proximity in time or space. Passion is a reaction to this proximity (or likelihood, if we prefer to express this relationship in formal terms). We can now better understand why Spinoza insisted, in the fourth part of his *Ethics*, that all passions derive from desire and why Hume preferred to focus on pleasure and pain in his empiricist analysis of the passions in the Second Book of his *Treatise of Human Nature*. When something happens to us, passion (rather than mere emotion or judgment) is a response to the closeness of the approaching solution to the problem. Avoidance or pleasure-seeking are *movements* and as such they operate upon distance. We may wish to avoid it, if we can, or we may want to see it realized. We may *hope* it happens or be in *despair* that it might. If something that we deem to be bad is likely to happen, we naturally fear that it will happen. We will become *angry* if indeed it does and we will need *courage* (Aquinas) if we are to face up to it.

For instance, in the distance I see that the road is blocked with a traffic jam. The question is whether it is inevitable that I too will become stuck in this traffic. I fear I shall. I hope for the contrary, of course, and I am angry if I cannot avoid it. But when the slowdown begins, I despair of not being able to get out of it. If things were necessarily bound to happen, passion would be uneconomical and useless—this is Spinoza's outlook in his deterministic approach to the world. And when the answer I want or reject comes closer to occurring, my passion, from mere evaluation of the problematic situation, increases and becomes more and more intense. In passions, the problem is taken into account, but also its likelihood to touch us by virtue of its being close to us: we fear a negative or unwanted answer all the more when its occurrence is more likely or comes closer, rendering the solution all the more unpleasant, making us angry, or if the answer is positive and desired, make us happy when it does occur. Pleasure and pain are also modulated by distance and change names accordingly. They are more physical when the distance is short and the body susceptible to being affected, but they are more abstract and intellectual when the problem to be confronted is very far, abstract, or unlikely. In the case of increased distance, we will instead speak first of joy or sadness and, at a greater distance, of happiness or unhappiness.

When we put these three components of the passions together, what do we notice? Judgment corresponds to *logos*; pleasure and pain correspond to *pathos* (modulated according to distance, hence the important role of the body in certain passions); and what we feel concerning the problem–solution relationship as a function of the distance corresponds to *ethos*. This latter relationship modulates the intensity of what we feel and not only the nature of *what* we feel.[6]

The parameter of distance is essential because it modulates the responses given to the speaker, while also influencing the way he addresses himself to his audience. The speaker is motivated by values, which provide him with arguments or premises for arguments. He usually assumes that these values are shared if no contestation arises.

---

[6] Fear is thus a response to a problem whose solution displeases us; fear becomes terror when this solution seems unavoidable and close; and hope rests on the possibility that it is still far away. Anxiety, or *angst* in the Kierkegaardian or existentialist sense, presupposes a degree of distance in which the object does not seem to count: it is a state of mind, of being-in-the-world with others, as Heidegger would put it. Thus we express the whole gamut of emotions of rejection of an answer to a problem which can cause us harm: we can speak of anxiety, fear, and terror as different ways of expressing distance from the object of this emotion. At a great distance, when the object is more or less precise or concrete, rather than being due to the fact of having to *exist* and confront problems in general, we are simply afraid that this or that might turn out to be the case. The sensation is here a judgment on a situation, rather than an affect turning into a vivid emotion or passion.

There is a link between values and emotions, conceived of as passions when the distance is short, and as mere feelings or personal opinions when the distance is greater. A simple formula serves to epitomize this link: values become emotions at a short distance and emotions turn into values (i.e. judgments) when the distance is long. They thus vary and transform into one another in an inverse relationship to distance. Values can be defined as *emotions without subjectivity* (for example: "family is a positive value for me" is an objective way of translating emotions such as "I would not like to see my parents divorcing," or "I respect my father," or "I love my children and I help as much as I can," and so forth), and conversely, *emotions (or passions) are values plus subjectivity*. What I hate and what I love are defined by what I value most, and this refers me back to the general values which are mine. Emotional language is another way of specifying "*this* is good, or *this* is bad."[7] Moreover, passions remain present at a wider distance under the attenuated form of general feelings or subjective judgments. They never completely disappear. Is this not the reason why we cling to our values so much?

By focusing on distance, rhetoric implies the intervening factor of emotions in setting values in motion. These emotions affect in a strong or weak way individual reactions to an answer or the question itself. This is the reason why resorting to emotions reinforces arguments and gives flesh to rhetorical speech, increasing (or decreasing) the impact they have on the audience.

Ethos and *pathos* in political and judicial rhetoric

Politics and law are important fields of rhetorical usage today. Rhetoric is omnipresent in advertising, in the media, or in social life, to say

---

[7] This view concerning the link between values and emotion is ancient, even if it has never been conceptualized in terms of distance. See Ch. Stevenson, *Ethics and Language* (New Haven, CT: Yale University Press, 1944) or E. Westermarck, *The Origin and Development of Moral Ideas*, 2 vols. (London: Macmillan, 1906).

nothing of its role in the humanities and the social sciences themselves. At stake here is not merely a question of language or arguments, but also a question of distance which is so important in the social sciences. In law, for instance, where formalism recreates the distance propitious to impartiality, rules serve as the general premises necessary to apply these rules to particular cases.[8] But law cannot be mechanically applied by the judge. The circumstances, the character of the accused, and more importantly, the qualification of the facts, count just as much. "What is the question at stake?" is really the question to be decided in court: was a murder committed or merely an act of self-defense? Has a right been violated or is it legally acceptable for A to have done X and so on? At a more general level, there is a link—and this link has always existed—between law and politics. Even the most totalitarian regimes have used law and tribunals to get rid of their opponents or as a means of punishment and repression (for example, Stalin and the trial of the Jewish doctors in 1952, or Hitler and the trials of the officers who had plotted his assassination in 1944). All political regimes endeavor to enshrine in law the unproblematic values of the community, even if in a democracy laws are meant to be limited to general principles, respectful of the values of freedom of expression and of thought. Politics wants to be translated into laws, and laws claim to be the expression of the fundamental moral values of the community. Political rhetoric arises in the irreducible gap between both.

Political debate arises from the divergence of opinions concerning what has to be done in society and with whom (if not, *for* whom). This divergence manifests itself through laws which are meant to be the solution to any debate that might arise. This situation can be rendered by Figures 8–11.

In politics, the *distance* between individuals is probably greater, since people seldom know one another, in contrast to what happens

---

[8] R. Alexy, *A Theory of Legal Argumentation* [1978] (Oxford: Oxford University Press, 1988); N. MacCormick, *Rhetoric and the Rule of Law* (Oxford: Oxford University Press, 2005).

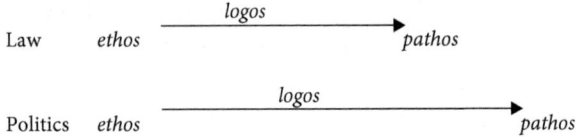

Figure 8 Distance in law and politics

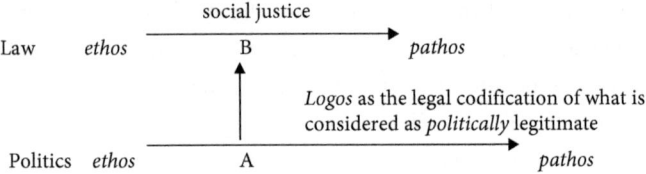

Figure 9 Translation of politics into law

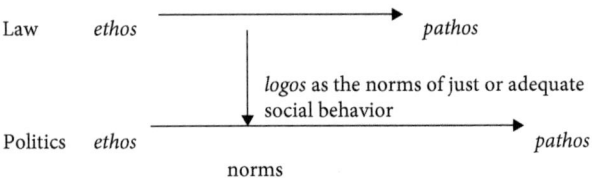

Figure 10 Translation of law into politics

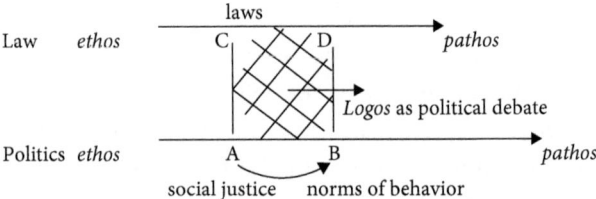

Figure 11 The space for political and legal debates

in court (Figure 8). But in politics, reactions are also more passionate and sometimes violent. The introduction of law into politics is intended to calm the conflicts and to diminish the violence associated with the dividing passions of the parties. Justice, and the courts more specifically, aim at creating distance between individuals, if only to defuse physical confrontation. Justice affirms its independence through its detachment, through its lack of passions for or against the opponents to be judged (i.e. separated), creating a minimal distance between them which is necessary to have a dispassionate debate. It therefore stages a formal ritual, including the wearing of formal clothes specific to tribunals. It is then logical that dictatorial regimes resort to courts in order to convey an impression of impartial sanctioning even when they are simply eager to punish and repress those holding adverse opinions.

A second graph (Figure 9) can help us to illustrate the relationship between law and politics. Politics aims at translating into law the decisions taken by the executive power once they have been submitted to the legislative assembly. But laws themselves evince political interests and values in general. Respect for the rule of law is in itself a political ideal and a value. This is one of the basic tenets of Dworkin's theory.[9] For him, "legality, alias the rule of law, is the political value that lies at the heart of any interpretative attempt to understand and characterize law."[10] But it also goes in the opposite direction: law—and it must provide arguments in order to achieve this goal—aims at giving each citizen an a priori sense of what is right, of what his or her rights are, as norms of social behavior and political exigencies (for example, the equal rights of man and woman inscribed in the law) (Figure 10). But, as we know, there is always a gap, wide or not, between the norms of behavior in our societies and the law itself (tax optimization, for example, is legally accepted but is politically disapproved of as a form of incivility, its goal being to avoid the due payment of taxes).

Political argumentation finds its source in such a gap, as illustrated by Figure 11. The space AB defines the space of argumentation in politics, where people debate what should be made mandatory but

---

[9] R. Dworkin "Hart's Postscript and the Character of Political Philosophy," *Oxford Journal of Legal Studies*, 24 (2004), pp. 1–37.
[10] MacCormick, *Rhetoric and the Rule of Law*, p. 28.

which is not yet the object of legislation. Conversely, politics questions what is legal but politically unacceptable by many or by some. The gap between what some groups or individuals believe to be extended social justice and the real norms of behavior which should be codified but which are not is what leads to political argumentation in society.[11]

In modern societies, in which there are elections, the distance between individuals of different ideologies, beliefs, and interests tends to increase. There is a necessity to overcome situations in which there are too many losers from decisions, in order to avoid an increase in social conflicts and their transformation into physical confrontations, sometimes giving rise to revolutions. This is why we can observe in recent times an increase in the emotional staging of the political problems met within society, notably through spectacle, mostly on television, of the ravages inflicted upon certain groups of people. Through television, we now live in an era of victims and under the tyranny of guilt and goodness, as the counterpart of a historical past of economic success ascribed to wrongdoings inflicted upon various classes and peoples, inside and outside of Europe, especially during the colonial era. Rational democracy has given place to an irrational "emocracy" (a contraction of "emotion" and "democracy") in which images play a major role, since they have a greater impact than any speech. One of the latest examples is the crisis of the migrants from predominantly Muslim countries, who are filmed drowning in the Mediterranean Sea or reaching shore with no food or water, and whose drowned children are shown as lifeless bodies lying on the beaches of paradisiac Greek islands. Debate about opportunity and feasibility is here replaced by a rhetoric of images meant to arouse (com)passion, distance being abolished by virtue of the images themselves, whose function is precisely to give a feeling of closeness. Emotions buttress and nourish values and, when well-staged, values transform themselves into emotions. Who would dare to manifest his or her disagreement in the face of the spectacles of

---

[11] See B. Barry, *Political Argument* (London: Routledge, 1965).

distress seen on television, when the aim of such a vision is to activate compassion and sympathy?

Political rhetoric is nonetheless more divided and divisive than legal argumentation, the traditional template of argumentation or dialectic in general, insofar as it can resort to images and dramatization as well as to argumentation. Politicians do not always resort to arguments when opposing one another. When addressing their own electors, they prefer rhetoric, sprinkling their speeches with keywords evoking or recalling the values or opinions to which they adhere and which are supposed to be those of their specific electors. This is why political rhetoric is generally compared to, if not associated with, advertising, which also uses arguments ("This washing product, as you can see, gives 'whiter' shirts than its competitor") as well as rhetoric, as we saw earlier with the example of Chanel N°5 and perfume advertising more generally.

11

The negotiation of distance or the embodiment of the interpersonal

Rhetoric is the negotiation of the distance between *ethos* and *pathos* on a given question (*logos*). In the preceding chapters, we have analyzed each component of the rhetorical relationship: *ethos*, *pathos*, and *logos*; argumentative discourse and the figures of speech; the question-view of language; and its *ad rem* or *ad hominem* strategies. Yet one element remains to be examined in our definition of rhetoric: the notion of distance as regulated by negotiation. This negotiation can be carried out in two ways: either by focusing on the question, as a measure of that distance, or by working on that distance itself, as in *ad hominem* arguments. Divisive questions exist, of course, and need to be "put on the table" and tackled head-on. Other questions are less divisive and some may even strengthen the social bond, as in formulas of politeness, or amiable discussions about the weather or the family, which aim at initiating a non-problematic conversation between strangers and thereby bringing them closer together or, at least, will diminish the potential problem each represents for the other. The negotiation of distance can also be achieved through an argument which unites individuals on a single answer, even if they were initially opposed to each other concerning this same answer. This is what agreement does. Rhetorically speaking, individuals are often close by virtue of sharing the same answers to implicit problems, openly discussed or not, without any real opposition, for example, when we politely discuss the weather. Aristotle called this kind of conversation *epideictic* discourse, thereby characterizing the fact that nothing problematic was at stake and that the goal of discourse was simply to be eloquent and pleasant.

When dealing with the problem of distance, what is fundamental is that we always have an idea of *who* our audience is, despite the fact that we never know exactly and entirely *what* this audience is. Even people we know quite well can, on occasion, surprise us. Individuals always retain a part of themselves which escapes us, a secret part of their person which remains hidden or inaccessible to others and even sometimes to themselves. There is a limit to our knowledge of what they really are and what they have in mind. What they are *effectively* lies beyond the knowledge we have been able to form about them in the various circumstances of life. The initial approach to other individuals is always a mixture of projection and of reality, of our own opinions and of our objective reading of them, if such a thing exists. This projective view includes our prejudices or preconceived ideas, which are usually based on induction. The "Other" is a projection of all the information we ascribe to other people, hence too our audience on the basis of what we see, observe, but also feel and hear about them.

This feature of rhetoric is called *projectivity*: we must have an idea of the audience to which we address ourselves in order to be able to please, persuade, or impress it. But we also know that there is a difference between what we think people are and what they really are. We have a *projective* idea of *pathos*, or our interlocutor, but she can never be *effectively* reduced to what we think of her. There is always some discrepancy between effectivity and projectivity. This explains why we are often surprised by what people are and do at certain moments in their lives, even when we are very close to them. There is always something which remains unperceived and which is ungraspable, something which could be called a sort of private or intimate domain. We are seldom fully aware of the deepest motives of other people, and these motives are often hidden even to themselves, when belonging to their unconscious. Is it not in this interstice between the projective ideas we form about others and the effective reality of what they are independently that the majority of our passions take shape? Do emotions not ensue from the numerous misunderstandings, disappointments, or hopes induced by the various harbingers, signs, and clues attached to the encounters we have with people? Suddenly individuals reveal themselves for what they really are, passing from love to hate and conflictual attitudes, and it is at this tipping point that passions become unavoidable. Strong reactions take place as if we were unhappy or indeed very happy, sometimes disappointed, sometimes regretful, or full of hatred. We cannot but respond to the discrepancy of projection and effectivity. That is why love is often blind (to the effective person) and, as much as hatred does, love magnifies its object.

Political rhetoric cannot be understood without the distinction between projective *pathos* and effective *pathos*. Many a politician has misjudged the opinions of his audience and, as a result, failed to be re-elected. A well-known example of this occurred in France when Lionel Jospin lost the 2002 presidential election after enjoying a successful term as prime minister, at least with respect to unemployment and economic growth. He nonetheless failed to be re-elected and was even overtaken by Jean-Marie Le Pen, the extreme right leader. The reason for his failure is today clear: he projected onto his electorate the image of a French people in need of a good accountant, failing to see that, in the presidential election, the French felt in need of a father figure rather than a good manager. Clearly, Jospin had projected onto the French people expectations that were not those of the real French people.

How does the dialectic of the projective and the effective work in rhetoric? It is in this very dialectic, composed of gaps and adjustments, that we find the notion of distance at work. Dialogue, confrontation, amid innocuous discussions all allow the speaker and the audience to express their respective standpoints, to come to know these standpoints more accurately, and to make them known to their various interlocutors. They thereby confirm, increase, or decrease the distance between the protagonists. Let us note that *ethos, pathos,* and *logos* have both a projective and an effective dimension: the speaker has an idea of who the audience is, of its composition, of its emotional interests, of its wishes, opinions, and problems. Through dialogue, the distance between the projective *pathos* and the effective *pathos* can be diminished, maintained, or strengthened and this is where the credibility and the authority of the speaker—linked to his status, personality, or expertise—play a major role in the interpersonal exchange. The audience responds and questions the speaker, and as a consequence the ideas it initially nourished concerning the speaker and his viewpoint change and become more precise, refined, and accurate, leaving less and less space for false interpretations and misunderstandings, which can then be corrected at different successive stages. If the distance between the projective and the effective has diminished, the conversation tends to converge toward a mere communication of information. This does not mean that confirming or increasing the social distance between the interlocutors was not the goal of their discussion; the latter only aimed at avoiding or suppressing false ideas concerning what the speaker wanted and expected the audience to discover about his real intentions. To negotiate the distance between individuals, as rhetoric does, is to convey a message about what people want others to think of a given question and also of what they themselves uphold. Reciprocally, the audience conveys the same idea to the effective speaker. As a result, an answer or even several answers ensue from the process and deal with the question at stake, broached at the outset of their linguistic exchange. How does the latter work? First, we must take into account the mutual distance between speaker and audience—we can express the distance with the graphic means of an arrow—which can be longer if the distance is greater or very short if people are closer. It can also become very short or null at the end of this exchange, as happens, for example, when a final agreement obtains. Second, the *ethos* has a *projective* view of *pathos* when he begins to speak, just as the *effective pathos* has a projective view of *ethos* when she responds to him. This can be expressed graphically as shown in Figure 12.

The projective *pathos* is the one the speaker imagines. But it is the real or effective *pathos* who responds, and who also has an idea in mind about what the speaker is (projective *ethos*). In the end,

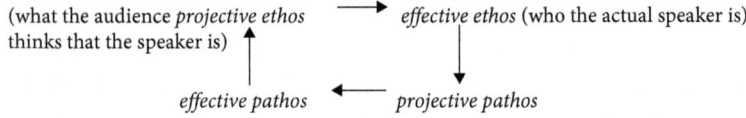

Figure 12 The projective and the effective: the arrows of distantiation

Table 11 The negotiation of distance: discrepancies and adjustments

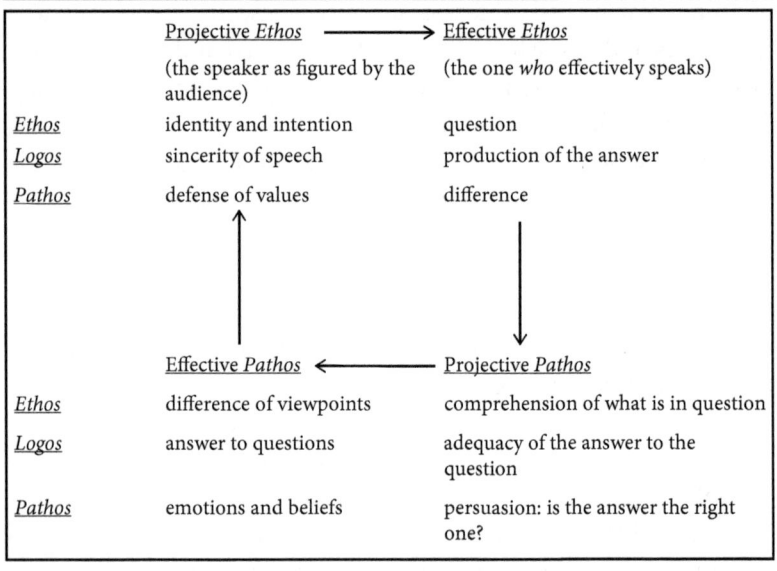

however, it will be the real or effective speaker who will address himself to the audience, on the basis of the (new) idea he himself forms about her, and so forth. This is a cobweb process.[1] Each time, then, what is at stake is an *ethos–logos–pathos* relationship. We can now fill in the gaps (Table 11).

[1] A cobweb is precisely a procedure of adjustment as in the following graph:

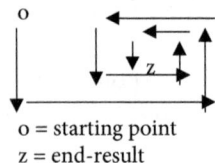

o = starting point
z = end-result

First (ideal) case: there is no gap or discrepancy. The question (*ethos*) raised gives rise to an answer (*logos*) and takes into account the difference between speaker and audience (*pathos*). The speaker really hopes and believes that his audience has understood what is in question (*ethos*-line, projective *pathos*), tested the rightfulness of the answer propounded (*logos*-line, projective *pathos*) to it and has been convinced or pleased (*pathos*-line, projective *pathos*). If the speaker has succeeded, there is no gap between what he believes and what the audience thinks. The difference of viewpoints (*ethos*-line, effective *pathos*) between the individuals is perceived and diminishes because of the acceptance of the answer (*logos*-line, effective *pathos*), and the answer stirs the targeted emotions and beliefs as aimed at by the speaker (*pathos*-line, effective *pathos*) when he has succeeded in convincing (and moving) the audience. This is due to the fact that the latter sees the speaker (projective *ethos*) as being a person animated with this or that intention (*ethos*-line, projective *ethos*) about which he is sincere and speaking the truth (*logos*-line, projective speaker), defending values which are, in this context, shared (*pathos*-line, projective speaker). Agreement ensues from these arguments or sympathy if the speech is found by the audience to be pleasant, as is the case in rhetoric.

We now have to complexify the situation. The cycle of discrepancies and adjustments at work as described in the table can reveal a greater distance, as indicated by the arrows →. A speaker addresses himself to his audience without necessarily knowing this audience closely. The arrow is quite short if he has a precise and adequate idea about what the audience thinks about the question raised (*ethos*-line, effective *ethos*), and how the answer must be produced in order to be right, true, and convincing as a solution (*logos*-line, effective *ethos*), given the difference (distance) between speaker and audience (*pathos*-line, effective *ethos*). Two cases are possible: the speaker is right and there is hardly any gap between what he thinks of his audience and the way it really thinks, *or* there is discrepancy at some level between what the speaker projects onto *pathos* and what *pathos* effectively is. We then move to the left of Table 11, and the distance which arises, weak or strong, is translated by the arrow which relates projective *pathos* to the effective.

Let us recall the initial case. The speaker has succeeded in avoiding any discrepancy between projective and effective *pathos*. As a result, both columns in Table 11 are in fact only one and each line of the first column is conflated with the corresponding one in the second column, being its translation by the audience. The question raised by someone does not raise any problem, nor does the answer, which may, in some cases, have been manipulated; nor, indeed, does the difference between the speaker and the audience raise a difference of values between them. Projective *pathos* and effective *pathos* are one. The understanding or interpretation of the question does not underline any difference of perspective. The adequacy of the answer is due to the fact that *pathos* considers the same answer as the adequate one and considers the speaker as having given a truly legitimate answer, to which she has nothing to add. As for persuasion, it is based on the real beliefs of and plays on the expected emotions entertained by *pathos*. The speaker has succeeded, or at least he is a very good manipulator.

Now, if there is a discrepancy between effective *pathos* and projective *pathos*, there will be a difference at some or all of the three levels, *ethos*, *pathos*, and *logos*, between the first and the second column. The greater the discrepancy, the longer the arrow. In the process, individuals may come to an agreement or be pleased by what is said. The arrows, then, diminish at each turn. In the end, however, perhaps after a long discussion aimed at setting the issues, agreement or persuasion occurs and the length of the arrows tend to diminish and eventually vanish after a "cobweb mechanism" of adjustment, where agreement is the punctual result. The two columns eventually become conflated. The arrows of distance remain operative in cases of disagreement, misunderstanding, or uneasiness with what is said, even if they have been diminished to some extent.

Protagonists may, however, be conscious that the gap between them will remain unbridgeable. As we have previously seen, different understandings reflect different perspectives; different answers lead one to modify (±), or add to (+), or contradict the given one (−).

Failed persuasion leaves the audience unsatisfied or even angry, subject to various emotions expressing what is felt. The effective audience may attribute this miscomprehension or disagreement to who the speaker is, to what his real opinion is, and to different if not opposing values. The cycle then goes on, beginning with a readjustment which leads the effective *ethos* to correct, change, or adapt his questioning, his answers, and his perception of the difference from his audience. Dialogue, inquiry, examination, and the search for another interpretation are the keywords which express the variability of responses symbolized by the arrows in the table.

Table 11 clearly respects what is meant by "negotiation of the distance" between individuals on a given question. It reveals that disagreement (or the uneasiness felt when an unpleasant speech is given, for instance) can bear on the values, on the answer, on the real difference of viewpoints on a given question between the speaker and his audience, as well as on these three elements simultaneously (as is often the case). Let us take the example of *logos*: the speaker thinks he has answered the question raised, but the effective audience or *pathos* does not think so and may reject the answer on the basis of sincerity, for instance, because it feels manipulated by the speaker. But it could also be because of the values embedded in the answer (*pathos*) or because of the person the speaker is or represents (*ethos*). Approval or rejection need not rely exclusively nor even mainly upon the validity of the argument (*logos*) or the eloquence used to speak, as in rhetoric *stricto sensu*. Lack of persuasion (projective *pathos* missed) can then stir different values and beliefs in the mind of the effective audience (third line in Table 11: *pathos*), after having led to disapproval.

All that has been said in this book on rhetoric as the negotiation of distance between individuals on a given question is epitomized by Table 11. In this table, we find all the components of our definition of rhetoric: questions, answers, speakers and interlocutors, arguments and figures of speech, possible manipulation and real sincerity, misunderstanding and disagreement, or the opposite. When we speak to another individual, instead of being two we are, in a sense, "four"; but when our exchange is over, only two *effective* persons remain, the speaker and the audience. The exchange has changed our ideas; its impact has brought about influence or persuasion, doubt or adherence, sympathy and communion among persons or precisely the opposite. Distance is at work here and is recognized as such, reaffirmed or provisionally suppressed during the time needed to deal with a question and to resolve it.

We could end our study of rhetoric in a sentence which recalls Cordelia in Shakespeare's *King Lear* (Act I, scene I, 87), when she says "I love your Majesty according to my bond, no more, no less": rhetoric is all that has been said so far, perhaps no more but certainly no less.

Conclusion

Rhetoric, as we have seen, is the negotiation of the distance between individuals, *ethos* and *pathos*, on a question (*logos*) which is more or less divisive, or more or less reductive of the distance between them. My treatise has been devoted to explaining the different concepts implied in this theory, given first in the form of a new definition, in which the new conception of rhetoric I advocate is implied. What are *ethos*, *pathos*, and *logos*? What is the role of questioning? What does the notion of distance imply and what does its negotiation mean? What is the role of emotions and values, and what are they precisely? Above all, the question has been to unify rhetoric as the rhetoric of conflicts—or argumentation, as in law and politics—and the rhetoric of figures, as in advertising or literature. The task seemed enormous; and without the conceptualization of the role of questioning as a unifying link, it would have been insurmountable. My conception of questioning stems from a general vision of philosophy, centered on questioning as a new foundation. Questions and answers here replace judgments or statements, hitherto considered as the basic units of thought. And now, for the first time in the history of philosophy, and in the history of rhetoric, preeminence is given to the question–answer difference. We debate problems, we discuss questions, we respond to others, while the distance separating us from one another is also very often the subject of literature. Distance itself, which defines our social life, is not only the object of politics and the aim of law when conflicts arise between parties, it is also what renders fiction, and works of art in general, enigmatic and transcendent, calling us into question and asking us to provide a response. Once again, from admiration to

What is Rhetoric? First edition. Michel Meyer
© Michel Meyer 2017. First published 2017 by Oxford University Press

rejection, from consent to dissent, the audience reacts with emotion and sometimes passion, something that the author, the speaker, the creator, has expected, if not calculated.

Due to the grounding role of questioning, rhetoric is a branch of philosophy, but it can be studied independently, as it was by Aristotle and Perelman. That is what has also been done here. We have seen that there is a relatively small number of possible audiences, based on four rhetorical operators, giving rise to four major classes of possible responses to a speaker. These operators have enabled me to provide an overarching rationality to the long list of arguments and figures we usually find in treatises on rhetoric. The time of scholastic catalogs of figures and arguments must be brought to an end if we want to give a well-established unity to rhetoric as argumentation and to rhetoric as figurative speech. There are correspondences between both forms of rhetoric because they represent, in fact, different strategies for confronting problems with the same underlying structure. Rhetoric is a way of dealing with questions raised in interpersonal relationships. It relies on values, including our interests and on emotions, and requires constant adjustment of distance between people: when the questions are too confrontational, we always answer them directly; but we answer them indirectly, through eloquence and elegance (two words with the same root), when we face a lower level of problematicity.

Rhetoric has now acquired influence in many areas of the humanities, to the extent of becoming, in the eyes of many, a kind of new matrix for the human sciences, one very much needed since the waning of structuralism. After all, in the human and social sciences we give arguments. But this is not the sole reason for adopting rhetoric as a new matrix. It seems that our unconscious is a codified language (Lacan), that our social life is as codified as our psychological life, and that we are always dealing with figurative speech, if only not to be aggressive in our dealings with others. The Other is undoubtedly in us, but it is also external as a question, if not as a problem. And from justice to family life, we cannot escape the problems others raise by their very presence. Once again, questioning is the core of the matter. Consensus is considered the ideal situation in our societies, but it is less and less the outcome in the concrete encounters of everyday life. We question because everything has turned out to be problematic in our Western societies, which have experienced an increased acceleration of history. As a consequence, old answers intermingle with new ones, leading to possible manipulation by means of false solutions which at first do not appear as such. This is why justification itself becomes a key problem, by bringing a rational solution to the possible confusions and amalgams. But without rhetoric, no selection is possible. We need rhetoric in public debate, in court, but it is also present in literature and art, which have become more and more figurative and enigmatic: music has become dissonant; painting, more and more abstract and conceptual; and poetry, more question-raising than ever. The reader is increasingly asked to offer an answer by herself to the question of the meaning of the world. Art and fiction become like water: we try to retain their signification in our hands, as though it were not already inexorably running out and flowing away.

We can no longer do without the question–answer difference. All our art is based on giving answers which express the problematic, asking us to make up for the evanescent meaning of a fractured world. If rhetoric is the discourse of the times, the concepts I have explicated and articulated in a general conception have enabled me to offer a rhetoric which goes far beyond the exigencies of the day. It integrates the various rhetorics given so far since Plato, Aristotle, and Cicero, into a single view which, relying on the constitutive role of questioning, I have called *problematology*.

The journey I have asked my reader to make with me has been a long one, in which I have articulated what came before with what must supersede it. As with everything new in philosophy, in linguistics, and in rhetoric, effort is demanded to follow the path dug into the past in order to achieve something new. But in order to impose itself as a full-fledged discipline, rhetoric needed such clarification and unification.

Glossary

Argumentation

To argue in favor of or against something is an attempt to answer a question by offering different answers pro and contra the solution proposed. In argumentation, agreement manifests itself as *one answer for two questioners* and consensus as *one answer to several questions*.

Ethos

In Greek, *ethos* refers to the speaker. Problematologically speaking, *ethos* is the stopping-point of questioning, because the speaker has the expertise (*Teknè*) or virtue to answer adequately and with sincerity. His virtues are marked by trustworthiness and authority.

Figures of speech, figures of thought

Figures can be divided into figures of language and figures of thought. Figures of language may be based on sound, grammar, and tropes, each of which is more problematic than the preceding type of figure. As a consequence, the most problematic—it is even its object—is the figure of thought, where the problem and often the type of distance are explicit. Both the problem and the distance can be minimized or amplified. Here rhetoric often overlaps with argumentation, since figures of thought can be used in both; their difference lies in the purpose of their use, i.e. the strategy to which their usage responds.

The four operators of rhetoric

Since Aristotle, rhetoric has been characterized by four operators: *identity*, *opposition*, and, in between, *difference* (or *similarity*), and *inference*. Symbolically, this sequence can be written as: $=$, $-$, $\pm$, and $+$. These four operators lie at the foundation of the basic classes of arguments, of figures, and of the number of possible audiences. How can an audience proceed if not by 1) approving and repeating what has been said ($=$); 2) rejecting in contradicting the speaker or finding a contradiction in what has been said ($-$); 3) modifying the initial statement ($\pm$) or 4) completing it through another one (+) (confirming or disconfirming it, according to the audience's initial standpoint).

The law of equivalence or the unity of rhetoric and argumentation

$a_1 \rightarrow q_1 \bullet q_2$ an answer is rhetorical if the question to which it literally corresponds is not the one it is meant to solve, but a different one, q_2, already implied in the fact of raising q_1 in a_1. We have two possible readings:

- an argumentative reading "a_1, therefore a_2"
- a figurative reading "a_1 is a_2" (as in rhetoric *stricto sensu*, as called the rhetoric of figures).

The law of inverse problematicity

The more a problem is literally expressed in a text, the more the text is itself literal in providing a resolution to the problem (as in love stories or thrillers). The less the problem is literal, the more the text is figurative and expresses itself enigmatically, asking the reader to make up for a meaning which is no longer given by the text. We find this law in many usages of rhetoric, such as literature and advertising. The specificity of literature lies in the auto-contextualization of this problematological differentiation.

Logos

In Greek, discourse or reason. Besides this ambivalence, *logos* is the place where questions and answers come to be expressed *and* differentiated.

Negotiation

The negotiation of distance between individuals needs a rhetoric to maintain this distance, or to increase it or reduce it.

Pathos

In Greek, *pathos* refers to the audience, but also includes the passions that define its response as an audience, particularly at a reduced distance where contact is more emotional, while at a wider distance passions become values by becoming more impersonal.

Principles of thought

Three basic principles underlie the functioning of thought and reason:

- the principle of contradiction: A *and* not-A is a contradiction because it is not an answer, but an alternative, i.e. a question. As an answer it is therefore invalid
- the principle of identity: *what* is in question in an array of sequential questions gives the identity of the problem
- the principle of reason: ultimately, the reason for any answer is a question.

These three principles help us define what the question is, what an answer is, and what renders the passage from one to the other possible.

Problematological and apocritical answers

An answer is at the same time *problematological* in virtue of its reference to the questions it evokes or suggests and *apocritical* by reference to the ones it solves.

Problematological difference

Compliance with the problematological difference is the basic imperative of thought. Questioning is a constant and constitutive feature of the human mind and only appears in a duality, the question–answer complex. Questions are always differentiated from answers, if only by being marked as such at the level of answers, from which they can also be rejected to constitute an order of questions per se (problematological level). This avoids any confusion between what the question is and what answers it (question-begging).

Problematology

A philosophical approach that puts questioning at the center of reflection, of perception, and in our relationship to the other and to the world. It has given rise to a new ethics, a new epistemology, and a new rhetoric, each of which has been articulated in a general view of philosophy with a new foundation. The question, "What comes first?" has only one possible answer, namely questioning itself. Any other answer, such as Being or the human subject, would be a self-defeating answer because it would, as an *answer*, already presuppose questioning and, as a result, would not be primary.

Rhetoric

Rhetoric is the negotiation of the distance between individuals, the speaker (*ethos*) and the audience (*pathos*), on a given question (*logos*).

Value and passion

Value is passion without subjectivity. It is the basis of decision for *ethos* at a distance from *pathos*. Passion is the opposite; it is a value completely "swallowed" by subjectivity and usually characterizes the nature of the relationship at a short distance, when people can be "touched," so to speak.

Bibliography

Alexy, R., *A Theory of Legal Argumentation* [1978] (Oxford: Oxford University Press, 1988).
Amossy, R., *L'argumentation dans le discours* (Paris: Armand Colin, 2012).
Angenot, M., *Dialogue de sourds. Traité de rhétorique antilogique* (Paris: Mille et une Nuits, 2008).
Anscombre, J. C. and O. Ducrot, *L'argumentation dans la langue* (Brussels: Mardaga, 1983).
Aristotle, *Categories*, tr. J. L. Ackrill in J. Barnes, ed., *The Complete Works of Aristotle* (Princeton, NJ: Princeton University Press, 1984).
Augustine, *The City of God*, bk. 14 (Harmondsworth: Penguin, 2003).
Aristotle, *Metaphysics*, tr. W. D. Ross in J. Barnes, ed., *The Complete Works of Aristotle* (Princeton, NJ: Princeton University Press, 1984).
Aristotle, *Rhetoric*, tr. W. Rhys Roberts in J. Barnes, ed., *The Complete Works of Aristotle* (Princeton, NJ: Princeton University Press, 1984).
Aristotle, *Topics*, tr. W. A. Pickard in J. Barnes, ed., *The Complete Works of Aristotle* (Princeton, NJ: Princeton University Press, 1984).
Austin, J. L., *Sense and Sensibilia* (Oxford: Oxford University Press, 1962).
Bailey, F. G., *The Tactical Uses of Passion* (Ithaca, NY: Cornell University Press, 1983).
Barilli, R., *Rhetoric*, tr. G. Menozzi (Minneapolis: University of Minnesota Press, 1989).
Barry, B., *Political Argument* (London: Routledge, 1965).
Barthes, R., *The Semiotic Challenge*, tr. R. Howard (Berkeley: University of California Press, 1994).
Beth, A. and E. Marpeau, *Figures de style* (Paris: Librio, 2005).
Billig, M., *Arguing and Thinking* (New York: Cambridge University Press, 1989).
Bitzer, L., "The Rhetorical Situation," *Philosophy and Rhetoric*, vol. 1 (1968), pp. 1–14.
Blair, A. and R. Johnson, eds., *Informal Logic* (Point Reyes, CA: Edgepress, 1980).
Booth, W. C., *The Rhetoric of Fiction* (Chicago, IL: University of Chicago Press, 1961).
Booth, W. C., *The Rhetoric of Rhetoric* (Oxford: Blackwell, 2004).
Borgès, J. L., *Labyrinths* (Harmondsworth, Penguin Books, 1970).

Breton, Ph., *L'argumentation dans la communication* (Paris: Editions la Découverte, 1996).
Brown, G. and G. Yule, *Discourse Analysis* (Cambridge: Cambridge University Press, 1983).
Burke, K., *A Grammar of Motives* (Oakland: University of California Press, 1969).
Campbell, G., *The Philosophy of Rhetoric* (Carbondale: Southern Illinois University Press, 1963).
Carrere, A. and J. Saborit, *Retórica de la pintura* (Madrid: Cátedra, 2000).
Cheng, A., *Histoire de la pensée chinoise* (Paris: Le Seuil, 1997).
Cicero, *De Inventione* [*On Invention*], tr. H. M. Hubbell (Cambridge, MA: Loeb Classical Library, Harvard University Press, 1949).
Cicero, *De Oratore* [On Oratory], tr. D. Sutton (Cambridge, MA: Loeb Classical Library, Harvard University Press, 1942).
Clarke, M. C., *Rhetoric at Rome* (London: Routledge, 1996).
Cockcroft, R. and S. Cockcroft, *Persuading People* (Basingstoke: Palgrave Macmillan, 2005).
Cohen, J., *La structure du langage poétique* (Paris: Flammarion, 1999).
Cole, T., *The Origin of Rhetoric in Ancient Greece* (Baltimore, MD: Johns Hopkins University Press, 1991).
Collingwood, R. G., *The Idea of History* (Oxford: Oxford University Press, 1996).
Conley, T., *Rhetoric in the European Tradition* (Chicago, IL: University of Chicago Press, 1990).
Corbett, E. and R. Connors, *Classical Rhetoric for the Modern Student*, 4th edn. (New York: Oxford University Press, 1965).
Crosswhite, J., *The Rhetoric of Reason* (Madison: University of Wisconsin Press, 1996).
Darwin, C., *The Expression of Emotions in Man and Animals* [1872] (London: Penguin Classics, 2009).
De Man, P., *Allegories of Reading* (New Haven, CT: Yale University Press, 1979).
De Man, P., *Blindness & Insight: Essays in the Rhetoric of Contemporary Criticism* (London: Methuen & Co., 1983).
Deonna, J. and F. Teroni, *The Emotions: A Philosophical Introduction* (London: Routledge, 2012).
Derrida, J., *Margins of Philosophy*, tr. A. Bass (Chicago, IL: University of Chicago Press, 1982).
Derrida, J., *Of Grammatology*, tr. G. Spivak (Baltimore, MD: Johns Hopkins University Press, 1976).

Derrida, J., *Writing and Difference*, tr. A. Bass (Chicago, IL: University of Chicago Press, 1978).
Descartes, R., *The Philosophical Writings*, tr. J. Cottingham et al. (New York: Cambridge University Press, 1991).
Dominik, W. and J. Hall, eds., *A Companion to Roman Rhetoric* (Chichester: Wiley-Blackwell, 2010).
Dow, J., *Passions and Persuasion in Aristotle's Rhetoric* (Oxford: Oxford University Press, 2015).
Dumarsais, C., *Traité des Tropes* [1730] (Paris: Flammarion, 1988).
Dupriez, B., *Gradus: A Dictionary of Literary Devices*, tr. A. Halsall (Toronto: University of Toronto Press, 1991).
Dworkin, R., "Hart's Postscript and the Character of Political Philosophy," *Oxford Journal of Legal Studies*, vol. 24 (2004), pp. 1–37.
Eco, U., *The Open Work*, tr. A. Cancogni (Cambridge, MA: Harvard University Press, 1989).
Ekman, P., *Emotions Revealed* (London: Weidenfeld and Nicolson, 2009).
Elsner, J., *Art and the Roman Viewer* (New York: Cambridge University Press, 1995).
Elsner, J. and M. Meyer, eds., *Art and Rhetoric in Roman Culture* (New York: Cambridge University Press, 2014).
Evans, J. D. G., *Aristotle's Concept of Dialectic* (New York: Cambridge University Press, 1997).
Fabre, M., *Philosophie et pédagogie du problème* (Paris: Vrin, 2009).
Fontanier, P., *Les figures du discours* [1830] (Paris: Flammarion, 1977).
Frank, D. and M. Bolduc, "Lucie Olbrechts-Tyteca's *New Rhetoric*," *Quarterly Journal of Speech*, vol. 96, no. 2 (2010), pp. 141–63.
Frege, G., *Translations from the Philosophical Writings*, ed. P. Geach and M. Black (Oxford: Blackwell, 1970).
Freud, S., "Negation" [1925], in *Metapsychology*, Standard Edition, vol. 11 (London: Penguin Books).
Fromilhague, C., *Les figures de style* (Paris: Nathan, 1995).
Gadamer, H. G., *Truth and Method* [1960], tr. J. Weinsheimer (London: Continuum, 2004).
Gardes Tamine, J., *Pour une nouvelle théorie des figures* (Paris: Presses Universitaires de France, 2011).
Genette, G., *The Architext* (Berkeley: University of California Press, 1992).
Genette, G., "Rhetoric Restrained," in *Figures of Literary Discourse*, tr. A. Sheridan (Oxford: Blackwell, 1982).
Golden, J. L., G. F. Berquist, W. E. Coleman and J. M. Sproule, *The Rhetoric of Western Thought* (Dubuque, IA: Kendall/Hunt Publishing Company, 2000).

Goldman, R., *Reading Ads Socially* (London: Routledge, 1992).
Greimas, A., *Stuctural Semantics*, tr. R. Schleifer (Lincoln: University of Nebraska Press, 1993).
Group Mu, *A General Rhetoric* [1970], tr. P. Burnell and E. Slotkin (Baltimore, MD: Johns Hopkins University Press, 1981).
Group Mu, *Rhétorique de la poésie* (Paris: Le Seuil, 1990).
Habermas, J., *Moral Consciousness and Communicative Action*, tr. C. Lenhardt and S. Weber Nicholsen (London: Polity Press, 1990).
Habermas, J., *On the Pragmatics of Communication* (MIT Press, 1998, repr. Oxford: Polity Press, 2003).
Habermas, J., "The Presuppositions of Argumentation," in S. White, ed., *The Recent Work of Jürgen Habermas* (New York: Cambridge University Press, 1988), pp. 55–8.
Hamblin, C., *Fallacies* (London: Methuen, 1970).
Hauser, G., *Introduction to Rhetorical Theory* (Prospect Heights, IL: Waveland Press, 1986).
Hill, Ch. and M. Helmers, *Visual Rhetoric* (Mahwah, NJ: Lawrence Erlbaum, 2004).
Hirschmann, A., *The Passions and the Interests*, Part One [1997] (Princeton, NJ: Princeton University Press, 2013).
Iser, W., *The Act of Reading* (Baltimore, MD: Johns Hopkins University Press, 1980).
Jauss, H. R., *Aesthetic Experience and Literary Hermeneutics*, tr. W. Godzich (Minneapolis: University of Minnesota Press, 1982).
Jauss, H. R., Aesthetische Erfahrung und literarische Hermeneutik (Frankfurt: Suhrkamp, 1991).
Jauss, H. R., *Toward an Aesthetic of Reception* (Minneapolis: University of Minnesota Press, 1982).
Johnson, R., *Manifest Rationality* (London: Routledge, 2000).
Johnstone, H. W., *Validity and Rhetoric in Philosophical Argument* (University Park, PA: Dialogue Press of Man & World, 1978).
Kafka, F., "The Test," in *Parables and Paradoxes* [1935] (New York: Schocken Books, 1975).
Kahn, C., "Questions and Categories," in *Questions*, ed. H. Hiz (Dordrecht: Reidel, 1978).
Kennedy, G., *The Art of Rhetoric in the Roman World* (Princeton, NJ: Princeton University Press, 1972).
Kennedy, G., *Comparative Rhetoric: An Historical and Cross-Cultural Introduction* (New York: Oxford University Press, 1998).
Kennedy, G., *A New History of Classical Rhetoric* (Princeton, NJ: Princeton University Press, 1994).

Knechtges, D. and E. Vance, *Rhetoric and the Discourses of Power in Court Culture* (Seattle: University of Washington Press, 2005).
Kopperschmidt, J., *Rhetorik* (Stuttgart: Kohlhammer, 1973).
Lanham, R., *A Handlist of Rhetorical Terms* (Los Angeles: University of California Press, 1991).
Lausberg, H., *Handbook of Literary Rhetoric* (Leiden: Brill, 1998).
Leith, S., *You Talkin' To Me?* (London: Profile Books, 2012).
Lukes, S., *Individualism* (Oxford: Blackwell, 1978).
McCloskey, D., *The Rhetoric of Economics* (Madison: University of Wisconsin Press, 1998).
MacCormick, N., *Rhetoric and the Rule of Law* (Oxford: Oxford University Press, 2005).
McCoy, M., *Plato on the Rhetoric of Philosophers and Sophists* (Cambridge: Cambridge University Press, 2008).
Mack, P., *History of Renaissance Rhetoric 1380–1620* (Oxford: Oxford University Press, 2011).
Mailloux, S., *Rhetoric, Sophistry, Pragmatism* (Cambridge: Cambridge University Press, 1995).
Mailloux, S., *Rhetorical Power* (Ithaca, NY: Cornell University Press, 1989).
Messaris, P., *Visual Persuasion* (Thousand Oaks, CA: Sage Publications, 1997).
Meyer, M., "Aristotle's Rhetoric," *Topoi*, vol. 31, no. 2 (2012), pp. 249–52.
Meyer, M., *Of Problematology*, tr. D. Jamison (Chicago, IL: University of Chicago Press, 1995).
Meyer, M., *Philosophy and the Passions*, tr. R. F. Barsky (University Park, PA: Pennsylvania State University Press, 2000).
Meyer, M., "Preface" and M. Meyer, "The Rhetoric of Roman Painting within the History of Culture: A Global Interpretation," in J. Elsner and M. Meyer, eds., *Art and Rhetoric in Roman Culture* (Cambridge: Cambridge University Press, 2014).
Meyer, M., "Questioning," in *Encyclopedia of Rhetoric*, ed. T. Sloane (Oxford: Oxford University Press, 2000).
Meyer, M., "What is the Use of Topics in Rhetoric?" *Revue Internationale de Philosophie*, vol. 4 (2014), pp. 447–62.
Mill, J. S., *A System of Logic* [1843] (New York: Cambridge University Press, 2012).
Mortara Garavelli, B., *Manuale di Retorica* (Milan: Bompiani, 1997).
Murphy, J., *Rhetoric in the Middle Ages* (Berkeley and Los Angeles: University of California Press, 1974).
Myerson, G., *Rhetoric, Reason and Society* (London: Sage, 1994).
Nietzsche, F., *Lectures on Rhetoric and Language* (Oxford: Oxford University Press, 1989).

Nussbaum, M., *Upheavals of Thought* (New York: Cambridge University Press, 2001).
Ottmers, C., *Rhetorik* (Stuttgart: Metzler Verlag, 1996).
Perelman, C., *The Realm of Rhetoric*, tr. W. Klubac (Notre Dame, IN: University of Notre Dame Press, 1982).
Perelman, C. and L. Olbrechts-Tyteca, *The New Rhetoric*, tr. J. Wilkinson and P. Weaver (Notre Dame, IN: University of Notre Dame Press, 1969).
Plato, *Gorgias*, tr. W. R. M. Lamb (Cambridge, MA: Loeb Classical Library, Harvard University Press, 1925).
Popper, K., *The Open Society and its Enemies*, vol. 1 (London: Routledge, 1962).
Quinn, A., *Figures of Speech* [1982] (London: Routledge, 2010).
Quintilian, *Institutes of Oratory*, tr. H. Butler (Cambridge, MA: Loeb Classical Library, Harvard University Press, 1921).
Reboul, O., *Introduction à la rhétorique* (Paris: Presses Universitaires de France, 1991).
Reboul, O., *La rhétorique* (Paris: Presses Universitaires de France, 1984).
Reding, J. P., *Les fondements philosophiques de la rhétorique chez les sophistes grecs et les sophistes chinois* (Berne: Peter Lang, 1985).
Rhetoric to Herennius [attributed to Cicero], tr. H. Caplan (Cambridge, MA: Loeb Classical Library, Harvard University Press, 1954).
Richards, I., *Philosophy of Rhetoric* (Oxford: Oxford University Press, 1936).
Richards, J., *Rhetoric* (London: Routledge, 2008).
Ricoeur, P., *The Rule of Metaphor*, tr. R. Czerny, with K. McLaughlin, and J. Costello (London: Routledge Classics, 2003).
Robertson Smith, W., *The Religion of the Semites* [1889] (New York: Meridian Books, 1956).
Robrieux, J.-J., *Elements de rhétorique et d'argumentation* (Paris: Dunod, 1993).
Rorty, A., *Essays on Aristotle's Rhetoric* (Oakland: University of California Press, 1996).
Schiappa, E., *Protagoras and Logos* (Columbia: University of South Carolina Press, 2003).
Siedentop, L., *Inventing the Individual* (London: Allen Lane, 2015).
Sloane, T., ed., *Encyclopedia of Rhetoric* (Oxford: Oxford University Press, 2001).
Solomon, R., *The Passions* (New York: Doubleday Anchor Book, 1977).
Stevenson, Ch., *Ethics and Language* (New Haven, CT: Yale University Press, 1944).
Suleiman, S. and J. Crossman, eds., *The Reader in the Text: Essays on Audience and Interpretation* (Princeton, NJ: Princeton University Press, 1980).

Tindale, C. W., *Acts of Arguing: A Rhetorical Model of Argument* (Albany: State University of New York Press, 1999).
Tindale, C. W., *Fallacies and Argument Appraisal* (New York: Cambridge University Press, 2007).
Tindale, C. W., *Rhetorical Argumentation: Principles of Theory and Practice* (Thousand Oaks, CA: Sage Publications, 2004).
Toulmin, S., *The Uses of Argument* [1958], 2nd edn. (New York: Cambridge University Press, 2003).
Toye, R., *Rhetoric: A Very Short Introduction* (Oxford: Oxford University Press, 2013).
Turnbull, N., *Michel Meyer's Problematology* (London: Bloomsbury Publishing, 2014).
van Eck, C., *Classical Rhetoric and the Visual Arts in Early Modern Europe* (New York: Cambridge University Press, 2007).
van Eemeren, F., *Strategic Maneuvering in Argumentative Discourse* (Amsterdam: Benjamins, 2010).
van Eemeren, F. and R. Grootendorst, *Speech Acts in Argumentative Discussions* (Dordrecht: Foris Publications, 1984).
van Eemeren, F. and R. Grootendorst, *A Systematic Theory of Argumentation* (New York: Cambridge University Press, 2004).
van Eemeren, F., R. Grootendorst, and F. Snoeck Henkemans, *Argumentation* (London: Routledge, 2002).
Vega y Vega, J. J., *L'enthymème* (Lyon: Presses Universitaires de Lyon, 2000).
Walton, D., *Informal Logic: A Pragmatic Approach* (New York: Cambridge University Press, 2008).
Walton, D., *Media Argumentation: Dialectic, Persuasion, and Rhetoric* (New York: Cambridge University Press, 2007).
Walton, D., *The Place of Emotions in Argument* (University Park, PA: Pennsylvania State University Press, 1987).
Walton, D., *Question-Reply Argumentation* (Westport, CT: Greenwood, 1989).
Walton, D., *Relevance in Argumentation* (London: Routledge, 2004).
Walton, D. and E. C. W. Krabbe, *Commitment in Dialogue* (Albany: State University of New York Press, 1995).
Walton, D., C. Reed, and F. Macagno, *Argumentation Schemes* (Cambridge: Cambridge University Press, 2008).
Wardy, R., *The Birth of Rhetoric* (London: Routledge, 1996).
Warning, R., *Rezeptionsästhetik* (Munich: Fink Verlag, 1994).
Weaver, R. M., *The Ethics of Rhetoric* (Chicago, IL: Henry Regnery Company, 1953).

Weaver, R. M., *Language is Sermonic* (Baton Rouge: Louisiana State University Press, 1970).
Weber, M., *Economy and Society*, 2 vols., ed. G. Roth and C. Wittich (Berkeley: University of California Press, 1978).
Wellek, R. and A. Warren, *Theory of Literature* (New York: Harcourt, Brace, 1956).
Westermarck, E., *The Origin and Development of Moral Ideas*, 2 vols. (London: Macmillan, 1906).
Whately, R., *Elements of Rhetoric* (Carbondale: Southern Illinois University Press, 1963).
White, H., *Metahistory* (Baltimore, MD: Johns Hopkins University Press, 1973).
White, S., *The Recent Work of Jürgen Habermas* (New York: Cambridge University Press, 1988).
Wilder, A. N., *Early Christian Rhetoric* (Peabody, MA: Hendrickson Publishers, 1999).
Willard, C. A., *A Theory of Argumentation* (Tuscaloosa: University of Alabama Press, 1989).
Woods, J. and D. Walton, *Argument: The Logic of the Fallacies* (Toronto: McGraw-Hill Ryerson Limited, 1982).
Yarbrough, S. R., *After Rhetoric* (Carbondale: Southern Illinois University Press, 1999).

Index

acceleration of history 19, 49, 171, 172, 183, 184, 227
acceptance 22, 58, 62, 66, 87, 122, 132, 134, 135, 154, 177, 178, 191, 221
acquiescence 167
addition 12, 73, 83, 86, 122, 123, 126, 129, 136-8, 142, 143, 149, 156, 208
addressee 86, 187, 194
adherence 54, 55, 106, 107, 125n9, 139-40, 224
advertisement 26, 27, 111, 112, 188, 189
advertising 11, 12, 26, 27, 110, 111, 112, 161, 187, 188, 210, 215, 225, 230
advocate 124, 167, 180, 225
Aeschylus 185
aesthetical personal ends 197
aesthetics 1, 181
affect xiii, xv, 28, 120, 167, 171, 180, 204, 207, 209, 210
affirmation xv, 103, 191
agreement xv, 3, 7, 9, 10, 13, 51, 54, 59-63, 65, 73, 78, 83, 87, 109, 122, 126, 129, 131, 133-5, 147, 155, 156, 191, 196, 204, 216, 219, 221, 222, 229
Aleixandre, V. 165, 177
Alexy, R. 211n8
allegory 129, 152, 178
allusion 33, 89
alternative 2, 10, 17-19, 21, 23, 25, 26, 33, 36-8, 42, 47, 53, 73-5, 96, 99, 108, 113, 114, 116, 117, 137, 139, 174, 179, 181, 201, 208, 231
ambiguity 24, 51-2, 124, 127, 128
amplification 44, 109, 111, 129, 147, 151, 155, 156
analogy 55, 129, 130, 132, 133, 136, 151, 156
analysis 9-11, 14, 27, 30, 32, 41, 45, 47, 48, 51, 52n39, 69, 72, 78, 81, 84, 87, 94, 126, 130, 150, 157, 160n1, 167, 170, 176, 181n3, 186n5, 199, 207n2, 208

Angenot, M. 63, 63n49
anger 28, 30, 110, 206-8
Anscombre, J. C. 73, 73n68
answer
  additional 134, 138
  apocritical 88, 159, 183, 231
  inferential 84, 85, 135
  obsolete xv, 2, 17, 19
  problematic xv, 49, 131, 145, 146, 227
  problematological 19, 34, 88, 93, 159, 178, 183, 187, 231
  qualifying 131
antistrophos 25
antithesis 125, 128, 129, 151, 152
antithetic responses 28
apocope 128
apocritical answers 88, 159, 161, 183, 231
apodicity 37
apodictic 17n4, 19, 34, 36, 37, 46, 54, 67, 115, 116, 117
apodicticity, *see* apodictic
apokrisis 88
apology 14
aporia 18
appearance 16, 45, 81
approval 62, 73, 107, 108, 122, 126, 127, 129, 131, 133, 134, 154, 155, 181, 204, 223
Aquinas, T. 44, 208
architecture 39n14, 166, 182, 185, 202
Architext, The 181n3
argue, *see* argumentation
argumentation xv, 1, 3, 5, 7, 10-12, 16, 20, 23-5, 29, 31, 32, 45, 48-50, 51n35, 53-5, 57-65, 58n44, 60n46, 64n50, 67-9, 68n54, 71-7, 71n61, 77n73, 79, 83, 84, 99-120, 122, 124, 129-40, 146, 147, 152, 154, 156, 190, 192, 193, 201, 203-15, 225, 229
argumentative xv, 4, 24, 31, 42, 46, 49, 50, 54, 59-61, 61n48, 63, 65, 67, 68, 69, 72-6, 83, 100-4, 108, 110, 112,

115, 125n9, 130–40, 143, 144, 155, 187, 188, 191, 192, 203–16, 226, 230
arguments
  ad hominem 65, 69n54, 73, 106–8, 110, 122, 123, 126, 130–3, 139–40, 156, 191, 216
  ad rem 106, 107, 110, 122, 123, 126, 130, 132, 139–40, 156, 216
  based on reality 55, 132, 133
  confirming the initial proposition by the consequences 155
  of difference 123, 123n2, 130, 131, 149
  distancing itself from the initial proposition 22
  of qualification (definition) 132, 134
  quasi-logical 55, 132, 133, 136, 150
  of rejection 77n73, 106, 133, 135, 209n6
  of similarity 122, 123, 123n2, 131, 142
  structuring reality 46
Aristophanes 185
Aristotle xv, 2–6, 9–11, 9n1, 15, 17–35, 30n8, 33n11, 35n13, 38, 40, 40n18, 43, 43n24, 44, 49, 54, 68, 73, 73n66, 78, 83, 89n5, 94, 94n7, 97, 112–14, 114n6, 118, 119, 125, 125n8, 133, 141, 142, 146, 146n9, 148, 148n10, 161, 166, 167, 170, 180n1, 181–3, 181n3, 185, 186, 192, 205–8, 207n4, 207n5, 216, 226, 227, 229
art xiii, xiv, xv, 39n14, 40, 41, 41n21, 72, 127, 161, 166, 167, 170–2, 175–8, 176n12, 176n13, 180–6, 190, 203, 204, 225, 227
articulate 35, 75, 119, 227, 231
assent 2, 54, 198
assertion 89, 102, 103, 129, 159, 171
assertoric 158
association 23, 100, 192
assumption 56
asyndeton 125, 127n13
audience 2, 14, 80, 100, 121, 131, 141, 160, 180, 190, 203, 217, 226
Augustine 44, 199, 199n6
Austin, J. L. 50, 84, 85n2, 182
authority 3, 4, 5, 39, 59, 77n73, 119, 132, 139, 193, 204, 219, 229
auto-contextualization 162–7, 187–9
autonomous 5, 29, 72
avoidance 125, 194, 208

background 26, 40, 70, 71, 81, 160
backing 67
Bakhtin, M. 163
Balzac, H. 158
Barilli, R. 15n2
Barnes, J. 9n1, 21n5
Barry, B. 214n11
Barthes, R. 72, 128, 130n15
beauty 2, 188
beginning 8, 11, 13, 26, 36, 40, 41, 44, 47, 62, 92, 97, 110, 114, 117, 124, 124n6, 148, 158, 167, 170n3, 173, 174, 223
belief 32–3, 32n10, 55, 62, 63, 66, 71, 132, 165, 168, 191, 195, 214, 220–3
benevolence 28, 207
Bitzer, L. 50, 53, 53n40
Blair, A. 50, 68
Blair, H. 45–6
Bolduc, M. 52n39
Bonaparte, N. 21
Booth, W. 51, 51n34
Borgès, J. L. 169, 170, 170n3, 177
Bourdieu, P. 198
Breton, A. 128
Brown, G. 160n1
Burke, K. 50, 69–72, 141, 149, 149n11, 155

Calvino, I. 165, 177
Campbell, G. 46
captivate 3, 168
captivating 2, 42, 80, 164–5
catachresis 144
catalog 11–12, 49, 128n14, 138, 141–2, 144, 147, 155, 192, 207, 226
category 55, 84, 89, 89n5, 132, 172, 176
catharsis 180
cause 25, 31, 40, 68, 97n10, 122, 132, 136, 149, 150, 150n12, 150n13, 197, 209n6
Celan, P. 165
Cervantes, M. 169–70
challenge xiv, 60, 130n15, 175n10, 190
character xvi, 2, 4, 27, 29, 45, 69, 74n69, 152, 161, 162, 164, 167, 169, 171–3, 176, 180–4, 211, 213n9
charm xiv, 3, 27, 42, 78, 109, 124
Cheng, A. 77n73
chiasm 128

INDEX   243

Cicero 6, 38, 39, 41, 41n19, 41n20, 41n22, 43, 52, 119, 124, 125n7, 143, 143n3, 143n4, 144, 145, 147, 180n1, 191, 227
cinema 184
circularity 98
claim xv, 5, 39, 51, 57–9, 76, 88, 94, 95, 116, 154, 175, 211
Clarke, M. C. 41n21
cobweb mechanism 220, 222
Cohen, J. 123n4, 144n7
coherence 193
Collingwood, R. G. 97n10, 168, 168n2
combination 49, 77
comedy 182–3, 185
commitment 139, 195
commonplace, see *topos*
communication 14, 51, 57–60, 66, 90, 92, 219
comparison 12, 55, 69, 77
compassion 28, 215
complementarity 7, 52n39, 93, 180–6
comprehension 183, 220
concession 65, 74, 84, 126, 131, 147, 151–2
conclusion 1–3, 12, 13, 21–5, 28–9, 31–6, 41, 43, 46, 52–4, 56, 59, 63, 65, 67, 68, 74, 75, 78–9, 88, 95, 100, 102–4, 113–15, 117, 139, 142, 143, 155, 168, 169, 177, 180, 192, 196, 200, 225–7
confirmation 152, 153
conflict xiv, 5, 45, 49, 53, 57, 59, 70, 71, 83, 106, 107, 140, 200, 201, 212, 214, 225
confrontation xv, 4, 22, 23, 25, 44, 60, 70, 83, 167, 183, 213, 214, 218, 226
Conley, T. 44n26, 45, 45n29
connectors (or connectives) 50, 73–6, 136–9, 152
consciousness 36, 56, 58n44, 178–9, 199
consensus 9, 58–60, 62, 64, 66, 226, 229
consequence 154, 155, 161, 162, 165, 169, 171, 173, 184, 196, 199, 219, 227, 229
consistency 94, 137, 160, 170, 171
constraints 11, 65, 68, 72, 76
contemporary rhetoric 35
contempt 28, 201, 206, 207
contestation 209

context 21, 24, 40, 81, 85, 86, 90, 102, 132, 137, 150, 158–64, 187, 221
contextuality (law of) 158–63
contradiction 18, 30, 31, 36, 37, 61, 62, 73, 86, 96, 121–2, 124, 128–32, 136, 170n4, 172, 196, 201, 229, 231
controversy 77, 83, 96, 115, 121
conventional 83, 104, 148, 149, 170
conversation xiii, 3, 7, 11, 20, 32, 82, 92, 108, 111, 119, 195, 216, 219
conviction 14, 32n10, 53, 63, 66, 111
co-text 158, 160–3, 187
counterpart 11, 19, 25, 26, 29, 43, 69, 172, 184, 214
courage 41, 183, 208
court xiii, 4, 5, 8, 25, 40, 57, 60, 62, 77n74, 107, 109, 110, 135, 140, 189, 211–13, 227
cowardice 159
credibility 39, 42, 193, 204, 219
Crossman, J. 175n9
Crosswhite, J. 51, 51n36
culture 77, 77n74, 176n13
cupidity 128, 199
cursor 74, 131, 149, 154, 155

Darwin, C. 205, 205n1
debate xiii, xiv, xv, 1, 3, 4, 8–10, 13, 17–19, 26, 33, 38, 41, 42, 44, 49, 53, 55–7, 59, 62, 63, 66, 78, 83, 85, 86, 96, 108, 109, 116–18, 124, 130, 135, 165, 175, 180, 189, 190–2, 195, 196, 199, 201–2, 211–14, 225, 227
deconstruction 36, 165, 176, 178
deduction 21, 24, 37, 55
defence 26, 64, 126, 129, 132, 136, 211
definition 6, 7, 9, 10, 12, 13, 20, 24, 29, 30, 32, 33, 35, 37, 39, 40n17, 79, 95, 97, 103, 108, 117, 123, 124, 126, 132, 133, 134, 136, 190, 195, 216, 223, 225
deliberation (deliberative) 33, 58, 114, 119
demand 22, 126, 197, 198, 201, 227
democracy 2, 17, 58, 77, 196, 197n4, 211, 214
demonstration 1, 48, 140, 187, 202
de Musset, A. 186
denial 87–8, 94, 128, 129, 147
derivation 144

244   INDEX

Derrida, J. 36, 72, 126, 126n10, 143n1, 176n14
Descartes, R. 17, 29, 36, 45, 46, 46n30, 47, 47n31, 47n32, 48n33, 55, 207, 208
description 115, 158, 160, 162
desire 7, 15, 60, 88, 112, 132, 193, 197–201, 206, 208
despair 207, 208
dialectic xiv, xvi, 3, 11, 20, 22–6, 32, 33, 44–6, 48, 77, 133, 163, 215, 218
dialogue 9, 12, 14–16, 59, 63n49, 72n62, 92, 96, 97, 99, 163, 167, 180, 191, 218, 223
dictionary 12, 130
disagreement xv, 5, 6, 9, 13, 25, 71, 106, 108, 122, 133–5, 155, 196, 201, 206, 214, 222, 223
disambiguation 52
disapproval 106, 127, 134, 154–5, 223
discourse xiv, 12–15, 17, 19–20, 23–6, 30, 32, 34, 36, 40–2, 44–9, 55, 61, 61n48, 62, 70–2, 77n74, 78, 80–92, 97, 100, 108, 109, 119, 132, 136, 139, 141, 142, 144, 146n9, 147, 151, 158–60, 160n1, 161, 162, 164, 166, 172, 180, 181–3, 187, 189, 190, 204, 216, 217, 227, 230
discussion 1, 9, 26, 43n24, 44, 58, 59, 62, 77n74, 83, 99, 104, 121, 167, 189, 197n4, 216, 218, 219, 222
dispositio 40, 47, 135
dissociation 54, 192
distance xiv, xv, xvi, 1, 6–10, 12–13, 25, 29, 32, 33, 70, 71, 79, 83, 103–10, 116, 119, 132, 135, 136, 139, 140, 150, 151, 164, 165, 167, 170, 171, 175, 176, 180, 181, 189–91, 204–9, 209n6, 210, 210n7, 211–14, 216–26, 229–30, 232
divergence 19, 43, 63, 211
division 11, 15, 24, 41, 43, 71, 145
doubt (doubtful, dubious) 8, 17, 46, 47, 52, 61, 64, 87, 137, 151, 152, 174, 182, 224
drama (dramaturgic) xvi, 167, 181–3
dramatization 27, 50, 69, 70, 215
Duchamp, M. 177
Ducrot, O. 50, 72–6, 152
Dumarsais, C. 45, 49
Dupriez, B. 151n14

Durkheim, E. 56
duties 8, 194, 197, 201
Dworkin, R. 213, 213n9

Eco, U. 182
Ekman, P. 205n1
Eliot, T. S. 173, 177
elocutio 41, 48
eloquence xv, 2, 3, 5, 14, 20, 23, 24, 26, 27, 41, 109, 111, 113, 141, 164, 185, 188, 223, 226
Elsner, J. 176n12, 176n13
"emocracy" 214
emotions xiii, xiv, xv, xvi, 3, 4, 12, 13, 16, 21, 23, 27–30, 32, 42, 44, 54, 59, 63, 65, 66, 68, 69, 78, 109, 110, 120, 139, 167, 180, 197, 201, 203–15, 205n1, 209n6, 210n7, 217, 221–3, 225, 226
emphasis 3, 14, 29, 38, 53, 78, 123
empiricist 46, 85, 208
emulation 28
enigma 25, 94, 96, 172, 177
enigmatic xv, 19, 25, 148, 149, 164–6, 170, 172, 184, 225, 227, 230
enthymeme 21–4, 27, 29, 83, 114, 119
envy 28
epagoge 133
epanorthosis 152
epic xiv, 3, 77, 170, 181, 182, 185
epideictic 4, 42, 119, 216
epistemic 60, 71
equality 71, 206, 207
equivocal 19, 177
ethics 4, 5, 14, 39, 45, 53, 57–9, 63, 94, 108, 208, 210n7, 231
ethos
    effective 218, 220–3
    projective 218–22
euphemism 151
Euripides 185
evaluation (of arguments) 69
exemplification 24, 129, 147, 152
exordium 8, 40, 187

fallacy 51, 61, 65
fear 28, 37, 132, 136, 138, 139, 183, 206–9, 209n6
feeling xiv, 12, 21, 27, 37, 42, 43, 46, 52, 81, 82, 139, 144, 150–2, 181–3, 191, 196, 203–15

figurative language 10, 48, 49, 83, 100, 105, 110, 111, 113, 141–4, 146, 164
figurativism 184–6
figures
  of language 125, 153, 156, 229
  of sound 122, 127, 128, 146–8, 153, 155
  of speech 3, 9, 11, 12, 32, 42, 45, 48, 51, 54, 83, 109, 122, 124, 126, 128, 130, 133, 141–57, 192, 207, 216, 223, 229
  of thought 122–5, 129, 145, 147, 151–6, 229
fine arts
  music 184, 186
  painting 182, 184–6
  sculpture 182, 184, 185
  theater 182, 186
Fontanier, P. 45, 49, 128n14
formalism 133, 211
Foucault, M. 36, 72
Frank, D. 52n39, 76n72
Frege, G. 84, 90, 91, 91n6
Freud, S. 36, 87, 88n4, 200, 201

Gadamer, H. G. 50, 76, 76n70, 163, 173n6, 173n7, 175, 175n11
Genette, G. 45, 45n27, 181n3, 182
genre 6, 13, 27, 39, 166, 172, 175, 176, 181, 182, 187
glossary 229–32
Golden, J. 14, 14n1, 111
Gradus: A Dictionary of Literary Devices 151n14
grammatology 126n10, 176n14
gratitude 3, 166, 188
Greek art (vases) 185
Greek rhetoric 39, 40
Greimas, A. 97, 97n9
Grootendorst, R. 50, 60, 60n46, 61n47, 64n50
ground 5, 12, 18, 22, 31, 44, 60, 91
Group Mu 11, 50, 72–6, 72n64, 73n65, 122, 123, 123n3, 123n5, 124, 127, 128, 145

Habermas, J. 10, 50, 57–60
hate 207, 210, 218
Hegel, G. W. F. 173
Heidegger, M. 36, 209n6
Helmers, M. 81n1
hermeneutics 50, 76–7, 171, 173–5, 178
Herodotus 185
Hill, Ch. 81n1
Hirschmann, A. 200n7
historicity 164
Hobbes, T. 29, 30, 94, 108, 201, 205
Homer 185
hope 62, 87, 127, 139, 207, 208, 209n6, 217, 221
Hugo, V. 186
humanism 17, 44, 45
Hume, D. 29, 46, 207, 208
hyperbole 152
hypothesis 137, 147
hypotyposis 129

identity xiv, xv, xvi, 31, 71, 73, 90, 93, 95, 97, 102–5, 121–33, 136, 149–52, 156, 168, 171, 172, 174, 183, 184, 195, 197, 198, 220, 229, 231
ideology 77, 214
image 9, 71, 81, 128, 129, 142, 146, 148, 198–200, 204, 214, 215, 218
impact xvi, 1, 3, 7, 9, 12, 13, 16, 23, 25, 28, 30–8, 50, 54, 73, 78, 85, 106–8, 114, 141, 142, 144, 156, 178, 180, 183, 191, 198, 203–10, 214, 224
implication 31, 102–4, 129, 132, 135, 137, 138, 144, 165, 170
implicit 18, 24, 26, 31, 36, 57, 59, 63, 66, 67, 74, 81, 82, 86–92, 95, 99, 100, 100n1, 101, 103n2, 104, 114–16, 118, 120, 122, 127, 129, 142, 143, 152, 158, 160, 187, 189, 192, 216
impression 29, 51, 56, 111, 204, 213
income 197–9
indignation 28
individualism 29n7, 205
induction 21–4, 133, 217
inference xiv, 11, 20–2, 31, 34, 51, 53, 67, 68, 72, 75, 83, 88, 99, 100, 102, 104, 113–18, 121–2, 123n2, 124, 129–33, 135, 137–9, 143, 149, 156, 165, 170, 171, 191, 192, 229
influence xiv, 11, 20–2, 31, 34, 51, 53, 67, 68, 72, 75, 83, 88, 99, 100, 100n1, 102, 104, 113–18, 121–2, 123n2, 124, 129, 130–3, 135, 137–9, 143, 149, 156, 165, 170, 171, 191, 192
informal logic 50, 67–9
information 142, 160, 163, 176, 217, 219

instance 9, 23, 26, 28, 31, 40, 42, 45, 51, 53, 74n69, 83, 85, 102, 105, 107, 112, 124, 127, 130, 137, 145, 152, 158, 162, 186, 188, 196, 202, 208, 211, 223
intention 3, 15, 51, 84, 138, 174, 198, 219-21
interaction 28, 133, 167, 182, 194
interpersonal 1, 2, 6-10, 32, 109, 116, 163, 181, 192, 204, 206, 216-24, 226
interrogatives (relative clauses) 89, 90, 92, 158, 169
inventio 40, 45, 46, 161, 186
inverse problematicity 12, 162-7, 187, 230
irony 70, 71, 128, 129, 149, 150, 152-5, 170
Iser, W. 50, 76n72, 175, 181
isotopia 97
Italian
 painting 184, 203
 Renaissance 17, 49

Jauss, H. R. 50, 76, 76n72, 163, 175, 175n10
Johnson, R. 50, 68, 69
Johnstone, H. W. 50, 71, 72, 72n62, 72n63
Joyce, J. 165, 177
justice 51, 145, 147, 196, 212-14, 226
justification 208, 227

Kafka, F. 165, 177, 178
Kahn, C. 89n5
Kennedy, G. 41n21, 77n75, 146n9
Kierkegaard, S. 209n6
Knechtges, D. 77n74
Kopperschmidt, J. 65, 66n51

language (*logos*)
 figurative 10, 48, 49, 83, 100, 105, 110, 111, 113, 141-4, 146, 164
 literal 123-5, 142
 question-view of 7, 11, 12, 80-98
Lanham, R. 128n14
laughter 183
Lausberg, H. 128n14
law (legal reasoning) 5, 6, 11, 12, 14, 25, 37, 39, 42, 53, 57, 62, 71, 104, 106, 108, 109, 118, 122, 129, 135, 158-64, 166, 187, 195, 198, 210-13, 211n8, 225, 230
legislation 214
legitimacy 4, 24, 181
Lévi-Strauss, C. 72
lexis 145
linguistics xiii, 1, 6, 51, 66, 72, 84, 90, 92, 99, 100, 142, 159, 160, 189, 219, 227
literality 102, 165, 166
literary criticism xiii, 1, 167-78
literature xiii, xiv, xv, xvi, 1, 3, 5, 12, 20, 72, 77, 83, 124, 142, 158, 161-8, 170-2, 176-8, 176n14, 180-90, 225, 227, 230
litot, *see* euphemism
logic 12, 34, 39, 50, 67-9, 108, 113-18, 115n7, 137, 138, 173, 195
logical inference 68, 114-17
Lukàcs, G. 163
Lukes, S. 29n7
lyric 181, 182, 185

Macagno, F. 68n54
MacCormick, N. 211n8, 213n10
Machiavelli, N. 200, 201
maintain 7, 8, 32, 49, 64, 97n10, 123n3, 160, 172, 189, 219, 230
Mallarmé, S. 165, 177
manipulation 2-4, 16, 17, 24, 26, 51, 65, 66, 146, 223, 227
mannerism 184
marker (argumentative) 72-6
Marx, K. 36, 77, 199, 201
matrix 1, 207, 208, 226
McCoy, M. 15, 16n3
meaning xiv, 14, 16, 18, 22-4, 31, 51, 59, 82, 84, 86, 88, 90, 91, 101, 102, 110, 121, 122, 124-7, 137, 143, 144, 146, 154, 163-76, 178, 189, 193, 227, 230
measure xiv, 6, 7, 139, 140, 198, 208, 216
memoria 41, 48
metahistory 71n60, 172n5
metalepsis 150n13
metaphor 2, 19, 45n28, 70, 71, 73, 77, 85, 108, 126n11, 129, 130, 142, 145, 146, 148-50, 153-5, 171, 172, 177, 183, 184, 189
metaphysics 35n13, 36, 39n14, 44, 94n7, 97n10
metaplasm 142
metapsychology 88n4

metarhetoric 50, 51
Methuselah 171
metonymy 70, 71, 125, 129, 149–51, 150n13, 153–5, 167, 192, 193, 203
Meyer, M. 24n6, 33n12, 78n76, 105n3, 176n13, 186n5, 207n2
Mill, S. 115, 115n7
mimesis 146, 166–8, 171, 178
mimetic 168, 170–2, 175
minimization 88, 109, 111, 129, 147, 151, 155, 156
mirror 146, 181, 186, 205
misunderstanding 50–2, 59, 63, 92, 206, 217, 219, 222, 223
modality 37, 84
modern rhetoric 10; *see also* Blair, H.; Whately, R.
modification of an answer 121
Montale, E. 165
Montesquieu 201
moral 4, 5, 56, 57, 58n44, 60, 61, 72, 94, 119, 201, 210n7, 211
Mortara Garavelli, B. 128n14
motives 14, 53, 54, 70n57, 70n59, 149n11, 155, 200, 201, 217
Murphy, J. 44n25
music 166, 172, 184, 186, 227
Myerson, G. 59n45

narratio 42
narrator 161, 164, 168, 170, 172
needs 8, 10, 93, 114, 148, 152, 172, 184, 197, 201, 230
negation
  connective 75
  denial 87, 88
  operation 87
negotiation xiv, xv, 6, 7, 9, 10, 12, 13, 25, 65, 79, 103, 104, 105, 180, 190, 197, 198, 204, 216, 230, 232
Nietzsche, F. 36, 189
nihilism 178
non-contradiction 94, 96
novel 160–3, 166, 167, 169, 172, 173, 177, 180, 182, 185
Nussbaum, M. 207n3

obviousness 22
Ockham, G. 89n5
Olbrechts-Tyteca, L. 52–7, 52n39, 54n41, 125n9, 133n2, 144n5, 144n6

opera 184, 186
operators 11, 73, 83, 84, 119, 121–33, 136–9, 149, 151, 154–6, 178, 226, 229–30
opinion 4, 9, 14, 17, 35, 57, 61, 63, 66, 74, 107, 108, 118, 130, 132, 135, 138, 139, 145, 149, 189, 193, 197, 197n4, 198, 201, 206, 210, 211, 213, 215, 217, 218, 223
opposition 11, 25, 49, 59, 61, 65, 71–3, 83, 106, 108, 114, 122, 123n2, 129, 131, 132, 134, 136, 147, 149, 152, 153, 156, 183, 191, 192, 216, 229
orator 38, 39, 39n16, 83, 109, 111
ornament 128, 144, 148

painting 39n14, 166, 176n13, 182, 184–6, 190, 202, 203, 227
paradox 17, 18, 23, 27, 29, 30, 34, 37, 129, 177, 177n15
paronomasis 127
Pascal, B. 32n10
passion 4, 12, 16, 21, 27–30, 139, 167, 198, 199, 200, 200n7, 201, 204–10, 212–14, 217, 218, 226, 230, 232
pathos
  effective 218–22
  projective 218–23
"pentad" 70
perception 80, 81, 223, 231
Perelman, C. 10, 17, 49, 50, 52–9, 54n42, 55n43, 81, 83, 109, 124n6, 125n9, 132, 133, 133n2, 143, 144, 144n5, 144n6, 150, 192, 192n1, 226
periphrasis 125
persuasion xiv, 1, 7, 14, 30–2, 32n10, 45, 46, 62, 65, 66, 68, 72, 78, 108, 220, 222–4
philosophy xiii, 1, 2, 14–17, 19, 24n6, 29, 30, 33–7, 42, 46, 49, 51–2, 51n38, 53, 53n40, 78, 85, 95, 96, 176n14, 179, 205, 207n2, 213n9, 225–7, 231
pity 28, 30, 183, 206
Plato xv, 2–4, 6, 10, 14–20, 16n3, 22–4, 33, 37, 38, 43, 78, 119, 146, 174, 182, 185, 227
pleasant 3, 9, 20, 24, 26, 27, 33, 40, 42, 43, 83, 109, 113, 119, 144, 156, 180, 188, 217, 221, 223
pleasure 23, 50, 112, 161, 166, 188, 191, 196, 200, 206–9

poetics 15, 44, 72, 124, 161, 166, 181, 181n3, 182
poetry 2, 3, 45, 77, 128, 152, 158, 163, 165–7, 172, 177, 181, 182, 186, 227
politeness 108, 216
political rhetoric 211, 215, 218
politics 1, 2, 3, 5–7, 11, 30, 35, 61, 94, 119, 166, 210–14, 225
Popper, K. 174n8
Pound, E. 165, 177
power 21, 22, 36, 38, 48, 69, 77n74, 78, 107, 111, 139, 149, 186, 197–201, 203, 213
praeteritio principii, see question-begging
pragmatics 12, 57–60
predicate 23, 89, 92–4, 116–18, 197
prejudice 4, 9, 30, 62, 65, 66, 217
premise 13, 21, 24, 64, 67, 68, 74, 100n1, 114–18, 129, 135, 192, 193, 195–8, 209, 211
presentation 41, 70, 165–8, 170–2, 178, 182, 185, 189
presupposition 22, 36, 58n44, 59, 60, 62, 63
principle
 of identity 95, 97, 231
 of non-contradiction 96
 of reason 95, 97–8, 97n10, 231
probability 1, 14, 46
problem xiv, 1, 17, 80, 109, 124, 135, 142, 159, 188, 193, 203, 216, 225, 230
problematicity level
 high 13, 88, 110, 113
 low 13, 83, 110, 130
problematological difference (or question-answer complex) 34
problematology 24, 24n6, 33, 33n12, 34, 53, 78, 78n76, 87, 96, 119, 165, 186n5, 227, 231
procedure 49, 63, 109, 132, 135, 146, 160, 187, 220
process 6, 10, 13, 15, 31, 51, 55, 59, 60, 62, 63, 70, 77, 80, 91, 94, 96–8, 100, 103, 117, 118, 133, 146, 161, 173, 174, 178–9, 183, 187, 191, 219, 220, 222
projective 142, 217–23
prolepsis 152
propaganda 2, 4
propositionalism 18, 19, 30–8, 84, 90, 95

prosopopoeia 152
Protagoras 14
prudence 138
psychoanalysis 2, 12, 81
psychology 1, 30, 205
public 1–2, 17, 35, 52, 140, 202, 227

qualification (requalification) 122, 123, 129, 132, 134, 136, 151, 153, 156, 211
question-begging 97, 231
questioning xiv, xv, 10, 11, 12, 19, 24, 30, 33–8, 75, 76, 78, 80, 81, 84, 86, 87, 89, 90, 97, 98, 98n11, 112, 116–19, 123, 145, 149, 159, 163, 166, 172, 173, 175–9, 223, 225, 226, 227, 229, 231
Quinn, A. 128n14
Quintilian 38, 39n16, 40, 42n23, 52, 70n58, 141, 143n2, 144, 146n8, 180n1

Ramus, P. 45, 46
rationality 19, 24, 34, 53, 54, 62, 63, 68n53, 69n55, 133, 141, 142, 145, 161, 200, 207, 226
reader xiv, xv, xvi, 70, 76, 77, 100, 126, 143, 146, 147, 161, 163, 164, 165, 168, 170–6, 178, 180, 181n2, 182, 189, 227, 230: see also *pathos*
realism
 in art 171, 172, 184, 186
 in literature 184, 185
reason 5, 6, 7, 16–19, 24, 31, 33–6, 38, 51, 53–5, 59, 73–5, 85–8, 95, 97, 97n10, 98, 102, 104–6, 110, 117, 125, 136–9, 143, 149, 150, 165, 169, 170, 179, 189, 199, 202, 207, 210, 218, 226, 230, 231
reception 12, 13, 50, 76–7, 174, 175, 175n10, 178
recollection (reminiscence) 14
Reding, J. P. 77n74
reference (meaning, denoting) 90
refutation 14, 23, 33, 41, 152
rejection xv, 61, 65, 73, 77n73, 106, 121n1, 122, 129, 133–5, 153, 154, 181, 191, 193, 204, 209n6, 223, 226
relativism 72
relevance 1, 73, 137, 187
Renaissance 17, 44, 45, 49, 184, 203

INDEX 249

reply 62, 75, 82, 123, 126
representation 70, 166–8, 170–2, 182, 185
requalification 122, 123, 134, 136, 153
resolution 9–11, 18, 25, 27, 31, 43, 45, 48, 70, 82, 99, 107, 111, 162–4, 168, 170, 171, 230
response 4, 9, 12, 20, 27, 28, 29, 32n10, 73, 82, 84, 85, 109, 110, 115, 116, 121–4, 131, 133–5, 140, 153, 161, 162, 164, 166, 167, 172, 173, 181, 184, 187, 191, 203–15, 225, 226, 230
retractation (recanting) 147, 152
rhetorical inference xiv, 114, 115, 117, 118
rhetoric
  of conflict (argumentation) 5, 225
  of figures (rhetoric *stricto sensu*) 230
  and logic 113–20
Richards, I. 50–2, 51n38
Ricoeur, P. 45n28, 126, 126n11, 143n1, 148
rights 57, 58, 194, 197, 201, 213
Robertson Smith, W. 194
Roman
  art 41n21, 176n12, 176n13, 180n1, 203
  rhetoric 3, 15, 38, 40–3
romanticism 186
Russell, B. 84, 85, 85n3

sadness 206, 209
Sartre, J. P. 81
Saussure, F. 72
scholastic 12, 17, 49, 51, 131, 141, 207, 226
science xv, xiv, 1, 2, 17, 19, 23, 24, 35–7, 47, 48, 70, 71, 80, 81, 90, 95, 108, 114, 173, 205
sculpture 166, 172, 182, 184, 185
Searle, J. 50, 84
seduction 1, 4, 26
Seneca 207
sequence, *see* succession (of answers, sequence)
Shakespeare, W. 127, 127n12, 224
Siedentop, L. 29n7
sign 82, 129, 133, 149, 151, 178, 191, 202, 203
Snoeck Henkemans, F. 64n50

society xv, 3, 4, 7, 19, 35, 39, 59, 59n45, 71, 154, 164, 176, 186, 192–6, 198, 199, 199n5, 200, 201, 211, 214
Socrates 14, 18, 22, 23, 31, 36, 38, 68, 105, 114, 115, 117, 118, 149
Solomon, R. 207n3
solution 9, 18, 19, 22, 23, 25, 27, 35, 36, 38, 40, 43, 48, 53, 77, 81, 82, 86, 96, 97n10, 102, 109, 111–13, 135, 152, 161, 164, 165, 173, 174, 179, 180, 188, 191, 207–9, 209n6, 211, 221, 227, 229
Sophist 14, 16
Sophocles 185
spectacle 26, 176, 186, 214
speechact 63
Spinoza, B. 29, 207, 208
starting-point 17, 26, 34, 43, 64, 113, 220
statement 21, 23, 34, 41, 48, 75, 84–91, 93, 97, 102, 105, 107, 117, 118, 121, 121n1, 122, 125, 127n13, 128, 129, 131, 133–8, 152, 159, 165, 169, 177, 192, 225, 229
status 1, 5, 8, 16, 28, 38–42, 91, 106, 112, 197–200, 219
Stevenson, Ch. 210n7
story 88, 164–9, 171, 172, 175, 177, 181, 189
strategy (rhetorical) 11, 25, 26, 32, 33, 42, 62, 65, 69, 70, 102, 105–11, 121, 139, 147, 191, 192, 204, 229
structuralism 72, 226
style 3, 5, 11, 20, 23, 24, 26, 27, 41, 42, 44, 46, 48, 50, 83, 104, 109, 111, 113, 119, 125n9, 126, 130, 131, 141–6, 146n9, 159, 164, 165, 167, 170n4, 183, 185, 186
succession (of answers, sequence) 136, 166, 186
suggestion 31, 34, 99, 100, 165
Suleiman, S. 175n9
suppression 18, 73, 123, 123n3, 123n4, 127–9
symbol (symbolic) 70, 101, 150, 151, 178, 184–6, 229
synecdoche 70, 71, 73, 129, 145, 149–51, 153–5

taste 3, 14, 46, 106–8, 193, 193n2
tautology 132, 169
teknè 161, 204, 229

Terence 186
terms of language 90
text 52, 76, 77, 80, 81, 143, 158, 160n1, 161–5, 167–9, 170, 171, 173–5, 178, 181n2, 187, 230
theater 3, 163, 170, 176, 178, 182, 186
threat 151
Thucydides 185
thymos 21
Tindale, C. W. 51, 51n35
topic 4, 6, 33, 73, 73n66, 97, 105, 108, 125, 129, 133, 135, 196, 205
topoï, see *topos*
topos 22, 76, 100n1, 104, 105, 135, 183
Toulmin, S. 17, 49, 50, 67–9, 67n52
tragedy 182, 183, 185
trial 5, 107, 135, 211
tropes 45, 70, 122, 125, 126, 129, 135, 145–51, 153, 154, 155, 229
truth-value 84, 85, 90, 91, 168, 169
truthworthiness 132, 229
Turnbull, N. 78n76

understanding xv, 7, 58, 60, 87–90, 96, 138, 163, 170, 171, 173, 174, 178, 182, 222
understatement 152
unity of rhetoric 11, 104, 230
utilitarianism 59
utility 142, 188, 201
utterance 31, 41, 76, 84–6, 88, 100, 102, 126, 135, 149, 150, 159

validity 17, 49, 51, 54–7, 58, 65, 69, 72n62, 72n63, 94, 95, 113–15, 117, 137, 154, 223

values 3, 4, 12, 13, 39, 41, 43, 45, 52, 54, 56, 62, 71, 77, 84, 85, 90, 91, 94, 129, 132, 136, 150, 168, 169, 181, 189–211, 210n7, 214, 215, 220–3, 226, 230, 232
Vance, E. 77n74
Van Eemeren, F. 50, 60–6, 60n46, 61n47, 61n48, 64n50
versification 126, 167
vice 135, 188, 206
viewer, *see* reader
virtue 5, 13, 26, 29, 39, 49, 57, 63, 73, 87, 89, 116, 122, 142, 148, 174, 176, 191, 194, 202, 204, 209, 214, 216, 229, 231
visual rhetoric 81, 81n1

Walton, D. 50, 68, 68n54, 132, 132n1
Warning, R. 76n71, 116, 136
Weaver, R. M. 50, 54n41, 70, 70n56, 144n5
Weber, M. 3, 58n44, 199, 199n5
Wellek, R. (and Warren, A.) 182n4
Westermarck, E. 210n7
Whately, R. 45
White, H. 71n60
White, S. 58n44
Willard, C. A. 50, 71, 71n61
wish 8, 17, 32, 34, 52, 114, 208
Wittgenstein, L. 49, 84

Yarbrough, S. 51, 51n37
Yeats, W. B. 165, 177
Yule, G. 160n1

zeugma 142